Data Analysis Using SPSS for Windows

Data Analysis Using SPSS for Windows

A Beginner's Guide

JEREMY J. FOSTER

SAGE Publications
London • Thousand Oaks • New Delhi

First published 1998

Reprinted 1999

SAGE Publications Ltd
6 Bonhill Street
London EC2A 4PU

SAGE Publications Inc
2455 Teller Road
Thousand Oaks, California 91320

SAGE Publications India Pvt Ltd
32, M-Block Market
Greater Kailash – I
New Delhi 110 048

British Library Cataloguing in Publication data

A catalogue record for this book is
available from the British Library
ISBN 0-7619-6015-5
        0-7619-6016-3 (pb)

Library of Congress catalog card number 98–61271

Typeset by Photoprint Typesetters, Torquay, Devon
Printed in Great Britain by The Cromwell Press Ltd,
Trowbridge, Wiltshire

SUMMARY OF CONTENTS

CONTENTS

PREFACE

This book is designed to teach beginners how to operate SPSS for Windows. You have some data and some questions such as 'How do I get a frequency table, an average, or a histogram?'. The book gives you the answers, explaining the commands you need, and showing you the output the commands provide. It is not a text in statistical analysis; I have assumed that the person who comes to SPSS is likely to know, at least in general terms, what statistical analysis they want to do. What they do not know is how to get SPSS to do it for them!

The book is intended for the individual student or researcher who has access to a PC with SPSS for Windows installed; moving between the computer and the written explanation is the only way to develop skill at using the program. A set of hypothetical data is used in explaining how to obtain the results you want from SPSS. Do please carry out the various examples and exercises: it is only by having hands-on practice that you will develop an understanding of the way SPSS works, and become its master.

SPSS is very efficient, but it is complicated. Do not become discouraged if at first you find it confusing: we all do! Once you have mastered the general principles, you will soon find that it is comparatively straightforward to obtain the results you want. And remember that when you are able to drive SPSS, you have enormous power at your disposal.

Jeremy J. Foster

ACKNOWLEDGEMENTS

Thanks are extended to SPSS UK Ltd for permission to use copies of SPSS for Windows screens.

SPSS is a registered trademark of SPSS Inc.

For information about SPSS contact: SPSS UK Ltd, St Andrew's House, West Street, Woking, Surrey GU21 1EB (phone: 01483 719200; fax: 01483 719290).

1

AIMS OF THIS BOOK

1.1 Versions of SPSS for Windows

The original edition of this book was written for SPSS/PC+, a DOS-based predecessor of SPSS for Windows. SPSS for Windows implemented a much simpler interface so that it became much easier to learn how to drive the system. The most recent version is number 8, but like version 7 this only operates under Windows 95. At the time of writing (early 1998) Windows 95 is not widely used in educational or public organizations, and they are using SPSS version 6 or 6.1. This book is based on these versions of the package. Versions 7 and 8 are operated in the same way as versions 6 and 6.1, but have a slightly different screen and some additional facilities.

1.2 How to use this book

This book is intended to show you how to operate SPSS for Windows so that you can analyse data which you want analysed. The fact that you are reading it means that you are thinking of using SPSS for Windows, and are probably aware that SPSS is a set of programs that allows you rapidly to analyse huge amounts of data, and that it lets you carry out in a few moments statistical analysis that would be impractical without the aid of a computer.

This is not a book on statistics. Although there are now a number of books which combine teaching statistics with teaching SPSS, this one assumes you know the analyses you want, if not how to obtain them. I have taken the view that learning statistics and SPSS together is risking overload, and that it is easier for the student to learn them one after the other. If you need a simple text on basic statistics, there are a number of excellent ones available (e.g. Hinton, 1995). There is a brief account of the basic principles of statistical analysis and various statistical procedures in chapter 2, but this is intended as a refresher rather than a full statistics course for beginners. Sections 8 and 9 in chapter 2 are intended to help you decide which analysis you require.

This book covers most of the facilities offered by the Base module of SPSS for Windows and some of the more advanced procedures which are provided by optional extra modules. I have structured the text by considering the questions that the user asks, moving from the simpler to the more complex procedures. (Manuals are often written the other way round; they explain the various commands one after the other, giving you the answer before you understand the question.)

Even the Base modules of SPSS offer you a very wide range of options when analysing your data. Saying that this book covers the facilities of the Base module, does not mean that I have attempted to describe every possible feature. There are thousands of different options which one can choose, and many of these can be explored at leisure once the basic mode of driving the package is understood. As in the previous editions, I have tried to explain the structure of the system and describe very fully how beginners can obtain the analyses they are likely to require. Once you have gained the fundamental skills, you can explore further facilities for yourself.

This book assumes you are sitting in front of a PC that either has SPSS for Windows installed on it or is connected into a network that makes the package available to you

The Windows environment has become so dominant in the PC world, that I have assumed that the reader is already familiar with it and with how to operate the mouse by pointing, clicking the mouse button, double-clicking (clicking twice in rapid succession) and click/dragging, which means you press the mouse button and while it is depressed move the mouse.

The first part of the book deals with general issues that are essential before you can use SPSS effectively. Chapter 2 is a summary of the principles of statistical analysis and can be skipped if you feel confident about what you want to do and why. In explaining how to use the package, I employ a set of hypothetical data, described in section 4.3, and referred to as salesq.

You need to know some basic information before you begin. I strongly urge you to read chapters 3 to 8 before doing anything else. You will then have the essential information you need before you can start using the package.

Chapters 14–20 deal with various types of statistical analysis, and provide an explanation of how to obtain them and how to read the printout. For this edition, all the examples have been re-analysed using SPSS for Windows version 6. The way to obtain a neat printout of the results is covered in chapter 21.

1.3 Conventions used in the printing of this book

Pressing the Enter key (also known as the Return key) is shown as ↵.

Your keyboard has a set of keys for controlling the movement of the cursor on the screen. They are labelled on the keyboard with arrows pointing up, down, left and right and are named in the text as up-arrow, down-arrow, left-arrow and right-arrow. The keys labelled PgUp, PgDn, Home, End, Ins are referred to by their names, as are the Esc (Escape), Alt and Ctrl keys.

There are two or three Del (Delete) keys. One, the backspace key, is on the top right of the main section of the keyboard and may be marked -Del or have a left-pointing arrow. There is another in the number keypad on the right of the keyboard which can also function as a decimal point key. For most purposes use the backspace -Del key, which deletes the character to the left of the position where the cursor is placed. If your keyboard has a grey key marked Delete it deletes the character at the point the cursor is placed when the key is pressed; characters to the right of the cursor position move left to fill the gap. The number keypad Del functions in the same way.

The Alt and Ctrl keys are rather like shift keys in that they modify the meaning of pressing an ordinary key if that key is pressed while Alt or Ctrl is depressed. When you need to press two keys together, for example the Alt and E keys, press down the Alt key and while it is depressed tap the E key, then release the Alt key. This is shown in the text as Alt+E, but remember it does not mean that you press the Alt key followed by the E key, and certainly does not mean that you press the + key: the Alt key must be held down when you press the E key.

1.4 Using floppy disks

Once installed, the various programs that make up SPSS are stored on the hard disk in their own directory. It is perfectly feasible to store the data that you want analysed and the results of the analysis on the hard disk, but hard disks can 'crash' (i.e. fail) so whatever is stored on them is lost. Furthermore, if you store your files on the hard disk they are not portable. But when stored on a floppy, they can be taken to any PC that has SPSS for Windows installed on it, and used on that machine. So you are not tied to one PC, and can make copies of your data and command files so that you have a back-up copy in case disaster strikes and your floppy gets damaged. I shall assume that you have a formatted floppy disk for storing your data, commands and the results of your analyses.

When you buy a new disk, it cannot be used until it has been formatted, a process which divides it into sections and creates a map telling the computer what is in the various sections. All this is electronic and invisible, of course. A disk needs to be formatted just once, and nowadays newly purchased disks are usually formatted when you buy them. If you do need to format a disk, insert it in the floppy disk drive and (assuming you are using Windows 3.1) select the Disk menu from Windows file manager. This has an option for formatting disks.

1.5 Chapter summary

- This book is based on versions 6 or 6.1 of SPSS for Windows.
- Before starting, read chapters 3 to 8.

THE BASICS OF STATISTICAL ANALYSIS

The main body of this book assumes that the user knows the statistical analyses that are needed, and describes the procedures for getting SPSS to provide particular statistics and apply specific statistical tests. The aim of this chapter is to remind readers of the principles of statistical analysis, so that they can decide which statistics they need for their particular sets of data. It is not intended as a substitute for a text on statistics, but should be seen rather as an aide-memoire for those who have temporarily forgotten what the various statistical procedures are used for.

2.1 Fundamental definitions

2.1.1 Population and sample

A population is an entire set of objects or people, such as the residents of France or Australian nine-year olds. A sample is a subset of a population, and in the majority of research analysis one works with a sample of a population. Usually one hopes to generalize from the sample to the population, as in opinion polls where perhaps 1000 people are asked for their opinion, the results obtained from this sample are generalized to the whole voting population of the country, and statements are made about the popularity of political parties in the country as a whole.

Whether it is valid to generalize from the sample to the population depends upon the size of the sample and whether it is representative of the population: does it have the same characteristics as the population of which it is a subset?

2.1.2 Descriptive and inferential statistics

Descriptive statistics are used to describe and summarize sets of data. They answer questions such as 'What was the average age of the patients who were admitted to the local hospital with a heart attack in the last six months?'.

Inferential statistics are used in generalizing from a sample to a wider population, and in testing hypotheses, deciding whether the data is consistent with the research prediction.

2.1.3 Scales of measurement

NOMINAL SCALES are where the numbers are used merely as a label. For example, we may code sex of respondent as 1 or 2, with 1 meaning male and 2 meaning female. The size of the numbers is meaningless, and 2 is not bigger or better than 1 (we could just as easily have used 1 to indicate female and 2 to indicate male).

Bear in mind that SPSS will happily give the mean of a variable measured on a nominal scale even though this is meaningless. There are examples in the scientific literature of eminent researchers making this mistake and reporting that the mean score on sex was 1.5. With nominally-scaled data such as sex, where respondents are 1, 2 or 3 (representing sex unknown), the mean of the scores is literally nonsense. But SPSS does not know that; it only knows there is a set of figures, so it does not object when it is asked for the mean even if it is not appropriate to do so. It is the user's responsibility to look at the results of the analyses intelligently!

ORDINAL (RANK) SCALES These have some correspondence between the size of the numbers and the magnitude of the quality represented by the numbers. A common ordinal scale is position in a race. One knows that the person who came first (position 1) was faster than the person who came second (position 2), who was in turn faster than the person who came third (position 3). But the numbers 1, 2 and 3 do not tell you anything about the size of the differences between the three people. The winner, number 1, may have been well ahead of numbers 2 and 3, or number 1 may have just beaten number 2 with number 3 trailing far behind.

INTERVAL SCALES These are where the numbers represent the magnitude of the differences. A frequently-cited example is the Celsius temperature scale, where the difference between 20 and 30 degrees is the same as the difference between 30 and 40 degrees. But note that the Celsius scale is not a ratio scale: something with a temperature of 40 degrees is not twice as hot as something with a temperature of 20 degrees.

RATIO SCALES These are where there is a true zero point and the ratio of the numbers reflects the ratio of the attribute measured. For example, an object 30 cm long is twice the length of an object 15 cm long.

The type of scale used in measuring a variable relates to other attributes one needs to bear in mind. Some variables, such as age, are continuous in that they can at least theoretically take any value between the lowest and highest points on the scale. They contrast with categorical or discrete variables which can only take a limited number of values. An example of a categorical variable is sex, since there are only two possible values.

Similarly, one can distinguish between different types of data: quantitative data is the result of measuring some variable on an ordinal, interval or ratio scale, whereas categorical or frequency data involves categorizing things and counting how many cases there are in each category. Many of the statistical procedures which apply to quantitative data cannot be used meaningfully with frequency data, and you need to decide which type of data you have before starting statistical analysis.

2.1.4 Parametric and non-parametric data and tests

The distinction between types of scale is important, as the type of scale determines which type of statistical analysis is appropriate. In order to use the parametric statistical tests, one should have used an interval or ratio scale of measurement. If the data is measured on an ordinal scale, use non-parametric tests. For nominal or categorical scales, some of the non-parametric tests, such as chi-square, are appropriate.

2.1.5 Dependent and independent variables

In experiments, the experimenter manipulates the independent variable, and measures any consequential alterations in the dependent variable. If the experiment has been designed and carried out properly, it is assumed that the changes in the dependent variable are the results of the changes in the independent variable.

The distinction between dependent and independent variables is not restricted to experiments. When correlational studies are performed, one also has a dependent variable and independent variables. For example, there has been a considerable amount of research into the factors associated with students' success and failure at their courses. This research has correlated students' study habits and personality to their course grades; the grades form the dependent variable, and the study habits and personality are independent variables.

2.1.6 Within-subjects and between-subjects comparisons

If scores on two or more variables come from the same respondents, comparing the scores involves related (within-subjects) comparisons. If the scores being compared were obtained from different respondents, they are compared using independent groups (between-subjects) procedures. In some studies, both related and independent comparisons are needed. For example, one might have data on men and women's ability to drive when they have had no alcohol and when they have had a certain amount of alcohol. If one used the same people in the no-alcohol and the with-alcohol conditions, alcohol would be a related subjects variable while sex of course is an independent groups (between-subjects) variable.

Different statistical tests are appropriate for within-subjects and between-subjects comparisons, and it is important to ensure one is using the proper test for the data being analysed.

2.2 Measures of central tendency: mode, median, mean

Given a set of scores or readings, one usually requires a single figure which indicates the 'typical' value of the set. There are three alternative figures one can use: mode, median and mean. Table 2.1 shows the scores of 22 respondents on an attitude-scale question, where the possible responses were coded as 1, 2, 3, 4 or 5.

The *mode* is the most frequently occurring value, in this instance 4.

The *median* is the value that divides the distribution of scores in half: 50% of the scores fall below the median and 50% fall above it. When the scores are in ascending order, if there is an odd number of scores, the median is the middle score. If there is an even number of scores, average the two middle scores. In Table 2.1, there are 22 scores, so the median is obtained by taking the average of the 11th and 12th scores; in Table 2.1 these are both 4, so the median is 4.

Table 2.1   *Scores on an attitude scale question*

Respondent	Response
01	1
15	1
19	1
02	3
06	3
08	3
11	3
17	3
21	3
22	3
04	4
05	4
09	4
12	4
13	4
14	4
16	4
18	4
20	4
03	5
07	5
10	5

The arithmetic *mean* is obtained by totalling the scores and dividing the sum by the number of scores. In Table 2.1, the total of the scores is 75, and the mean is therefore $75/22 = 3.41$.

2.3 Measures of variability

2.3.1 The concept of variability

An important feature of a set of data is the spread or variation of the scores in the set. We need to be able to express the variation within a set of scores as well as the central value (mode, median or mean) of the set. Table 2.2 shows the number of customers visited by male and female sales personnel.

Table 2.2   *Customers visited by male and female personnel*

Males		Females	
Respondent number	Number of visits	Respondent number	Number of visits
2	46	1	43
3	48	6	72
4	83	7	42
8	28	11	39
9	41	14	33
10	76	15	36
12	30	16	79
13	68	18	48
17	38	19	58
21	39	20	60
		22	40

2.3.2 Range; interquartile range

The *range* of a set of scores is simply the difference between the highest and lowest scores. So for the males in Table 2.2, the range is $83 - 28 = 55$, and for females the range is $79 - 33 = 46$. Range gives an indication of the spread of the scores, but of course it depends completely on just two figures from the whole set, the highest and the lowest. One very low or very high score will produce a large increase in the range, and this might be quite misleading.

One alternative measure is the *interquartile range*. As mentioned earlier, the *median* is that score which divides the set into two halves, with half the scores falling below the median and half the scores falling above it. The median is the 50th percentile, which means 50% of the scores fall below it. We can also have a 25th percentile, which is the score below which 25% of the scores fall, a 75th percentile, a 90th percentile, etc. The interquartile range is the difference between the 25th and 75th percentiles. The interquartile ranges for the two sets of data shown in Table 2.2

are 34 for males and 21 for females. The semi-interquartile range is the interquartile range divided by 2.

Unlike the range, the interquartile range is not affected by a single score which is much greater or much less than the others. But it does use only two figures from the set to express the variability in the set, and so ignores most of the numbers.

2.3.3 Variance and standard deviation

A better measure of variation would be one that used all the numbers in the set, not just two of them. This problem is tackled by looking at the mean of the set of scores, and taking the difference between each score and the mean. If one adds these deviations from the mean, the total is zero: so this figure is not going to be very helpful as an indication of the variation in the set of scores! The way round this is to square each of the deviations, which gets rid of all the negative numbers, and then add them up to obtain a sum of squared deviations. In order to get an idea of the variation in the set, it is sensible to take the average of the squared deviations. The sum of the squared deviations divided by the number of values in the set, n, is known as the *variance* of the set of scores.

(Note: If you are using data from a sample as an estimate of a wider population, then divide by $n - 1$ to obtain a better estimate of the population variance.)

The square root of the variance is the *standard deviation*, and is the number used to express the variation in the set of scores.

2.4 Frequency distributions

2.4.1 Histograms and barcharts

A frequency distribution shows the number of times each score occurs in the set of scores under examination. Figure 2.1 shows as a histogram the frequency distribution of the scores in Table 2.1.

Histograms and barcharts are graphical displays of the frequency distribution of the scores. A histogram is used for a continuous variable, and a barchart for a categorical variable. In a barchart the bars are separated to indicate that they represent different categories. In SPSS, any category which is empty (has a frequency of zero) will not be shown in a barchart.

A frequency distribution can be symmetrical or skewed. Figure 2.1 is skewed – the scores tend to be piled up at one end of the scale. If a distribution is roughly symmetrical, the mean can be used as the measure of central tendency, but if it is skewed the median should be used rather than the mean. A normal distribution, which is symmetrical,

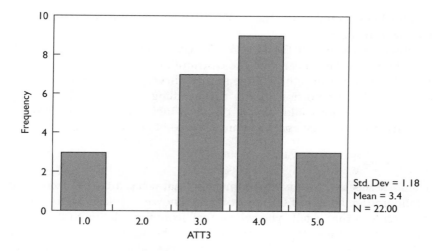

Figure 2.1   *Example of a histogram showing distribution of scores on a variable*

has a skewness statistic of zero. Kurtosis measures the extent to which observations are clustered in the tails.

2.4.2 The normal distribution curve

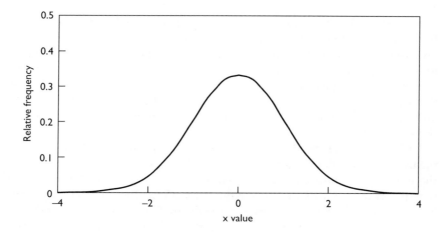

Figure 2.2   *The normal distribution curve*

The normal distribution curve, illustrated in Figure 2.2, is fundamental to statistical analysis. A perfect normal curve is symmetrical, with the 'middle' being equal to the mean. The skewness is zero and the kurtosis statistic is also zero.

One can measure off the horizontal axis in standard deviations (sd) from the mean. Very nearly all the distribution lies between -3 sd and $+3$ sd from the mean. Tables of the normal curve, found in most statistics texts, give the proportion of the curve falling above and below any position on the horizontal axis. From such tables, it is easy to find the proportion of the curve between any two points on the horizontal axis.

2.4.3 z scores

When a series of scores is transformed so that it has a mean of zero and a standard deviation of 1.00, the scores are known as z-scores. The benefit of a z-score is that it tells you where that score lies relative to the mean: a negative z indicates that the score is below the mean and a positive one that it is above the mean. From normal curve tables, one can find just where any z score stands in relation to the population. For example a z score of $+1.50$ has 5.9% of the distribution above and 94.1% below it, so this means that someone who has a z score of $+1.5$ has surpassed 94.1% of the population. If you want to compare scores from different tests, you can do so if you express the scores in z units.

2.5 Standard error and confidence limits

Inferential statistics involve estimating the characteristics of a population from the data obtained from a sample of that population. For example, one uses the mean of the sample to estimate the population mean. If one took a large set of samples from the population, the means of the samples would form a normal distribution. The standard deviation of that distribution is given by taking the standard deviation of the sample and dividing it by the square root of n, the number in the sample. This is the standard error.

The standard error allows one to state the probability that the true mean of the population is within specified limits. From the properties of the normal distribution, it can be deduced that there is a 95% probability that the true mean of the population is within plus or minus approximately 2 standard errors of the sample mean. Suppose you have taken a sample of 100 subjects from a population and found that the mean of the sample is 50, and the standard deviation is 15. The standard error is 1.5 (15/square root of 100). One can conclude that the true mean of the population has a 95% probability of being within the limits 50 $\pm$ two standard errors = 50 $\pm$ 3, i.e. between 47 and 53. So the 95% confidence interval means that there is a 95% probability that the true mean is between the limits specified.

2.6 Statistical significance and testing hypotheses

2.6.1 Statistical significance of the difference between means

The data in Table 2.3 shows the number of customers visited by the sales personnel of two employers (labelled 2 and 3). The question that the researcher asks is: is there a statistically significant difference between the mean number of visits of the two groups of sales personnel?

Table 2.3   Customer visits by sales personnel from two employers

Employer 2		Employer 3	
Respondent number	Number of visits	Respondent number	Number of visits
2	46	4	83
5	71	6	72
8	28	10	76
11	39	13	68
14	33	16	79
15	36	19	58
20	60		
21	39		
Mean:	44.00	Mean:	72.67

In Table 2.3, employer group 2 has the smaller mean, and so you might wish to conclude that these people made fewer visits. But look at respondent number 5 in employer group 2 and respondent 19 in group 3: the group 3 member has a smaller score than the group 2 member. So if you took just those two scores, you could not say that group 2 had the lower score.

If there were no difference between the two groups, their mean scores would be the 'same'. This does not imply, of course, that they would be identical, because responses almost always show some variance (variability). This random, unexplained variation is due to chance. For example, the variation in the scores for employer group 2 in Table 2.3 is variation due to chance. The mean for respondents 2, 5, 8 and 11 in group 2 is 46 and the mean for respondents 14, 15, 20 and 21 from the same group is 42. The difference between these two means is simply due to chance, random variation. It arises even though both these subgroups come from one 'population' (the complete set of scores given by employer group 2 respondents).

Our question now is: is the difference between the means of group 2 and group 3 also simply due to chance? If the difference between the means of group 2 and group 3 is the result of chance, then groups 2 and 3 are samples from the same 'population', just as respondents 2–11 and 14–21 of employer group 2 are samples from one population.

To decide whether groups 2 and 3 are samples from one population or are 'really' different and come from different populations, one applies a test of statistical significance. The significance tests let you estimate how likely it is that the data from the separate groups of respondents come from one population. If it is unlikely that they came from the same population, you can conclude that they didn't, and that they came from separate populations.

In the significance testing of differences we look at the difference between the sets of scores and compare it with the amount of variation in the scores which arises due to chance. If the chance variation is likely to have produced the difference between the groups, we say the difference is non-significant, which means the difference probably did arise from chance variation. We have to conclude there is no 'real' or statistically significant difference between the groups, and they are both from the same underlying population.

2.6.2 Significance level

If the difference between two groups is likely to have arisen from chance variation in the scores, we conclude there is no real 'significant' difference between them. On the other hand, if the difference between the groups is unlikely to have been brought about by the chance variation in scores, we conclude there is a real, statistically significant difference between the groups.

But what do we mean by likely? It is conventional to use the 5% probability level (also referred to as alpha-level): what does this mean? If there is a 5% (usually written as 0.05) or smaller probability that the difference between the groups arose from chance variation, we conclude it did not arise from chance and that there is a 'real' difference. If there is more than 5% (0.05) probability that the difference arose from chance, we conclude the difference is not a real one.

You may well ask why we use 5%; and the answer is that it is merely convention. We could use 10% (0.10), 1% (0.01), 0.5% (0.005).

2.6.3 Type I and type II errors

A significance test allows us to say how likely it is that the difference between scores of groups of respondents was due to chance. If there is a 5% or smaller probability that the difference is due to chance variation, we conclude that it was not caused by chance. But we can never be sure: there is always a possibility that the difference we find was due to chance even when we conclude that it was not. Conversely, we may find a difference and conclude that it is not significant (that it was due to random or chance variability in the scores) when in fact it was a 'real' difference. So there are two types of error we may make. These are referred to as type I and type II errors.

A type I error occurs when we reject a null hypothesis when it is true, i.e. we say there is a 'real' difference between the groups when in fact the difference is not 'real'. The probability that we shall make a type I error is given by the significance level we use. With an alpha or significance level of 5%, on 5% of occasions we are likely to make a type I error and say the groups differ when they do not.

We can reduce the probability of making a type I error by using a more stringent level of significance: 1%, say, rather than 5%. But as we reduce the chances of making a type I error, we increase the likelihood that we shall make a type II error, and say there is no difference between the groups when there is one.

2.6.4 Directional (one-tailed) and non-directional (two-tailed) hypotheses

Referring back to Table 2.3, the aim of the study was to test the hypothesis that there is a difference between the scores of the two groups of respondents. (The null hypothesis is that there is no difference between the scores of the two groups.)

Note that the hypothesis is that there is a difference. It does *not* say employer group 3 will score higher or lower than group 2, merely that group 3 and group 2 will differ. This is a non-directional or two-tailed hypothesis: group 3 could score less than group 2 or group 3 could score more than group 2.

If we had stated the hypothesis that group 2 will score less than group 3 (i.e. if we predict the direction of the difference between the groups), then we would have had a directional or one-tailed hypothesis. Similarly, if our hypothesis were that group 2 would score more than group 3, this would also be a directional hypothesis since we would still be predicting the direction of the difference between the groups.

The distinction between directional and non-directional hypotheses is important when applying significance tests. Most SPSS printouts show the non-directional (two-tailed) probability of the calculated statistic. If you have stated a directional hypothesis before examining the data, you can use the one-tailed probabilities, which are the two-tailed probabilities divided by 2.

2.7 Interpreting the outcome of a significance test

Understanding what a significance test tells you is the most important part of statistical analysis: doing all the proper tests and getting the correct answers is no good if you then misunderstand what the outcome means! Unfortunately, in the drive to do the computations, some investigators forget that the interpretation is the rationale for the whole procedure. So try to remember some basic principles:

1 If the test tells you the difference between groups is not significant, you must conclude there is no difference, even though the mean scores are not identical.
2 If the difference between groups is statistically significant, this does *not* necessarily mean that it is practically meaningful or significant in

the everyday sense. For example, in a study of people's ability to remember car licence plates, one group's score remained the same on two test occasions so the increase was 0, whereas another group's score increased from 3.22 to 3.42, an increase of 0.20; the difference was statistically significant. But it is a subjective judgement, not a statistical one, as to whether the increase of 0.20 for the second group has any practical importance.

3   If you are analysing the results of an experiment, remember that the assumption behind the experimental method is that one can conclude that significant changes in the dependent variable are caused by the changes in the independent variable. But the validity of this assumption depends on one having used a properly designed and controlled experiment: just because one has a significant difference between group A and group B does *not* mean you can necessarily conclude the difference was due to the changes in the independent variable. If the experiment was confounded, and the different groups differed systematically on another variable in addition to the independent variable, no clear explanation of the differences in the dependent variable can be given. The statistical significance of the result does not by itself give grounds for concluding that the independent variable brought about the changes in the dependent variable.

4   Avoid the temptation to take the level of significance as an index of the magnitude of the experimental effect. By convention one usually uses the 5% significance level, but one can use a more stringent one, and find that a difference between groups is significant not only at 5% but also at 1% or 0.1%. Even eminent researchers have been known to argue that a difference significant at 1% is somehow more 'real' than one significant at 5%. This is *not* a valid interpretation. If the result of your analysis is significant at the level you are using (usually 5%), just accept that and do not give in to the temptation to conclude that a difference significant at 1% is 'better'.

2.8 Parametric and non-parametric tests

Parametric significance tests rest upon assumptions that the data has certain characteristics. The assumptions for using parametric tests are:

1   Observations are drawn from a population with a normal distribution. (Note that the population is normally distributed, not necessarily the sample of scores taken from it.)

2   The sets of data being compared have approximately equal variances. (This is referred to as homogeneity of variance.) If the groups are of equal size ($n_1 = n_2$), then this assumption is not so important. If the groups being compared have an n of 10 or less, it is acceptable for the variance of one group to be up to three times as large as that of

another. With larger groups, you can still use the parametric tests if one group has a variance double that of another.

3   The data is measured on an interval or ratio scale.

If the data does not meet these assumptions, you can convert the data into a non-parametric form and then apply one of the non-parametric tests. The commonest way of converting data into a form for non-parametric analysis is to rank it.

2.9 Selecting the appropriate test

When analysing data it is vital that you use the appropriate form of significance test. To decide which test is the appropriate one, you have to be able to answer a number of questions:

1   Does the data consist of frequency counts?
2   Are you looking for a difference between sets of scores or a relationship between sets of scores?
3   Are you using data from different sets of people or different data obtained from the same people?
4   How many sets of scores are you analysing?
5   Are the dependent variables measured on an ordinal scale or are they measured on an interval or ratio scale? (Is a non-parametric or a parametric test appropriate?)

When you have answers to all these questions, you can use Figure 2.3 to help you identify the analysis you need. But the questions are not always easy to answer! If you feel you need some help, try Exercise 2.1 which will give you some practice.

Exercise 2.1

1   A recent survey asked a group of men whether they thought 'adult' films should be shown uncut on TV. Data was reported for different age groups, and 75 men under 60 said 'yes' while 35 said 'no'. For those over 60, 30 said 'yes' and 50 said 'no'. Which type of analysis is needed?

2   Jones wanted to know whether people remembered more from a weather forecast which they heard on the radio or from one they saw on the television. She had two sets of respondents: one watched a TV forecast and the other listened to it on radio. She then gave all the participants a test to see how much they remembered. Which type of analysis is needed?

3 King carried out research into the effects of playing computer games on sporting performance. She measured 50 people's skill at kicking a football at a target, asked them to play a computer game for three hours, and then measured their football kicking skill again. Which type of analysis is needed?

4 Lovell was also interested in the effects of computer game playing on football kicking accuracy. He used two age groups: boys aged 10 and boys aged 15. In each age group, he had two subgroups. One of the subgroups was assessed for kicking accuracy, played a computer game for three hours and was assessed again. The other subgroup was assessed, then spent three hours having normal lessons and was assessed for kicking skill. Which type of analysis is needed?

5 Mycroft wanted to know whether managers who report high levels of stress at work drink more. He asked 50 managers to answer a questionnaire which gives a score on stress level between 10 and 100, and also to record how much they drank during a two-week period. Which type of analysis is needed?

6 Harris investigated whether children from large families did less well at tests of reading than children from small families. He obtained reading test scores from 500 children and also found out how many brothers and sisters each child had. Which type of analysis is needed?

2.10 Chapter summary

- A population is an entire set, a sample is a subset of a population. Descriptive statistics are used to describe sets of data. Inferential statistics are used in generalizing from a sample to a wider population and in testing hypotheses.
- Some variables are continuous, others are categorical or discrete.
- There are four types of measurement scale: nominal, ordinal (rank), interval and ratio. The type of scale determines which type of statistical analysis is appropriate.
- If scores on two or more variables come from the same respondents, you are dealing with related (within-subjects) comparisons. If the scores being compared were obtained from different respondents, use independent groups (between-subjects) procedures.
- Ensure you appreciate the distinction between directional and non-directional hypotheses and how to interpret the outcome of a significance test.
- Use Figure 2.3 to help you select the appropriate test.

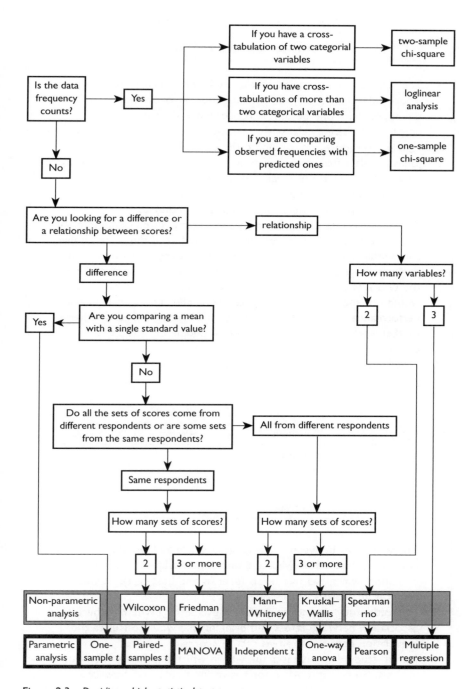

Figure 2.3 *Deciding which statistical test to use*

Answers to Exercise 2.1

1   The two-sample chi-square test is used with nominal (frequency) data
    where subjects are assigned to categories on two variables, and so is
    the appropriate one here. It is concerned with answering the
    question: Is there a relationship between the two categorical variables
    (age and response 'yes' or 'no' in the example).
2   Jones has data from two groups of respondents, and the data (scores
    on a memory test) are measured on an ordinal or possibly an interval
    scale. So she needs a test to compare two sets of scores and would
    use the independent t-test or the Mann–Whitney test.
3   King has two sets of scores and a variable measured on an interval
    scale. The two sets of scores were obtained from the same people,
    so a within-subjects t-test would be the first choice. Note that this
    study as described uses a very weak experimental design, and even if
    the two sets of scores were found to be significantly different this
    would not show that the computer game affected football kicking
    performance. There needs to be a control group to see whether
    football performance alters even when people do not play a
    computer game.
4   Lovell's study is an improvement on that of King because a control
    group was used. The table of data would look like this:

		Performance measured at	
Age group	Condition	Pretest	Post-test
10	computer game		
10	no computer game		
15	computer game		
15	no computer game		

There are two between-subjects factors: age and whether or not a
computer game was played, and one within-subjects variable: test
condition, which has two levels (pretest and post-test). So this
requires an analysis of variance.
5   Mycroft's study was concerned with establishing whether there is an
    association between stress and drinking. He would calculate the
    correlation between the two sets of scores.
6   Harris' study demonstrates the way in which alternative methods of
    analysis can be appropriate for answering a research question. He
    could see whether there is an association between number of siblings
    and reading attainment by correlating these two variables.
    Alternatively, he might set the data out in a table like this:

Number of siblings	Mean reading performance
0	
1	
2	
3	
4 or more	

There are five means to compare so a one-way analysis of variance would then be appropriate.

STARTING OUT

3.1 What is SPSS?

SPSS is a suite of computer programs, which has been developed over many years. The original SPSS and SPSSx were only available on mainframe computers. The Windows PC version is now one of the most widely-used programs of its type in the world. The most recent version is number 8, but this only operates under Windows 95. As Windows 95 is not yet widely used, this book is based on SPSS version 6 or 6.1.

All users will have the Base system of whichever version of SPSS they have available. In addition, one can purchase extra modules which provide additional analytic procedures, and some of the more commonly used ones are described in this book.

Even the Base system consists of a large set of programs, but the user does not need to know much about the actual SPSS programs; the important thing is learning to drive rather than learning how the car works! It is, however, important to understand the general characteristics of the structure of the package and the files that are used and created by it.

Like earlier versions, SPSS for Windows consists of a number of components. First, there are the programs making up the package itself; these read the data, carry out the analysis, produce a file of the results. The normal user needs to know little about these programs, just as a driver needs to know little about the structure of the internal combustion engine or the physical characteristics of a differential. Second, there are the numbers that the user wants analysed, and these have to be entered into a data window and saved as a data file. Third, there are the commands which tell the package which analyses the user wants performed on the data. Fourth, there are the results of the analysis.

Entering the data, providing the instructions on which analyses to perform, and examining the output can all be carried out on screen, with the data, commands and results being available in separate windows at the same time.

Figure 3.1 indicates the way in which the files are organized. (In this book it is assumed the data and command files are stored on a floppy

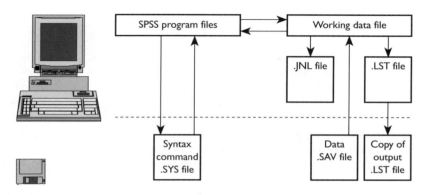

Figure 3.1 *Diagram of the structure of SPSS for Windows files*

disk, and that one of the output files, the .LST file is also sent to the floppy disk.) Essentially, SPSS itself sits on the hard disk. In order to use it you must provide it with data to be analysed, which is entered into a table presented on the screen and is then stored in a data file which has the filename extension .SAV. When you want the data to be analysed, you have to tell SPSS which analysis you want done, by issuing commands. The commands can be entered by selecting from the Window menus, and they can be pasted into a syntax window and stored in a syntax file. It is not essential to save one's commands in a file, but I strongly urge you to do so. You can tell SPSS to print each procedure or command it is following in the output file as it does it. This is extremely useful when you are analysing a complex set of data, and the way to turn this facility on and off is described in section 7.1.

When SPSS for Windows runs, it either reacts to the commands selected from the menus directly and applies them to the data in the table or it reads the commands from the syntax window and responds to them by applying them to the data.

When it is running, SPSS for Windows creates two output files. One holds the results of the analysis it has performed and is put into a window on the screen initially entitled !Output1. You will almost always want to save this file, and it will be saved with the filename extension .LST.

The other output file is named SPSS.JNL, and records a list of the commands which SPSS carries out. Every time you use SPSS for Windows, the record of the commands you use is added to the end of the .JNL file, so over a series of sessions it can become very lengthy. You can turn off the process of recording the journal file, or you can ask the system to record only the .JNL file for the current session, overwriting any previous version. You can also have the .JNL file stored on the floppy disk rather than the hard disk. To do any of these, you use Edit /Preferences: the way to achieve these alterations to the way the .JNL file is saved will be clear once you have experience at using SPSS for Windows.

3.2 Naming files

SPSS will automatically give data files the extension .SAV, output files the extension .LST, syntax files the extension .SPS and chart files of graphs the extension .CHT. The way file names are structured in Windows 3.1 is a hang-over from an operating system known as Microsoft DOS. In DOS, a filename could only consist of a maximum of eight characters followed by a full-stop and then a three character extension, and this pattern is also true of filenames in SPSS if you are using Windows 3.1. (As Windows 95 supports long filenames, these can be used if you have SPSS version 7.)

You will find in practice that with SPSS version 6, the restrictions on filenames are a real nuisance, because you will be doing a number of analyses on a set of data and it is very easy to lose track of all the files you create on the way. I have found it helpful to save the files created in each SPSS session using names which indicate the date when they were created. So, for example, if you are working on September 15th, save the syntax file with the name sep15.sps, the output file with the name sep15.lst. Then when you come back later and have to find a particular file on a crowded disk at least you know that the syntax stored in sep15.sps produced the output stored in sep15.lst. In addition, you will know that the files named sep15.sps and sep15.lst are a pair and different from those named sep20.sps and sep20.lst. Another worthwhile tip is to be sure to keep all the files referring to one set of data in one directory, separate from the files referring to another set of data.

One note of warning: do ensure that you keep the correct filename extensions for the type of file you are saving. So all syntax files must have the extension .sps, all data files the extension .sav and all output files the extension .lst. If you fail to do this you will have a chaotic situation, have great difficulties finding the files you want and may well lose vital files altogether.

3.3 Essential terminology for all SPSS users

You need to appreciate some of the terminology that is used when explaining how the package operates.

THE CASE When you approach SPSS, you have some data to be analysed, and this is in the form of responses or scores from a number of different respondents. A respondent may be a person or an organization such as a hospital ward or a school. (You might be dealing with the records of number of patients treated over a given period or the exam successes of each of 200 schools, for example.) Each respondent is known as a *case*, and the results from one case (respondent) form one line in the data file. In SPSS for Windows, the data from one case forms one row in a table.

VARIABLES AND LEVELS   You will have a number of items of data from each case, such as the respondent's age, sex, income, score on an intelligence test, number of heart attacks, etc. Each of these is a score on a *variable* (age, sex, income, etc.). Each variable has to have a name, which cannot be more than eight characters long and must not contain a space. (So you could name a variable intell, but not intelligence since the full word has more than eight letters. And you cannot call a variable score 1, as that contains a space; you would have to use score1 or score_1 as the name.) In SPSS for Windows version they are automatically named var0001, var0002, etc. until you rename them (which you should always do).

When you tell SPSS to analyse the data from the data file, you have to tell it which variables to analyse, by indicating their names. So if you have a variable which indicates the respondent's gender, you might name this variable sex. Then when you want to analyse the responses on this variable (for example, to find out how many respondents were male and how many female), you have to tell SPSS to analyse the variable sex, i.e. you use the name that has been given to that variable.

It is important to be clear about the difference between variables and levels of a variable. The variable is whatever aspect of the respondent you have measured: age, sex, number of times admitted to hospital, intention to vote for a particular party, etc. The levels are the number of alternative values that the score on the variable can take. For example there are two levels of the variable sex: male and female. Age can have many levels; if you record the age in years, it can vary from 0 to about 105, so there would be 106 levels. Usually, age is put into categories such as 0–20, 21–40, 41–60, over 60, and in this particular case this gives four levels of the age variable. (It is quite simple to enter the actual ages into SPSS and then have the program code the values into a smaller number of categories, using the RECODE procedure described in chapter 12.)

SYSTEM-MISSING AND USER-DEFINED MISSING VALUES   You need to appreciate the concept of the system-missing value, and how it differs from a user-defined missing value. When you enter data into the Data Editor table, if you leave empty one of the cells in a column or a row that contains data, the empty cell will be filled with a full-stop (period). This cell will be detected as containing no data, and SPSS for Windows will give it the 'system missing' value. So the system-missing value is automatically inserted when a number is expected but none is provided by the data.

But when some respondents have not answered all the questions asked, or have failed to provide a measure on one of the variables, it is sensible (for reasons that will become clear later) to record a no-response by entering a particular number. So one might record male as 1, female as 2 and then use 3 to indicate that the person failed to indicate their sex. The value of 3 on the variable sex would then be a user-defined 'missing value'. Of course one has to tell SPSS that this value does represent 'no response': how to do this is explained in section 5.6.

When choosing a number to represent 'data missing', it is essential to use a number that cannot be a genuine value for that variable. If one wanted to define a missing value for age, for example, one would use a number that could not possibly be genuine, such as -1 or 150.

CASE NUMBER   When entering data from a set of respondents, it is always worth inserting a variable that represents the identification number of the respondent. You can then readily find the data for any respondent you need, and check the entries against the original record of the responses. This identification number has to be entered as a 'score' on a variable, just like any other.

But SPSS also assigns its own identification number to each case, numbering each case sequentially as it reads the data file. This is the $casenum variable, which you may see listed when you ask for information about the variables in the data file. The first case in the data file, which may have any user-defined identification number you wish, will have the $casenum of 1, the next one will have $casenum 2 and so on. Do not rely on $casenum for identifying cases in the data file, as it can change if you put the cases into a different order. Use an ID number variable as well!

PROCEDURES   When SPSS analyses data, it applies a *procedure*: for example, that part of SPSS which calculates a correlation coefficient is one procedure, the part which reports the average score on a variable is another. Most of this book is concerned with explaining how you decide which procedure you want in order to achieve a particular type of analysis, and how you run that procedure on your data.

3.4 What you need to run SPSS for Windows

Assuming SPSS for Windows is installed on your hard disk, there are seven things you need to know in order to use it:

1   how to get to the SPSS programs;
2   how to create and save a file of data to be analysed;
3   which analyses you want done;
4   how to obtain the commands (procedures) which do those analyses;
5   how to get SPSS to apply the commands to the data file;
6   how to save the contents of the output (.LST) file on the floppy disk;

7 how to save the commands in a syntax file.

These requirements are covered in the following chapters. To begin, how do you get into SPSS for Windows (and how do you get out of it)?

3.5 Getting to SPSS for Windows

If you are using Windows 3.1, the first task is to run Windows, so you are looking at the Program Manager screen. This may contain a group icon labelled SPSS V6.0 or SPSS V6.1. Open the group by double-clicking on it; it will contain a number of icons, including SPSS, Sample Data and Sample Chart. (Sample Data and Sample Chart are used in the manual for SPSS for Windows to explain how the package operates.) To start the package, double click on the SPSS icon. (As it is possible to rename groups and move applications from one group to another, the arrangement on your system may not be the same as the original one. You will need to ask locally if you have problems initiating SPSS for Windows.)

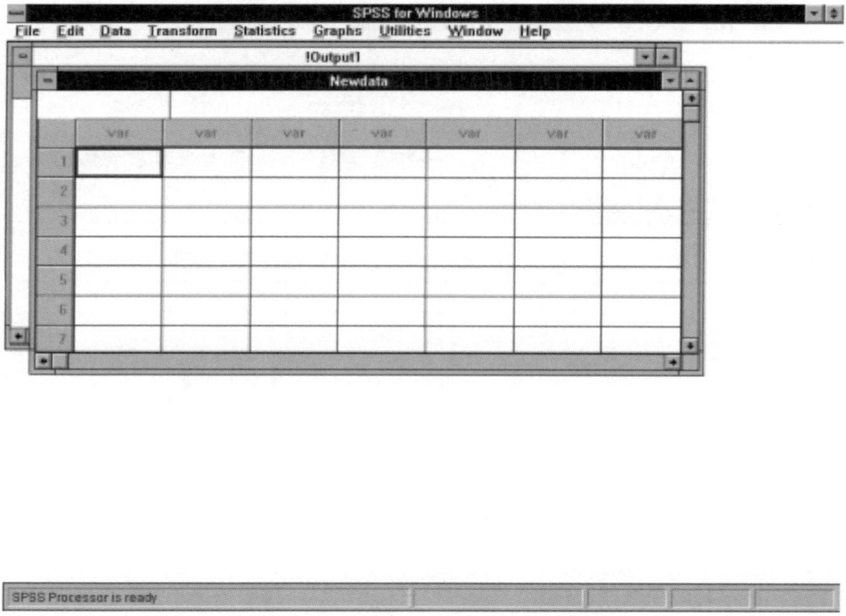

Figure 3.2   *The screen when SPSS for Windows version 6 is started*

If you are using version 6 you will be presented with the screen shown in Figure 3.2; users of version 6.1 are presented with the screen illustrated in Figure 3.3. The screen for SPSS version 7 is shown in Figure 3.4. The next sections of this chapter describe the use of windows and

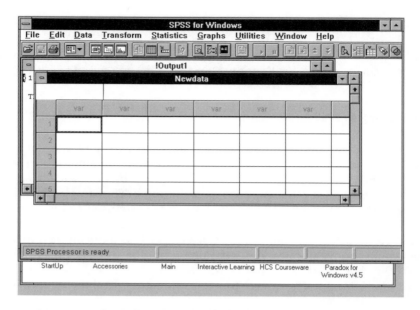

Figure 3.3 *The screen when SPSS for Windows version 6.1 is started*

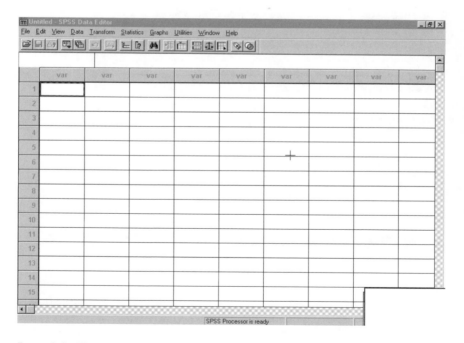

Figure 3.4 *The screen when SPSS for Windows version 7 is started*

dialogue boxes; if you are familiar with using these, go straight to section 3.9.

3.6 The components of a window

The *title bar* of a window is at the top and includes the window's title. At the left edge there is a control-menu box, and clicking on this will open the control menu, which can also be opened using Alt followed by Spacebar on the keyboard. The control-menu entries allow you to restore a window to its previous size, move it via the keyboard, alter its size, reduce it to an icon, enlarge it to its maximum size or close the application.

At the right edge of the title bar there are the minimize and maximize buttons which allow you to reduce the window to an icon or enlarge it to its largest possible size. You can alter the size of a window more precisely by placing the mouse pointer in the bottom right corner and using the click/drag technique to reduce or increase the size of the window. The position of a window on the screen can be altered by click/dragging the title bar.

The *menu bar* is the bar below the title bar. It includes a number of menu headings (such as File, Edit). Each menu can be opened by moving the mouse cursor over it and clicking the left mouse button, or by using the keyboard: while holding down the Alt key press the letter key corresponding to the underlined letter in the menu's title. To select one of the entries in the selected menu, put the mouse cursor over it and click the mouse, or type in the underlined letter of the entry name (you do not press Alt for submenu entries). A menu is closed by moving the pointer so it is outside it and clicking the mouse button.

Some windows in SPSS for Windows have an *icon bar*. This contains some command buttons and/or icon buttons (command buttons with an icon rather than a verbal label to indicate their function).

The *scroll bars* are used to reveal information that is outside the limits of the window. You can scroll the information by clicking on the scroll arrows at the end of the scroll bar, click on the space between the scroll box (which shows which part of the file is being shown in the window) and the arrows, point at the scroll arrow and hold the mouse button down, or by click/dragging the scroll box to position the window where you want it to be in the file.

3.7 The components of a dialogue box

A example of a dialogue box is illustrated in Figure 3.5. *Dialogue boxes* are presented when you have to enter information about the task to be performed. They have a number of components.

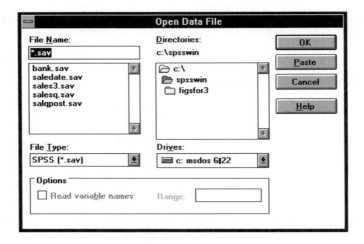

Figure 3.5   *Example of a dialogue box*

Scroll bars are provided down the side and (when needed) along the bottom when a window or a drop-down list box cannot show all the information available.

Text boxes are areas where you type in text from the keyboard. Move the pointer into the text box, and an insertion point (flashing vertical bar) appears. Anchor the insertion point by clicking the mouse, and then type in material.

List boxes display a list of options; if there are more options than can be shown, the box has scroll bars which you use to scroll the list. To select one of the options, click on it: it will be highlighted. To select a number of adjacent items, use the click/drag technique to highlight the set of options you want. To select a number of non-adjacent items, hold down Ctrl while you click on each one you wish to select.

Drop-down list boxes show a selected option, but if you click on the down-pointing arrow at the top right of the box, a list of alternatives will be revealed. You can select one of these by clicking on it. A double click will insert the selected entry in the text box at the top of the list, or you can click in the text box at the top of the list to insert the highlighted item into it. A double click on the entry in the text box invokes that item.

Check boxes are small squares adjacent to a label indicating their function. By clicking on them, you either delete or insert an X into the box. If there is an X, the option is in force, and if the box has no X it is not.

Command buttons are shaded rectangular areas which you click on to initiate an action or to reveal another dialogue box. Those buttons not available at the present time are dimmed.

Most dialogue boxes in SPSS for Windows contain a Help button; clicking on this will open a window showing information about the topic with which the dialogue box is concerned.

Option buttons (sometimes known as radio buttons, these are circular) are organized in sets. The members of a set are exclusive: if you click on one of them, any other previously selected one will be deselected, since only one of the set can be operative at any one time.

3.8 Using the keyboard if there is no mouse

IN THE WINDOWS

- To move to the menu bar, press Alt or the F10 key.
- To move along the menu bar, use the left or right arrow keys.
- To move down a menu, use the down arrow key.
- To select an item in the menu, have the cursor over it and press the ⏎ key on the keyboard.
- To cancel a selection, press Esc.
- To open Help, press F1.

IN THE DIALOGUE BOXES

- Move between items with Tab (to move forward) or Shift+Tab (to move backward).
- To move up or down a list, use the down arrow and up arrow keys.
- To move up or down a list of radio buttons or check boxes, use the down arrow and up arrow keys.
- To select an item, use the underlined letter in the item name.
- To select a highlighted item, press the ⏎ key on the keyboard.
- To activate the OK or Continue buttons, use the Tab keys to highlight them and press the ⏎ key on the keyboard.
- To cancel and close the dialogue box, press Esc.
- To open Help, press F1.

3.9 The SPSS for Windows version 6 or 6.1 screen

When SPSS for Windows first starts, it presents the screen shown in Figure 3.2 if you have version 6.0, or Figure 3.3 if you have version 6.1. (If you are using version 7, the screen is as illustrated in Figure 3.3.) In both cases there are three major components: the Application window, the Output window and the Data Editor window, titled Newdata. These are seen as lying one on top of the other, the Application window being the rear one that fills the screen, and the other two lying on top of it.

THE APPLICATION WINDOW   The top line contains the usual Windows control box in the top left, the title bar showing that it is SPSS you are using, and the two boxes in the top right corner for minimizing or maximizing the size of the window. The second line is the Menu bar, and lists a number of Menu headings from File to Help. The File menu is used for retrieving and saving files, and therefore controls the way the package interacts with the hardware. The Window menu is used to alter the way that the items on the screen are organized and displayed, and the menus between these two, Edit to Utilities are used to have the package perform operations on the data. The Help menu provides access to information which can assist you to use SPSS for Windows; further information on Help is given in section 3.12.

As is generally true in Windows, the contents of the menu are revealed by moving the mouse pointer to the menu heading and clicking; items in the drop-down menu which is then revealed are selected by clicking on them. (If you select a drop-down menu and it is not the one you want, just click outside it and it will be folded up.) Entries in the drop-down menu which have an arrow against them lead to further menus; those with . . . against them lead to a dialogue box.

Each menu heading in the menu bar has an underlined letter in its title; this indicates that one can reveal the drop-down menu by holding down the Alt key on the keyboard and while it is depressed tapping the underlined letter. So to have the Help drop-down menu revealed, hold down Alt and tap the H key on the keyboard. The items in the drop-down menu also have an underlined letter which can be used to select that entry without using the Alt key.

The bottom line of the Application window, the status bar, presents messages indicating what the package is doing. When first started, it reads 'SPSS Processor is ready'.

The main difference between the screens of SPSS version 6 (Figure 3.2) and version 6.1 (Figure 3.3) is that version 6.1 has an icon button bar below the menu bar. Many operations can be carried out by pressing the appropriate icon button. To see what each button does, put the mouse cursor over it; a description of the button's function will appear in the status bar at the bottom of the screen. The functions of the icon buttons, reading from the left, are:

- Open a file
- Save a file
- Print
- Recall a dialogue box
- Cycle through the output windows
- Cycle through syntax windows
- Cycle through chart windows
- Go to chart (activates the chart corresponding to the next chart line in an active output window)

- Go to output (from an active chart window)
- Go to data editor
- Go to case number
- Display variable information
- Search for text in output or syntax
- Show syntax chart (the technical structure of syntax commands)
- Open glossary
- Send output or syntax to this window
- Run highlighted command
- Pause or scroll output
- Go to previous page in output window
- Go to next page in output window
- Go to previous output block
- Go to next output block
- Find data value in selected variables
- Insert case in the Data Editor
- Insert variable in the Data Editor
- Display values or value labels in the Data Editor (the button toggles between the two alternatives)
- Use defined variable sets.

The meaning of many of these buttons will only become clear when you have had some experience with the package. The two buttons you need to locate at the outset are the ones for sending output or syntax to this window, and the Run button which has a small right-pointing arrow in the lower right corner. All the others carry out commands which can be accessed in other ways, using the menus.

THE OUTPUT WINDOW   The second window shown in Figure 3.2 or 3.3 is entitled !Output1. The results of the analyses are put into this window, and the contents can be examined, edited, and the file then saved. When the package is started up, the window contains the first line of the output file, giving the date and stating that the file comes from SPSS. The output window has a number of buttons (Pause, Scroll, etc); their function is described in chapter 7.

At start up, the output window is behind the Data Editor. To make it active and bring it to the front, move the mouse pointer on to the title bar (!Output) or the scroll bar down the side, and click. When the Data Editor needs to be made active, clicking in its title bar or in its scroll bars will bring it to the front.

The output window has scroll bars down the right side and along the bottom, so one can move the contents of the file within the window to reveal parts of it not otherwise visible.

THE DATA EDITOR WINDOW   The window at the front of the screen in Figure 3.2 or 3.3 is the one where you insert the data to be analysed.

Initially it is titled Newdata, and contains no figures, but it can be seen to be a table with columns headed var and rows labelled 1, 2, etc. Like the Output window, it has scroll bars down the right side and along the bottom, so one can move the contents of the file within the window to reveal parts of it not otherwise visible.

ACTIVE AND DESIGNATED WINDOWS When using SPSS for Windows, you can have a number of output windows and a number of syntax windows on the screen simultaneously. (No syntax window is shown when the package first begins, but they are used for recording the commands you use in analysing the data.) For the moment, assume you have two output windows visible. One of these is the one that will receive the results of the analysis you are performing, and this is known as the *designated* window. It is identified by having a ! before its verbal title, so the title reads !Output1.

The *active* window is the one that is currently selected: it is the 'front' one, with the darkened (blue) title bar. You can make any window currently on the screen the active window by clicking in it: it will then come to the 'front'. Note that the active window is not necessarily the same as the designated one: you might have a data window as the active window, but a different one, such as an !Output1 window, as the designated one, the one that will receive the results of the analysis you are currently performing.

3.10 Rearranging the screen windows

When you first start SPSS for Windows, the windows are arranged to overlap, like a stack of cards. The 'front' window is for data input, and is entitled Newdata; behind that is the output window, !Output1, and the largest window, at the 'back' of the stack is the Application window, titled SPSS. This stacked arrangement is known as cascading. If the screen becomes cluttered, and you cannot see the window you want, you can have the cascade re-arranged by clicking on the Window menu heading in the menu bar of the Application window, and selecting the Cascade option.

You may want the windows arranged side-by-side. This is known as the tile arrangement, and can be selected from the Window menu of the Application window. When the windows are tiled, they are narrower than usual. You can scroll the contents of the window with the scroll bars along the bottom and down the right-hand side. If you want one of the windows to fill the screen, click on the small square button with an upward pointing arrow in the top right of the window (the maximize button). This covers up the other windows, but they can be revealed by clicking on the double-headed arrow button in the menu bar or by using the Window /Cascade or Window /Tile commands from the menu bar.

3.11 Leaving SPSS for Windows

To leave the package, you can either double click on the control box at the left edge of the application window title bar, or select

```
File
    Close
```

from the application window menu. In either case you will be asked whether you wish to save the files that are at present in use: the data file, output file, and any syntax and chart files that are present.

3.12 On-screen help for SPSS for Windows

Selecting Help from the menu bar of the Application window or by clicking on the Help button in the dialogue boxes opens a Help window, in which information about the operation of SPSS is displayed. (Pressing the F1 key on the keyboard will also open Help.) The information presented will be relevant to that part of the package you were in when you requested help. So clicking on the Help button in the Frequencies dialogue box will present information about the Frequencies command, whereas the Help menu of the Application window enters the help files from the beginning. You can also access help information about the menu commands of the Application window by pressing Shift+F1.

Help is displayed in a hypertext form: key words are shown underlined and in a different colour, and by clicking on them, a fuller explanation of their meaning is shown.

You close the Help window in the usual windows way by double-clicking on the close box in the left corner of the title bar.

MOVING AROUND IN THE HELP FILE   The menu bar of the help window contains these entries:

```
Contents   Search   Back   History   << >>
```

- To see a list of the help topics, click on Contents. You can then move to one of the topics by clicking on it.
- If you want an explanation of a particular word, select Search; this invites you to enter a word, and will show an index of topics. You can select a topic and if you press the Go To button the help information will be displayed.
- To see the help page that you have just been looking at, select Back, which displays the previously viewed page of help.
- To obtain a list of the help pages you have viewed previously, so you can return to any one of them by double-clicking on its name, click the History button.

- << shows the previous page in the help file. This may not be the one you last looked at.
- >> shows the next page in the help file.

3.13 Saving, editing, copying parts of Help

The Help window has a main menu bar of

```
File    Edit    Bookmark    Help
```

so you can save the Help window's contents as a file, edit it, insert a bookmark to allow you to get back to a particular point, print parts of which you want a hard copy, copy parts of the Help information to another file or ask for help on Help!

You can copy some of the Help information to another window, or to another application outside SPSS, such as a Windows word processor. This is achieved by selecting Edit /Copy . . . from the help window menu bar, which opens a dialogue box. You then select the text to be copied (using the click/drag technique) and click on the Copy button. The text you had highlighted is copied to the Windows clipboard. If you make another window active by clicking in it, you can paste the help information into it: click at the point where you want the text inserted, and then select Edit /Paste from the Application window menu bar.

Edit /Copy pastes the copy of the help information to the Windows clipboard, so you could close SPSS for Windows, open another Windows application, such as Word for Windows or Windows Write, and then use Edit /Paste to paste the help information into a Word for Windows or Write file.

3.14 Seeing a list of all the files on your floppy disk

Select File /Open /Data from the Application window and replace .SAV in the File Name text box by typing *.*. Open the Drives drop-down list and click on the icon for drive a:. All the files on the floppy will be shown in the file list, and you can scroll down it using the scroll bar.

3.15 Stopping SPSS

If you have launched the package on some lengthy analysis and suddenly realize it is the wrong one or there is some error and you want to stop the run, select from the menu

```
File
    Stop SPSS Processor
```

If you need to get out of a dialogue box, pressing the Cancel button will take you back to the position you were in previously.

3.16 Seeing what facilities your SPSS for Windows contains

From the File Manager of Windows, access the SPSS for Windows Setup procedure by double-clicking on the Setup icon in the SPSS group. The Setup window displays the procedures installed. (If the Setup icon is not shown in the SPSS group, you will need to seek local advice. If you are using a network Setup may have been disabled to prevent computer vandals disrupting the package.)

3.17 Upgrading to SPSS for Windows from SPSS/PC+

Users familiar with SPSS/PC+ will probably find that after an initial feeling of confusion the Windows version is easy to use, and that the transfer up from earlier versions is comparatively painless. The way that SPSS operates does not appear to have altered very much; there are some additional facilities, and the main contrast is the interface to the user. After a little practice, one appreciates how much easier it is than the previous interface, even though one is presented with so many choices that at first one feels overloaded with options.

There are a few points worth bearing in mind when making the transition to SPSS for Windows, particularly regarding the files. Figure 3.1 demonstrates that the file structure for SPSS for Windows is similar to that for SPSS/PC+, but that the filename extensions are different: .LIS has been replaced by .LST, and .JNL (for Journal) replaces .LOG. Command files, now known as syntax files, automatically have the extension .SPS. Perhaps the most notable feature is that in SPSS for Windows, data files created by saving the table in which data has been entered are system files; these have the extension .SAV, whereas previously the extension was .SYS.

Some of the names given to procedures in the menus have been changed. For example, the EXAMINE procedure of SPSS/PC+ is EXPLORE in SPSS for Windows. (In fact this difference is only in the menu entries: when EXPLORE is invoked, the SPSS processor is actually running EXAMINE, as is shown in the status bar at the bottom of the applications window.)

Upgraders should note that some of the facilities available are not accessible from the SPSS for Windows menus, but have to be written into syntax files. So if you are looking for a particular subcommand and cannot find it, it is probably accessible but only indirectly. Paste the commands into a syntax file, as described in chapter 7, and then edit them. Help on the structure of syntax file commands is available from the Syntax button of the Syntax window.

The output generated by some procedures is not identical with that obtained from those same procedures in SPSS/PC+, but in most cases the differences are unimportant or self-explanatory.

Finally, SPSS for Windows has much more sophisticated facilities for dealing with some kinds of material – graphs is the obvious example.

3.18 Chapter summary

- SPSS data is stored in a file with the filename extension .SAV.
- Tell SPSS which analysis you want done by selecting commands from the Window menus and pasting them into a syntax window. Run the commands from the syntax window.
- Tell SPSS to print each procedure or command it is following in the output file (see section 7.1).
- If you are working on, say, September 15th, save the syntax file with the name sep15.sps, the output file with the name sep15.lst.
- Each respondent is known as a *case*, and the results from one case (respondent) form one line in the data file.
- The variable is whatever aspect of the respondent you have measured. The levels of a variable are the alternative values that the score on the variable can take.
- The system-missing value is automatically inserted when a number is expected but none is provided by the data.
- When some respondents have failed to provide a measure on one of the variables, record a no-response by entering a particular number to represent 'missing value'.
- The SPSS for Windows screen has three major components: the Application window, the Output window and the Data Editor window.
- If you have SPSS version 6.1, ensure you can locate on the icon button bar the buttons for sending output or syntax to this window, and the Run button.
- If the screen becomes cluttered, re-arrange it by clicking on the Window menu heading in the menu bar of the Application window and selecting the Cascade option.
- To leave SPSS, select from the application window menu

```
File
     Close
```

- To stop SPSS, select from the menu

```
File
     Stop SPSS Processor
```

CRUCIAL PRELIMINARIES

4.1 Know what you want to find out

SPSS provides the opportunity to carry out a wide range of statistical procedures very rapidly and with little effort. The danger is that because it offers such power, the researcher is tempted to comb the data: 'Let's do a factor analysis / multiple regression / 100 *t*-tests . . . and see what happens'.

It must be emphasized that there are real dangers in this approach. First, there is the statistical problem of interpreting significance levels when one has done a series of significance tests after the data has been given a preliminary examination. Practically, there is a risk that you obtain masses of output which overwhelm your ability to interpret and understand them: faced with a 4-inch pile of listing paper, many researchers, after the first flush of enthusiasm, have regretted their unrestrained proliferation of analyses!

SPSS offers the facility for obtaining plots and test statistics which may be unfamiliar to you. Do be very wary of obtaining analyses which you do not understand. If you have never heard of Lilliefors, you will only confuse yourself by being presented with it. Decide before you get to the computer what you want to find out, which statistical analyses you wish to apply. The power of the program is not a substitute for clear thinking. Without a definite idea of what you are looking for and how to find it you are likely to generate confusion rather than understanding. Section 2.9 is intended to help you decide which analyses you need, and therefore which SPSS procedures you require, in order to obtain the results you want from your data.

4.2 How to find answers to questions you are asking

HOW MANY RESPONDENTS GAVE THAT RESPONSE? In many types of investigation, the investigator wants to know *how many* respondents gave a particular answer or response. For example, how many cases in the data file were female, how many were female and under 40 years of age? Answers to this kind of question are provided if you use the FREQUENCIES procedure (chapter 14).

You may want to obtain a table showing the number of cases that had certain scores on one variable subdivided according to their scores on another variable. For example, suppose you want a table showing the number of males and females coming from the North and the South. This type of table is provided by CROSSTABS (section 14.4).

Having produced a table showing the number of people of each sex coming from each part of the country, you might ask whether there is a significant relationship between these two factors: do proportionally more men than women come from the North? To see whether this type of relationship exists with frequency data, you need the chi-square test, which can be obtained within the CROSSTABS procedure (section 14.5).

HOW ARE THE SCORES DISTRIBUTED? WHAT ARE THE PERCENTILE SCORES? If you want to see how the scores are distributed (perhaps to see whether they form a normal distribution?) or discover the percentile scores, use EXPLORE (chapter 9).

AVERAGES: WHAT ARE THE MEANS AND MEDIANS? You may want to know what was the average score on a certain variable: what, for example, was the average age of all the cases in the data file? This data can be found using DESCRIPTIVES (chapter 15). Note carefully that if you want the means of subgroups of respondents, such as the average age of males and then of females, you need the MEANS procedure (section 15.3).

AVERAGES: WHAT ARE THE MEANS FOR SUBGROUPS OF RESPONDENTS? If you want the average score of subgroups of respondents, such as the average age of men and of women, or the average income of people aged below 40 and the average income of people aged over 40, then you need the MEANS procedure (section 15.3).

IS THERE A SIGNIFICANT DIFFERENCE BETWEEN SCORES? A large part of statistical analysis is involved with evaluating the differences between sets of scores, and determining whether they are statistically significant. The concept of statistical significance is summarized in chapter 2, and identifying the particular test for a specific question is explained in section 2.9. Chapter 16 covers the *t*-test and analysis of variance for comparing means of sets of scores.

IS THERE A SIGNIFICANT DIFFERENCE BETWEEN NON-PARAMETRIC SCORES? If you need to use non-parametric analysis, the NPAR TESTS procedure (chapter 18) offers a number of tests, including the Kruskal–Wallis, Mann–Whitney and others.

ARE TWO SETS OF SCORES CORRELATED? As scores on one variable increase, do scores on another variable increase or decrease? This type of question is asking whether there is a correlation between the scores on the two variables, and is answered by using the CORRELATIONS procedure (chapter 17). Rank correlations are also obtained from COR-RELATIONS. If you have to rank the data, you use RANK (chapter 11).

HOW WELL CAN I PREDICT ONE SCORE FROM RESPONDENTS' OTHER SCORES? You may want to investigate whether responses on test1 and scores on test2 predict scores on test3, and this is a problem in multiple regression, which is dealt with using the REGRESSION procedure (chapter 17).

HOW DO I ANALYSE SUBGROUPS OF RESPONDENTS SEPARATELY? You will frequently want to analyse the data for just some of the respondents: perhaps compare the scores on test1 and test2 only for people aged over 40, for example. To do this, you have to tell SPSS which subgroups you want to select, and then which analysis you wish to be carried out. You can use SELECT IF or SPLIT FILE (chapter 13).

HOW CAN I CALCULATE 'NEW' SCORES, SUCH AS EACH RESPONDENT'S AVERAGE ON A NUMBER OF VARIABLES? You will often find that you want to obtain a 'new' score from the data provided by your respondents. Suppose, for example, that you have scores on test1 and test2; you might want to find the average of these two scores for each respondent. To do this, use the COMPUTE procedure (chapter 12).

HOW DO I PUT THE SCORES INTO A PARTICULAR ORDER? This is achieved using the SORT procedure (chapter 11).

CAN I CHANGE THE WAY DATA IS ENCODED? Suppose you have asked your respondents to indicate their age in years, and you find that their ages vary from 16 to 85. To make the data more manageable, you might decide that you would like the respondents grouped into different age groups of 16–35 years, 36–55 years, 56 and above. This can be achieved using the RECODE procedure (chapter 12).
   To transform scores into ranks, use RANK (chapter 11).

HOW DO I OBTAIN GRAPHS? The graphing facilities for SPSS for Windows are considerably more sophisticated than for previous versions, and allow you to create barcharts, histograms, box plots, line graphs, area charts and pie charts, using the GRAPHS procedure (chapter 10).

HOW DO I GET A NEAT TABLE OF THE RESULTS? SPSS has a procedure called REPORT which allows you to generate clean displays of tables and output (chapter 21). Alternatively, you can transfer your output file to a word processor and edit it there (section 7.8).

I HAVE DATA IN DIFFERENT FILES — HOW DO I MERGE THEM INTO ONE?
The procedures needed are covered in chapter 6.

4.3 The data used in this book

The data file is simply the stored record of the numbers (data) which are to be analysed. The way you create a file of your data is described in chapter 5. In explaining how to create, store and use a file of data, it is helpful to have an example to refer to, and I shall be using the data described here.

Imagine that we have carried out a piece of research in which we gave a questionnaire to each of a group of 22 salespeople. They were employed by three different employers, and the respondents were asked their sex, the name of their employer, the area of the country they work in (either North or South), and then three questions intended to reveal their attitude towards their job. Each of these questions (numbers 5–7 in Figure 4.1) invited a response on a scale from 1 to 5. The questionnaire also asked the number of customers each salesperson had visited during the previous month, the total sales for the previous month, the sales for the current month and the date the respondents started working for their company. Figure 4.1 shows an example of a completed questionnaire from one respondent, and in all there are 22 questionnaires like this.

When encoding these responses for SPSS, all the responses were encoded as numbers. Although the respondents indicated whether they are male or female, the answers were expressed as a number, with 1 representing male and 2 representing female. Similarly, each employer was given a number, and the respondent's employer was recorded as 1, 2 or 3; the value 1 was used to represent Jones and Sons etc. The area of work was also coded numerically, with 1 for North and 2 for South. (It is straightforward to have the verbal meanings of the numbers displayed in the printout or on the screen.)

Although this type of investigation may not be of any interest to you, the kind of responses obtained are similar to those yielded by many kinds of research. Essentially, we have series of numbers. Here they are used to represent sex, employer, area of country, attitude expressed on each of three questions, three performance measures (customers visited, last month sales, current month sales), and the date when the person started with the company. We could have data on socio-economic status, number of children, or a thousand other things which can be represented as numbers.

4.4 Numeric and string (alphanumeric) variables

SPSS does accept alphanumeric (known as string) data, in which the data is coded in the data file not as a number but as a series of letters (or

Sales Personnel Questionnaire

Where there are alternative answers, please underline the one relevant to you. For the other questions, please fill in your answer.

Respondent number: 01

1 What is your name?   K Smith

2 Are you male or female?   M   F

3 What is the name of your employer?   (1)   Jones and Sons

                                         (2)   Smith and Company

                                         (3)   Tomkins

4 In which area of the country do you work?   North   South

Please indicate your response to the following three questions by underlining one of the numbers, using the following scale:
   1 means that you strongly agree with the statement;
   2 that you agree with it;
   3 that you are uncertain;
   4 that you disagree;
   5 that you strongly disagree with the statement.

5 In general I enjoy my job   1   2   3   4   5

6 In my company, hard work gets rewards   1   2   3   4   5

7 I often wish I was doing a different job 1   2   3   4   5

8 How many customers did you visit last month?   43

9 What was your total sales value last month?   3450.60

10 What was your total sales value this month?   4628.90

11 Enter the date you started working for your present employer:

                                  01 day 06 month 88 yr

Figure 4.1 *Completed sales personnel questionnaire*

letters and numbers). If the data contains any letters, it is a string variable. SPSS divides string variables into two types: short ones, which have eight characters or less, and long ones.

There are some drawbacks to using string variables. First, typing in strings takes longer than typing in numbers. Second, there are limitations on what SPSS can do with string variables: one cannot use them in most statistical procedures. Consequently, it is usually more convenient to use numerical coding of all variables. For example, when recording a respondent's sex you might code male as 1 and female as 2. (It is simple to have the printout show that a score of 1 on sex means male and a score of 2 means female.)

Bear in mind when using numbers instead of a string label, such as coding male as 1 rather than 'm' and female as 2 rather then 'f', that the numbers are merely labels and form a nominal scale.

If you are using a string variable in your data file, you have to tell SPSS that the variable is a string by using the Define Variable dialogue box, as described in section 5.5. You can convert a string variable into a numeric one using the Automatic Recode procedure described in section 12.7 or by using Compute If: covered in section 12.3.

4.5 Chapter summary

- Decide before you get to the computer what you want to find out, what statistical analyses you wish to apply.
- The data described in section 4.3 is used from now on to explain how SPSS operates.
- It is usually more convenient to use numerical coding of all variables rather than have string variables.

5

THE DATA FILE

In SPSS for Windows, data is entered into the table which is automatically presented in the Data Editor (Newdata) window. When putting data into the Data Editor, each row of the table should contain the results from one respondent; SPSS refers to each line as a case.

Each column contains the results on one variable; for example the second column, var00002, might contain the data indicating the respondent's sex. The cell entries are values, usually numbers. (If you wish to use letters, refer to section 4.5.)

If you do not want the grid lines separating the cells in the Data Editor window, turn them off by selecting the Utilities menu: the drop-down menu includes a Grid Lines option, and selecting it turns the lines off or on.

5.1 Entering data into SPSS

To enter data, ensure the Data Editor window is active; if necessary, click on its title bar

Check that the top left cell is highlighted. If it is not, press the Ctrl+Home key combination to move the cell selector to this cell

Type in the first set of numbers for the first case of your data set: I advise you always to have an identification number as the first 'score' for each respondent.

Press the right arrow key or the down arrow key or ↵ on the keyboard. If you press the right arrow key, the cell selector moves to the next cell on the right of the one you have just been addressing. It is usually more convenient and less prone to error to enter the data for each respondent rather than each variable, so pressing the right arrow key is normally the easiest procedure. If you press Enter or down arrow, the cell selector will move down to the cell below the one you have just been addressing.

The first cell will now contain the figures you typed in, and the column will now be headed var00001. Type in the figures for the second cell, press the right arrow key and continue until all the figures have been

entered in the appropriate row and column positions. Each time you put
a number into a column for the first time, the column will be given a
label: column 2 is labelled var00002, column 3 is var00003 and so on.

Exercise 5.1: Entering a set of data into the Data Editor

The data I shall use to explain how SPSS for Windows operates has been
described in chapter 4 and will be referred to as salesq (for Sales
Questionnaire). The table of data is shown in Table 5.1, and your first
task is to enter it into the Data Editor. Put the first number (1, the id for
the first respondent) into the top left cell of the table, the number 2
(representing the sex of respondent number 1) into the top cell of the
second column. Then continue entering numbers until all the data has
been put into the table. The complete number for sales_1 (3450.60 for
the first case) goes into one cell in column 9 of the table. The three sets
of numbers representing the date started go into separate columns, so
you will have 13 columns of numbers altogether.

   The variables (with their names shown in brackets) are, reading from
left to right: id, sex, employer (empl), area, response to question 5 (att1),
response to question 6 (att2), response to question 7 (att3), customer
visits (cust), sales for last month (sales_1), sales for the current month
(sales_2), day of date started (dstd), month of date started (dstm) and
year started(dsty). The abbreviated variable names are shown in the table.
(Remember that variable names cannot exceed eight characters in
length.)

   If some data were missing, you would just leave that cell empty. There
are no empty cells in the salesq data, but if respondent number 5 had
failed to indicate their sex, for example, you could just skip over that cell
when entering the data. It would contain a full-stop, which is the 'system-
missing' value. This is the value that SPSS inserts into any empty cell in a
column that contains data. It allows the program to keep track of the
occupied cells – even those that are left with no data being entered have
some content. (The notions of the system-missing value and user-defined
missing values are explained in section 5.6.)

5.2 Correcting data

If you need to make corrections to any of the cell entries, simply move
the cursor to that cell (most easily done by clicking on it), type in the
correct numbers and press ↵ or an arrow movement key.

   If you want to alter one number in a long numerical entry, click on the
relevant cell. The cell contents are reproduced in the line below the title

Table 5.1 *Data from the sales questionnaire study*

ID	SEX	EMPL	AREA	ATT1	ATT2	ATT3	CUST	SALES_1	SALES_2	DSTD	DSTM	DSTY
1	2	1	1	4	5	1	43	3450.60	4628.90	1	6	88
2	1	2	2	4	4	3	46	4984.42	5136.78	8	6	90
3	1	1	2	2	3	5	48	10432.82	10589.54	9	6	90
4	1	3	1	2	3	4	83	8235.21	9621.21	1	6	90
5	3	2	2	2	2	4	71	6441.38	6388.32	8	6	90
6	2	3	2	3	3	3	72	6497.05	4400.50	9	6	90
7	2	1	2	3	2	5	42	3835.26	2209.76	1	6	90
8	1	2	2	4	5	3	28	3819.00	4238.50	8	6	90
9	1	1	1	2	3	4	41	5723.52	5508.90	9	6	90
10	1	3	2	1	2	5	76	7937.45	8120.54	8	6	90
11	2	2	1	2	3	3	39	4582.44	5709.00	9	6	90
12	1	1	1	2	3	4	30	2005.30	3215.35	1	6	90
13	1	3	2	2	2	4	68	8914.50	9156.45	3	6	91
14	2	2	2	1	2	4	33	3124.20	2200.59	5	6	91
15	2	2	2	5	4	1	36	4222.45	3300.50	3	6	91
16	2	3	1	2	2	4	79	8881.28	10120.00	31	5	91
17	1	1	2	3	4	3	38	3449.35	4120.54	5	6	91
18	2	1	1	2	3	4	48	7882.60	8007.50	31	5	91
19	2	3	1	4	3	1	58	8779.00	8508.60	3	6	91
20	2	2	2	1	3	4	60	5822.68	4305.40	31	5	91
21	1	2	2	3	4	3	39	4004.80	4407.54	3	6	91
22	2	1	1	2	3	3	40	5886.40	7200.48	5	6	90

bar of the window; click at an appropriate position in this cell editor line, and you can edit the entry. To insert it in the table, press ⏎ or use the mouse to select another cell in the table.

INSERTING ROWS OR COLUMNS IN THE TABLE Rows can be inserted into a table by selecting a cell in the row below the one where you want a row inserted and then using from the menu bar

```
Data
    Insert Case
```

A column is inserted by selecting a cell in the column to the right of where you want one inserted, and then choosing from the menu bar

```
Data
    Insert Variable
```

COPYING OR MOVING DATA IN THE TABLE To copy or move cells, select them using the click/drag technique and while they are highlighted select Edit from the menu bar of the Application window. If you are copying the cells (so they are repeated elsewhere), click on Copy. If you are moving the cells from one place to another, click on Cut. Then move the cursor to the point where you want the cells to be repeated or inserted, click to select that cell and select from the menu bar

```
Edit
     Paste
```

You can paste the copied or cut cells to an area outside the current table, but any empty cells that result will be filled with the system-missing value, the full stop.

To move a complete column or row, insert an empty column or row as described above. Highlight the column or row you want to move by clicking in the area showing the variable name or the row number, select

```
Edit
     Cut
```

and then click in the empty column or row you obtained when you inserted a variable or case. Select

```
Edit
     Paste
```

and the column or row you cut earlier will be inserted.

DELETING ROWS (CASES) OR COLUMNS (VARIABLES)   Click on the case number on the left side of the row, or on the variable name at the top of the column and from the menu bar choose

```
Edit
     Clear
```

5.3 Moving around in the data table

With a large table, you will want to be able to move around it rapidly. The Home key takes you to the first cell in a row, End to the last cell in a row, Ctrl+up-arrow to the first row of a column, Ctrl+down-arrow to the last row of a column. Page Up and Page Down scroll up or down one window-height, and Ctrl+Page Up or Ctrl+Page Down scroll one window left or right.

TO GO TO A PARTICULAR VARIABLE   Select Utilities /Variables from the Application window menu, highlight the variable in the list presented in the box then revealed, and click on the Go To and Close buttons.

TO GO TO A PARTICULAR ROW   Select

```
Data
     Go To Case
```

Enter the case (row) number in the text box, and click on OK and Close. Note that the case number is the number of the row, $casenum, not any identification number that you may have entered as a variable. If you want to find the row of data for a particular respondent, use the procedure described in the next paragraph.

TO GO TO A PARTICULAR SCORE OR TO A PARTICULAR RESPONDENT Select a cell in the column containing scores on the variable, and select from the menu bar

```
Edit
     Search for Data
```

You can then enter the value to be searched for in the text box of the Search for Data dialogue box, and click on the Search Forward or Search Backward buttons. (Clicking on Cancel will remove the dialogue box after the search has been made.) This technique can be used to find a particular respondent, so long as you have given each a unique identification number (id), as I recommend you always do. Put the cursor at the top of the column containing the id numbers and then select Edit /Search for Data. If you put the id number of the respondent you want in the Search text box and click on Select Forward, the row for that respondent will be found in the Data Editor.

5.4 Saving the data file

SAVING THE DATA FILE FOR THE FIRST TIME Once you have entered the data, the first thing to do is to save it so that if anything goes wrong later you have a copy you can use. In most cases you will want to save the file on a floppy disk, so make sure your formatted disk is inserted into drive A. To save the file on the floppy disk, follow these steps:

Check that the Data Editor is the active window, with the title bar in colour or darkened. From the Application window menu bar, select

```
File
     Save As
```

You will be presented with the Save Data As dialogue box shown in Figure 5.1. This offers many options that as a beginner you will not need, but there are five things you must do:

- Type in the filename which you want the file to be called (for example, salesq.sav). Remember that the main part of the name cannot exceed eight characters and must not contain any spaces, full stops, commas.
- Open the Drives drop-down list and click on the icon for drive a:. This means the file will be stored on the floppy disk.

- If you open the drop-down menu for Save File as Type, it lists a number of file formats. Select the one you want. Unless you have a reason for doing otherwise, use the SPSS format.
- Move the pointer so it is over the button marked OK at the upper right, and click.
- The data file will then be stored on your floppy disk, with the name SALESQ.SAV (if you used the filename MYDAT, the file will be MYDAT.SAV). The name will now appear in the Title bar of the Data Editor window.

If you think you made a mistake, just repeat the steps given above, checking that you are making the right selections at each point.

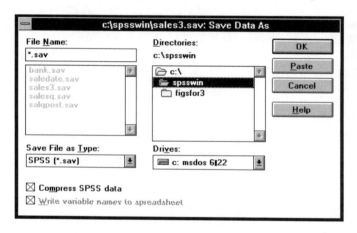

Figure 5.1   *The Save Data As dialogue box*

SAVING THE DATA FILE FOR THE SECOND TIME   When you are working on a data file and have saved it once, or are working on a file that you have retrieved from disk, you can save the file under the same name as it already has by simply selecting

```
File
    Save
```

from the Application window menu bar. The version you are now saving will over-write the previous one. If you want to keep the old version and the current one, use File /Save As (as described above), and type in a different name from the current one. For example, suppose you have made some changes to SALESQ.SAV and want to keep both the original and the altered versions; you would save the current version under a new name by typing in a name such as SALESQ2, and the file will then be saved as SALESQ2.SAV.

Exercise 5.2: Save the data

Save the file as salesq.sav, following the procedure described above.

5.5 Assigning names and labels to variables and values

VARIABLE NAMES   Variable names are used by SPSS to refer to the variables (columns) when it is processing the data. Left to itself, SPSS names the variables (columns) as var00001, var00002 and so on, which is not at all informative when you are looking at the table. So you need to insert meaningful names into the column headings.

When deciding on a variable name, it is sensible to use one that reminds you of what the variable actually is. So you would call sex 'sex', and age 'age'. But variable names cannot be longer than 8 characters, cannot contain a blank space between characters, must not end in a full stop (although one can be enclosed by characters), must not use punctuation characters such as ! or *. Also, the name can only be used once. We have two sets of sales figures in the data file used in this book, but cannot call them both sales; instead they are named sales_1 and sales_2. Note that case is ignored, so SALARY, salary and Salary are all the same to SPSS and cannot be used together in one set of variable names.

It is important to distinguish between variable names, variable labels and value labels. The variable name is used by SPSS when identifying which variables it is to analyse, and as explained cannot be more than eight characters long, cannot contain a space, etc. So sales_1 is an acceptable variable name but sales*1 or sales 1 are not. Variable labels are added to the output and serve to explain what the variable is. They are not restricted in the way variable names are since they can be up to 120 characters, can contain any characters or spaces. So for the variable which is named sales_1 you could have the label 'Sales for previous month'.

Value labels, on the other hand, are added to the output to explain what a particular value or score on a variable denotes; so the printout will show, for example, that a score of 1 on the variable sex indicates 'male'.

ASSIGNING VARIABLE NAMES AND VARIABLE LABELS   To name the variable and/or assign a variable label, click on one of the cells in the column containing the data on that variable, and from the menu bar of the Application window select

```
Data
    Define Variable
```

Clicking on this entry yields a dialogue box (Figure 5.2), with the cursor already positioned in the text box marked Variable Name. Type in the new name of the variable.

To change the name of a variable, repeat the process of naming the variable by opening the Define Variable dialogue box and typing the new name into the Variable name text box.

To assign a variable label, click on the Labels button in the bottom area of the Define Variable dialogue box. This will reveal another dialogue box, headed Define Labels (Figure 5.3). Type the label into the text box to the right of Variable Label:, and click on the Continue button. This will return you to the Define Variable box, and the label will be shown on the relevant line of the centre part of the box, the area marked as Variable Description. Click on OK, and the name and label will be assigned. The column containing the data on that variable will now be headed with the variable name you assigned.

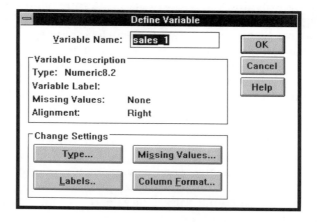

Figure 5.2   *The Define Variable dialogue box*

ASSIGNING VALUE LABELS   To give labels to each value (score) on a variable, you use the Define Labels box (Figure 5.3), obtained from the Define Variable box by clicking on the Labels button as explained above. Move the pointer so it is in the Value text window, click the mouse to anchor the cursor, and type in the value. Then type the label into the Value Label text box and click on the Add button. For example, to insert the value label 'male' for the score of 1 on sex, you would type 1 into the Value box and male into the Value Label box, then click on the Add button. The result, 1='male' appears in the list box to the right of the Add button.

If you need to change one of the labels, get to Figure 5.3 and click on the label in the list that is shown. Enter the new label in the Value Label

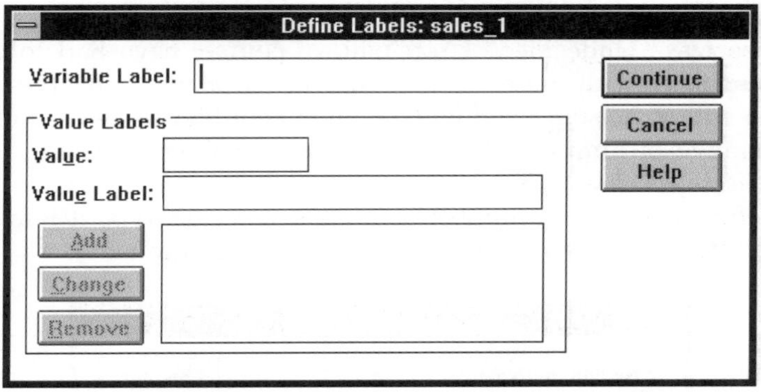

Figure 5.3   *The Define Labels dialogue box*

box and click on the Change button. You delete a label by clicking on it in the list box, and then click on the Remove button.

If you are using SPSS version 6.1, once you have assigned value labels you can readily switch between seeing the numbers or their label equivalents by clicking on the last icon but one in the Data Editor's menu bar.

Exercise 5.3

Assign names to each of the variables in salesq, using the names shown just above the first row of numbers in Table 5.1: id, sex, empl, att1 and so on. Assign variable labels: 'Employer' to empl, 'Customer visits' to cust, 'Start day' to dstd, 'Start month' to dstm and 'Start year' to dsty. Assign value labels to sex: 1 represents 'male' and 2 represents 'female'. Finally, assign value labels to area: 1 represents 'North', 2 represents 'South'.

5.6 When data is missing: Missing Values

When a respondent fails to provide a response on a variable it is important to encode the fact that there is no response, using a separate number which is defined as indicating 'missing value'. You inform SPSS of the missing value for a variable through the Define Variable box (Figure 5.2), which is obtained by selecting Data /Define Variable from the Application window menu bar. When presented with the Define Variable dialogue box, click on the Missing Values button. This exposes the Define Missing Values box shown in Figure 5.4. You can enter up to three different values each of which will be classed as missing (i.e. not a genuine data value). Having a number of different missing values can be useful: you may have one number to represent 'no response given', another to represent 'response was "Don't Know"', another to represent 'response was "Undecided"'. You will, of course, have had to encode these responses with the relevant numbers when you enter the data in the data editor. As suggested by the contents of Figure 5.4, you can also have a range of numbers defined as missing values or a range plus a single discrete value.

To define a particular number as a missing value, type it into one of the Discrete missing values boxes and click on Continue.

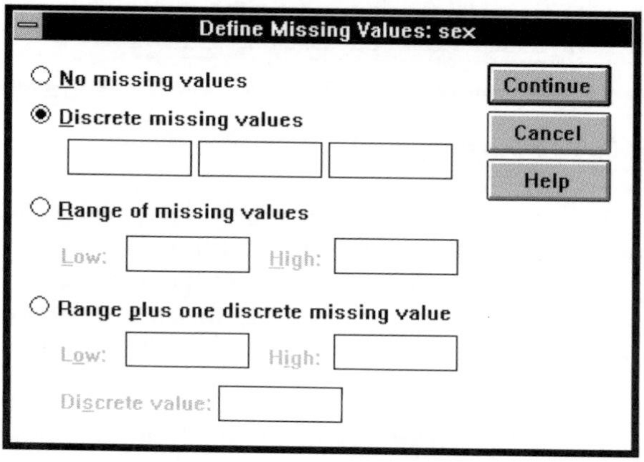

Figure 5.4   *The Define Missing Values dialogue box*

Exercise 5.4

Using the technique described above, tell SPSS that a score of 3 on sex is a missing value (i.e. signifies that the respondent's sex is unknown).

5.7 Setting the column width of a variable and aligning entries in a column

When you have selected Data /Define Variable from the menu, and obtained the Define Variable dialogue box (Figure 5.2), the Variable Description area provides further information about the variable. Type shows whether it is a numeric variable (i.e. numbers only), a date variable, a string variable (meaning it includes letters rather than just numbers), or one of a range of other types. It also indicates the width of the variable as it is displayed in the table.

In Figure 5.2 the variable has a width of 8.2: this means the numbers displayed in this column can be up to 8 characters wide, including the decimal point, and there are 2 decimal places allowed. So the largest number which could be shown in this variable column is 99999.99. Until you change the settings, the variable is numeric and its width is set at 8 with 2 decimal places. This default setting is altered by clicking on the Type button in the Change Settings area of the Define Variable dialogue box. If you do alter the variable's column width, the altered settings are lost when you leave SPSS: they are not saved when you save the file.

The width settings only control the width as displayed on the screen, and not the way the variable is stored in the program, where numeric variables are 40 characters wide with up to 16 decimal places. So although you may type in a number like 44.444, the table may only show 44.44; but in carrying out calculations the program uses the full number, with (in this example) three decimal places.

The Alignment entry in the Variable Description area of the Define Variable box tells you how the entries in the column will be aligned; for numeric variables, the conventional setting is right aligned. It can be changed to left aligned or centred by selecting the Column Format button from the bottom of the box and clicking the relevant radio button in the Define Column Format dialogue box.

5.8 Using templates to assign value labels etc. to a number of variables

You may have a large number of variables for which you wish to assign the same value labels, missing values, column width, alignment specification or some combination of these features. It is tedious to go through the process of defining these attributes for each one, and you can use a template to do it for you. You create a template from

```
Data
      Templates . . .
```

in the Application window menu bar, which exposes a Template dialogue box. Clicking on the Define button allows you to access Define Template buttons, and from them you can enter the settings you want. You can then save the template by clicking on the Add button. In the Template dialogue box you can give your specification a particular name or have it as the default template.

Having specified a template, you will want to apply it to a number of variables. When in the Data Editor, select the variables to which the template is to be applied by dragging along the row so that entries in the appropriate variables are highlighted. Then click on Data /Templates . . . and select which attributes of the template you wish to apply by clicking on the relevant items from the list provided in the Apply area of the box. You can apply any combination of Type, Value Labels, Missing Values,

Column format specifications. Then click on the OK button, and the highlighted variables in the Data Editor will have the designated template attributes applied to them.

Exercise 5.5

Make any adjustments you wish to the variable names, column widths, value labels features of the data in salesq and then save it again.

5.9 Retrieving data files

RETRIEVING A .SAV DATA FILE   To retrieve a data file from your floppy disk, select from the Application window menu bar

```
File
     Open
          Data
```

You will be presented with the Open Data File dialogue box shown in Figure 5.5. Assuming the data file you want is on the floppy disk and has been saved previously by SPSS, open the Drives drop-down list and click on the icon for drive a:. All the files on drive A, the floppy disk, ending with the .SAV extension will be listed in the files list. Click on the name of the file you want to retrieve, and it will appear in the File Name box. Click on the OK button on the right hand side of the dialogue box. The file will then be put into the Data Editor window, and its name will be the title of that window.

RETRIEVING A DATA FILE WITH A FILENAME EXTENSION OTHER THAN .SAV Select from the Application window menu bar

```
File
     Open
          Data
```

You will be presented with the Open Data File dialogue box shown in Figure 5.5. If the data file has a filename extension other than .SAV, you need to replace the .SAV in the Name text box with the appropriate extension. For example, you may have a .sys file called PROJDAT.SYS that you saved in SPSS/PC+. The easiest method of retrieving such a file is to replace the .SAV in the File Name box of Figure 5.5 with *.*, as the * is a wild card symbol and means 'any letters'. Open the Drives drop-down list and click on the icon for drive a:. All the files on the floppy

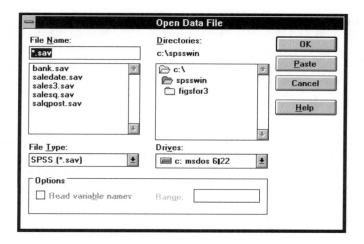

Figure 5.5 *The Open Data File dialogue box*

disk will be shown in the file list, and you can use the scroll bars to scroll down the list. When PROJDAT.SYS is visible, click on it and it will appear in the File Name text box. Then click on the OK button.

When you are faced with the Open Data File dialogue box, you will see that you can import files from other packages, such as Excel, dBase, Lotus 1-2-3. How to import Excel files is described in section 5.11 below.

5.10 Importing data prepared in a word processor

Data can be prepared outside SPSS for Windows. If possible, it is better to prepare the data in a spreadsheet rather than a word processor and then import it into SPSS. You can then use the spreadsheet to do some tasks such as graph drawing, and the data in a spreadsheet will already be organized into columns and rows. Importing from a spreadsheet is explained in section 5.11 below. But you can use a word processor to prepare the data, save it in ASCII format and then import it into SPSS. When writing the data in a word processor, use a tab between each of the variables if possible; this makes it simpler to import it into SPSS.

IMPORTING A TAB-DELIMITED FILE If data is prepared in a word processor with scores on the variables separated by tabs and the file saved in ASCII format, the data files can be imported into SPSS by selecting from the menus

```
File
    Open
        Data
```

Open the File Type drop-down menu. From the list of file types, choose Tab-delimited and type the name of the file into the File Name box. If the file is on a floppy disk, open the Drives drop-down list and click on the icon for drive a:. Select the file to be imported from the list of file names or type the name in so that it appears in the File Name text box. Click on OK.

IMPORTING A TEXT FILE WITHOUT TABS   If you are preparing the data in a word processor but not using tabs to separate the different variables, use a fixed width font and ensure the data is lined up in columns in a consistent way. For example, make sure that for all respondents id is in columns 1 to 3, age is in columns 5 and 6 and so on, and also make sure the data is right-aligned. This means that if id numbers run from 1 to 100, the number 1 is put in column 3, the number 10 is put in columns 2 and 3 and the number 100 is in columns 1, 2 and 3. This is easier to do if you make all the data for any one variable the same length, so that for id 1 would be typed as 001, 10 as 010.

The text file of the data can be imported into SPSS for Windows by selecting

```
File
     Read ASCII Data
```

If the file is on a floppy disk, open the Drives drop-down list and click on the icon for drive a:. Select the file to be imported from the list of file names or type the name in so that it appears in the File Name text box. Click on the Define button. Here you have to specify the name of the variables. If the data for each case extends over more than one line you must indicate which line of the case has the variable you are defining, by entering the line number in the box marked Record. You must also indicate the columns in the ASCII file which each variable occupies. (In salesq for example, id is in columns 1–2, sex in column 4 and so on.) The type of data must be specified in Data Type. (For the beginner, the default Numeric, as is, will be appropriate but other types are available in the drop-down list.) Then click on the Add button, and the informa-tion you have provided will appear in the Defined Variables list.

When you have entered the specifications for all the variables, click on OK. The file will be read and the data will appear in the Data Editor window: before you do anything else, check that the data is as you expected!

5.11 Transferring data files to/from other packages such as Excel

Data files can be saved in a number of formats so they can be read by other packages such as Excel, Lotus, dBase. The options are offered when

you select File /Save As for a data file and open the drop-down menu
Save File as Type. Similarly, data files from these other packages can be
read into SPSS for Windows. This is extremely useful, since you can
prepare the data in a program such as Excel and do not need a computer
with SPSS installed.

If you are preparing the data in MSWorks or Excel, ensure the
spreadsheet file is saved in the format for Excel 4 or lower, not Excel 5 or
7. SPSS version 6 will not read Excel 5 or 7 files.

When preparing the spreadsheet file of the data, you can put variable
names into the first row of the sheet and these can then be imported and
will form the column names in the SPSS file.

When you have an Excel 4 file to import, select

```
File
    Open
        Data
```

The usual dialogue box is presented. Open the drop-down list of file
types and select Excel, and open the Drives drop-down list and select the
icon for drive a:. Enter the name of the Excel file into the File Name text
box either by typing it in or by selecting it from the file list. If the Excel
file contains only the data, clicking on OK will load the file into SPSS. If
you have written the variable names into the first row of the Excel table,
check the option Read variable names in the Options section of the
dialogue box before clicking OK. The data will be imported into SPSS
with the variable names already assigned.

Whenever importing data from another package, check the data
carefully so that you can be sure the transfer has been accurate and
complete.

5.12 Printing the data file

Check the window to be printed is the active window and select

```
File
    Print . . .
```

from the Application window menu bar. The Print dialogue box will
appear, with the name of the file to be printed in the title bar. By default,
one copy of the whole file will be printed. To print more than one copy,
type in the number required in the Copies box. Click on OK.

If you do not want the grid lines printed, remove them from the Data
Editor window before you select File /Print. With the data editor active,
select Utilities /Grid Lines from the Application Window menu, and the
dialogue box gives you the option of suppressing these lines.

If you have assigned value labels to the data so that, for example, a value of 1 in the variable sex has the label 'male' and value 2 has the label 'female', you can have these labels printed instead of the numbers when you print out the file. To do this, ensure the Data Editor is the active window, and select Utilities / Value Labels. Then print the file as explained above.

5.13 Chapter summary

- When putting data into the Data Editor, each row of the table should contain the results from one respondent or case.
- Always have id (identification number of the case) as the first variable.
- Rows or columns can be inserted anywhere in the table.
- To save the file on the floppy disk, use Save As.
- Assign variable names and variable labels to the data.
- Assign value labels when appropriate (e.g. to show 1 represents 'male').
- When data is missing use Missing Values.
- Use templates for defining a number of variables.
- Ensure you can retrieve a data (.sav) file.
- Ensure you can print the data file.

MERGING DATA FILES

6.1 When do you need to merge data files?

You may find that you have two sets of data, in separate files, that you want to merge to form one file. There are two situations where this is likely to happen. First, you have collected data from a sample of respondents, and later obtain data from some more respondents which you want to add to your first set. The obvious way of doing this is to retrieve the original data file and simply add the new cases on the end, but this is not always feasible. (Perhaps you have the data from 1000 children in Mexico, and a colleague has data from 1000 children in Poland. Both of you have written a file containing the data you have collected, neither of you wants to type in another 1000 cases!) You can merge the two data files using Add Cases as described below.

The second situation where you want to merge data is when you have data from a set of respondents, and then obtain another series of responses from the same respondents. For example, imagine we surveyed 500 adults on their alcohol drinking behaviour six months ago and yesterday. We want to add the data we collected yesterday to the file of their responses of six months ago, so we can look at changes in drinking behaviour over the six month period. We are not adding new cases to our data file, only adding new data to existing cases. We could go back and add the new data to our data file, but it may be that we have the two data sets in separate files and want to merge them. For this type of situation, use Add Variables (section 6.3).

6.2 Adding cases

Suppose we have a file which contains data on additional respondents to be added to salesq, and this additional data, shown in Figure 6.1, has been saved in a file called extra.sav, with the same names for the variables as were used in salesq.

```
23 1 1 1 3 2 3 055 03800.50 010691
24 2 2 2 4 2 4 060 04780.60 030690
25 2 1 2 3 2 5 078 06782.00 040690
```

Figure 6.1   *Additional data from three respondents to be added to the data file*

To add these cases to salesq, retrieve salesq so it is in an active Data Editor window. From the menus, select

```
Data
     Merge Files
          Add Cases
```

This opens a dialogue box entitled Add Cases: Read File. Specify the file to be read (extra.sav in this example) in the File Name text box, and click on the Continue button.

This reveals another dialogue box (Add Cases From), and variables in the two data files which match are listed in the text box headed Variables in New Working Data File. So if both data files have a variable called sex, this will be listed in this box. The dialogue box also has a list of variables in a text box headed Unpaired Variables. Those variables followed by a * are present in the current, open data file, and those variables followed by a + are present in the external file (extra.sav in this example). These are variables which do not have the same name in the two files. You can make a pair of them, so a variable called sex in the current file can be matched with a variable called gender in the external file, by clicking on these two names and then on the Pair button. (If the two variable names are not adjacent, hold down Ctrl while you click on the names.) If necessary, variables in the Unpaired Variable list can be renamed by selecting them and clicking on the Rename button.

If you want the merged file to include a variable that only exists in one of the files being merged, select its name and click on the right arrow button to add it to the list of Variables in New Working Data File.

When the definition is complete, Paste the command into a syntax window and run it. A file called Newdata will appear in the Data Editor. Save this file, but before carrying out any analysis check it carefully to see that the new cases have been added accurately.

6.3 Adding scores to existing cases: Add Variables

This procedure merges two data files that contain different data on the same respondents. Imagine we have additional data for the respondents recorded in salesq: perhaps we now have their date of birth as a six-digit number like this: 050870, representing 5th August, 1970. This data has been assigned to three variables: dobd (day), dobm (month) and doby (year), and is stored in a data file (addat.sav). An example of the data for the first two respondents is:

```
01 120870
02 221070
```

We want to add this additional data on each respondent to the salesq file. First, the data in both files must have been sorted into the same order on the key variable which will be used to ensure the data is assigned to the correct case: this is one reason for having identification numbers (id) in data files such as salesq. Having sorted both salesq and addat.sav by id, ensure one of the files is in the active Data Editor. (Assume for this explanation that salesq is the active file.) From the menu select

```
Data
    Merge Files
        Add Variables
```

Enter the name of the other file (addat.sav in this example) in the File Name text box. Then click on Continue.

Any variables which appear in either of the data files are shown in the New Working Data File list of the dialogue box entitled Add Variables From. Those variables followed by a * are present in the current, open data file and those variables followed by a + are present in the external file (addat.sav in this example). Any variables which appear in both of the data files are shown in the Excluded Variables list, since one does not want them to appear twice in the merged file.

If the second file (addat.sav) has data on every case in the current file (salesq), you can click on Paste and run the syntax. The two sets of data will be merged and seen in the Data Editor window. Save the data file and check it carefully for accuracy before analysing it.

If the external file (addat.sav) does not have data for every one of the cases in the current file (salesq), see the next section.

6.4 Add Variables with incomplete data

Suppose we have a set of additional data, the marital status of some of the respondents in salesq. The variable is named as marst, and 1 means unmarried, 2 is married. The data is shown in Figure 6.2, the first two digits being the respondent's id (identification number). This data has been saved in a data file called marry.sav.

Marry.sav has scores on marst for five respondents. (Note that in marry.sav the respondents are not in the same order as in the original data file; this is so you see how to cope with this situation.)

When one merges the data from the two files, it is obviously essential that the data from marry.sav is added to the appropriate persons in

```
06  1
03  2
05  2
18  1
11  2
```

Figure 6.2 *Additional data on the respondents to be added to the data file*

salesq. There must be some way of identifying which lines from salesq match which lines from marry.sav, and in this example the variable id, referred to as a key variable, lets us do that because id is included in both the data files.

The key variable must have the same name in both files, but you can if necessary use the Rename facility to bring this situation about by clicking on the variable name in the list of variables and then on the Rename button in the Add Variables From dialogue box. Then ensure that both data files have the cases sorted on the key variable (id, in this example); if necessary, retrieve each file, sort the data and then save the file.

Once the files have been sorted on the key variable, the procedure for matching salesq and marry.sav is to select from the menu

```
Data
    Merge Files
        Add Variables
```

When faced with the Add Variables From dialogue box, click on the key variable name (id in our example) in the Excluded Variables list, click the button entitled Match cases on key variables in sorted files and then enter the key variable into the Key Variables text box by clicking on the right arrow button. Then click on Paste.

When the syntax is run, the files will be merged and the new merged set of data will appear in the Data Editor window where you can inspect it to ensure the data has been matched correctly. Then save the new file.

6.5 Chapter summary

Use Merge Files when you have sets of data from different respondents in separate files that you want to merge to form one file or when you want to merge additional data for the same respondents which has been stored in a separate file.

RUNNING A SIMPLE ANALYSIS AND OBTAINING THE OUTPUT

7.1 Setting output page length, page width and inserting commands in output

SPSS is set up so that it assumes that you are using a non-A4 page, and it is sensible to alter the settings to the paper size you are actually using, which will usually be A4. SPSS is very prolific with paper, and will waste a huge amount by inserting page breaks at very frequent intervals. While you are carrying out analyses you can save a few trees by turning off this wasteful feature. Furthermore, if you are going to use a word processor to format and print the output files, it is wise to set the page width of the output to an appropriate amount.

The output from SPSS often contains tables, and these have borders made up of either lines or typewriter characters; if your printer cannot deal with lines (you find that unexpected characters such as lines of 'd's or '3's appear), you need to set the border to be typewriter characters. How to set these features is explained below.

It is extremely useful, when you are trying to follow a series of complicated tables and statistics, to have the output contain the commands used to obtain it. To have the commands inserted in the output, use Edit /Preferences as described below.

Select from the menu of the application window

```
Edit
     Preferences
```

This presents the dialogue box shown in Figure 7.1. Press the Output button in the bottom right and the Preferences: Output window shown in Figure 7.2 will be revealed. To have the commands printed in the output as they are processed, check the entry Commands in the area headed Display. To stop SPSS inserting page breaks in the output, set the page length to 'Infinite' by selecting that option in the area headed Page

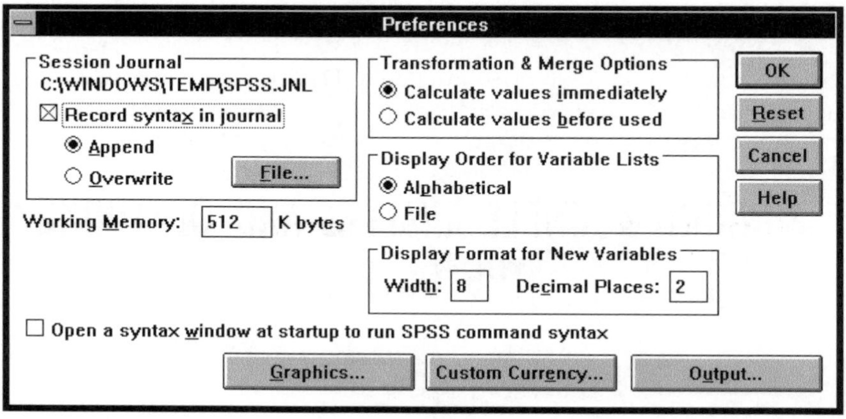

Figure 7.1   The Edit /Preferences dialogue box

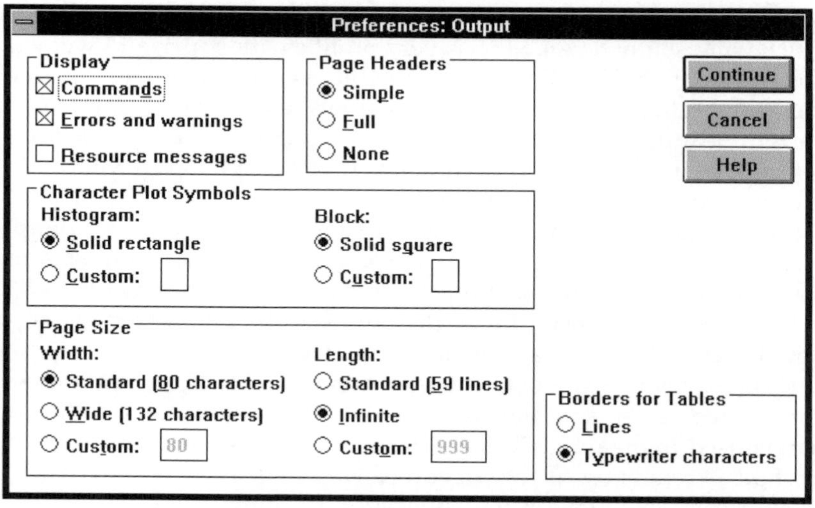

Figure 7.2   The Preferences: Output window for setting page length and width

Size. If you want to set the page length to A4 paper, click on the Custom option in Page Size and type 70 into the text box beside it. To alter the page width from the default value, select the Custom option and type in a figure for the width of the page. The width is measured in characters, and a full width is 80. If you want the borders of output tables to be typewriter characters, select that option in the area headed Borders for Tables.

7.2 Using the menus to analyse the data

Once you have a data file open (an active Data Editor window containing data) and have decided which analyses you require, you are ready to run SPSS. Most of the analyses can be obtained by selecting from the menus in the Application window.

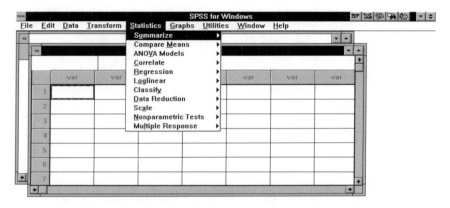

Figure 7.3 *The Statistics drop-down menu*

Clicking on the Application window Statistics menu reveals the drop-down menu shown in Figure 7.3 with some or all of these options:

```
Summarize
Compare Means
ANOVA Models
Correlate
Regression
Loglinear
Classify
Data Reduction
Scale
Nonparametric Tests
Multiple Response
```

Each entry has an arrowhead to show that there is another menu which can be obtained by clicking on the entry or by pressing the key of the underlined letter. The analyses under these headings are described later in this book except for those under the Loglinear and the Classify entries. Classify leads to discriminant analysis.

The Summarize entry, for example, has a submenu containing these entries:

```
Frequencies ...
Descriptives ...
Explore ...
Crosstabs ...

List Cases ...
Report Summaries in Rows ...
```

The . . . indicates that if you select that entry, a dialogue box will be revealed in which you enter more details about the analysis you want.

Exercise 7.1

We want to find out for the data in the data file salesq.sav the number of males and females and the number of people from each area, i.e. we want to know how many cases there are for each level of the variable sex and for each level of the variable area. This information is obtained using the Frequencies procedure. So click on Statistics /Summarize /Frequencies, and a dialogue box (Figure 7.4) will appear.

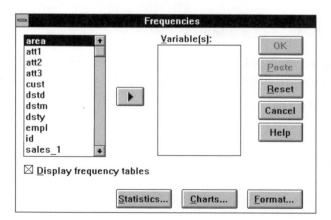

Figure 7.4   *The dialogue box for Frequencies*

Dialogue boxes for the statistical procedures have a common format. In the left-hand box, which has no title but is known as the source variable list, there is a list of the variables in the data file; the variable

---

names are those which are given at the top of the columns in the Data Editor, so will be var00001, var00002, etc. unless you have assigned variable names as explained in section 5.5.

You have to tell SPSS which variables you want analysed. To do this, select each variable by clicking on its name, which will then be highlighted. Then click on the button marked with a right-pointing arrow, and the variable will appear in the right-hand box, the one headed Variable(s). Select whichever variables you want to analyse in this way. If you want to select a number of variables, you can use the drag method of selecting a set in one movement; pressing on the arrow button will transfer the names of all the variables in the set to the Variable(s) box.

If you make a mistake, and have selected a variable you do not want to analyse, you remove it from the Variable(s) box by clicking on it; the arrow on the arrow button will become a left-pointing one, and clicking on that will remove the highlighted variable from the list and return it to the left-hand box.

In our example, click on sex in the left-hand box and then on the right-pointing arrow; then click on area in the left-hand box and on the right-pointing arrow again. The variable names sex and area will appear in the Variables(s) box.

Now click on the OK button at the top right of the dialogue box. (For the moment ignore the other buttons down the right-hand side and along the bottom of the dialogue box.) The FREQUENCIES procedure will run, and a message to this effect will appear briefly in the status bar at the bottom of the Application window. The results will appear in the output window, !Output1. It is as simple as that!

The result of running this example is shown in Figure 7.5. The table shows the frequency of males, females and sex unknown (missing),

```
SEX
                                                    Valid     Cum
Value Label             Value  Frequency  Percent   Percent   Percent
male                      1        10       45.5     47.6      47.6
female                    2        11       50.0     52.4     100.0
                          3         1        4.5     Missing
                                   -------  -------  -------
                        Total      22      100.0    100.0

Valid cases    21     Missing cases    1

- - - - - - - - - - - - - - - - - - - - - - - - - - - - - -
AREA
                                                    Valid     Cum
Value Label             Value  Frequency  Percent   Percent   Percent
North                     1         9       40.9     40.9      40.9
South                     2        13       59.1     59.1     100.0
                                   -------  -------  -------
                        Total      22      100.0    100.0

Valid cases    22     Missing cases    0
```

Figure 7.5 *Output from running Frequencies for sex and area on the data in salesq.sav*

corresponding to values 1, 2 and 3 on the variable sex. It also shows the frequency of each level (1 and 2) on the variable area. (Further explanation of the output from Frequencies is provided in section 14.1.) You can scroll the output, using the scroll bars on the right-hand side of the Output window.

Exercise 7.2

Now try a second example, to obtain the mean and standard deviation of the number of customer visits (the variable is labelled cust) for the data in salesq. Means can also be obtained via the Frequencies procedure, so select from the Application window

```
Statistics
      Summarize
            Frequencies
```

The dialogue box may still have sex and area listed in the Variable(s) box. Remove them by clicking on them and pressing the left-pointing arrow button. Select cust from the source variable list, and click on the right-pointing area so that cust appears in the Variable(s) box.

  To obtain the means using Frequencies, you need to request them by clicking on the button labelled Statistics . . . at the bottom left of the dialogue box, which reveals another dialogue box illustrated in Figure 7.6. This is where you indicate the statistics you want: click on the word Mean in the area labelled Central Tendency, and on the words Std. deviation in the area labelled Dispersion. As you click on these, the small squares next to the words will have a cross put into them to show they have been selected. If you click on the wrong thing, just click on wrongly-selected item and the cross will be removed from its indicator square to show it is not selected. (Clicking the Cancel button will cancel all the selections you have made and take you back up one level, to the Frequencies dialogue box.) Now click on Continue in the upper right of the dialogue box, and you will be returned to the Frequencies dialogue box; click on the OK button. The Frequencies procedure will run, the results again appearing in the !Output! window. The output is illustrated in Figure 7.7; the mean and standard deviation of the data on the cust variable are shown after the frequency table.

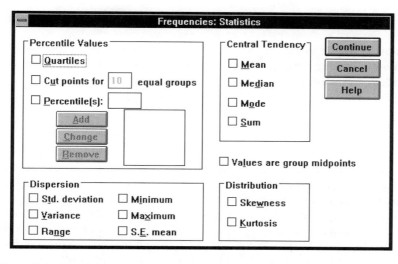

Figure 7.6 *The dialogue box for indicating the statistics required under Frequencies*

```
CUST        Number customer visits
```

Value Label	Value	Frequency	Percent	Valid Percent	Cum Percent
	28	1	4.5	4.5	4.5
	30	1	4.5	4.5	9.1
	33	1	4.5	4.5	13.6
	36	1	4.5	4.5	18.2
	38	1	4.5	4.5	22.7
	39	2	9.1	9.1	31.8
	40	1	4.5	4.5	36.4
	41	1	4.5	4.5	40.9
	42	1	4.5	4.5	45.5
	43	1	4.5	4.5	50.0
	46	1	4.5	4.5	54.5
	48	2	9.1	9.1	63.6
	58	1	4.5	4.5	68.2
	60	1	4.5	4.5	72.7
	68	1	4.5	4.5	77.3
	71	1	4.5	4.5	81.8
	72	1	4.5	4.5	86.4
	76	1	4.5	4.5	90.9
	79	1	4.5	4.5	95.5
	83	1	4.5	4.5	100.0
	Total	22	100.0	100.0	

```
Mean          50.818      Std dev        17.012
Valid cases      22       Missing cases       0
```

Figure 7.7 *Output from running Frequencies for cust on the data in salesq.sav with mean and standard deviation requested*

7.3 Pausing the output

When output is generated, it scrolls through the output window, but clicking on the Pause button in the output window menu bar will suspend the scrolling. To return to scrolling, click on the Scroll button.

7.4 Sending the output to a different output window

When SPSS for Windows starts, it always creates an output window entitled !Output, and the results of any analysis will be put in that window. You can open another output window, by selecting

```
File
    New
        SPSS Output
```

A number of output windows can be open simultaneously, but only one of them, known as the designated window, can receive output. You know which is the designated window because it has an exclamation mark before the title in the title bar. To make an output window the designated window, ensure it is active by clicking in it. If you are using SPSSv6 click on the ! button in the second line of the window; if you are using SPSSv6.1, click on the ! icon button in the icon bar (it is immediately to the left of the run button). Any fresh output that you generate will be appended to the bottom of the file in the currently-designated output window.

7.5 Saving an output file

SAVING THE OUTPUT FILE FOR THE FIRST TIME   As you have seen, the output is displayed in an output window. By default, this will be saved on the hard disk when you leave SPSS, with the name Output1.LST. It is almost always more convenient to save it on a floppy. Check that the output window is active and select from the Application window menu bar

```
File
    Save As . . .
```

The dialogue box you will see is similar to that for saving the data file. Enter the name of the file into the File Name box, ensuring that it has the extension .LST. Open the Drives drop-down list and click on the icon for drive a:. Click on the OK button.

SAVING A PREVIOUSLY SAVED OUTPUT FILE AFTER EDITING IT   Any changes you make to an output file you have retrieved from disk will be lost unless you save the file. Ensure the window is active and select from the Application window

```
File
```

To save the current version of the file, overwriting previous ones, select

Save SPSS Output

The new version will be saved on the same drive from which it was retrieved.

To save the current version while keeping the previous one, select

Save As . . .

which will present the Save As !Output dialogue box. Type in a new name for the output file in the File Name text box; remember it must not be more than eight characters before the full stop, must not contain a blank space and must end in .lst. To save the file on the floppy disk, open the Drives drop-down list and click on the icon for drive a:. Click on the OK button.

SAVING A PART OF THE OUTPUT FILE If you want to save just a portion of the text output file, highlight the area to be saved, using the click/drag procedure. Then go through the steps explained above for saving an output file. You will be asked to confirm that you want to save only the marked area; click on Yes to do so. If you click on No, the whole file will be saved.

7.6 Editing the contents of the output window

Although you may find it simplest to edit a .LST file by loading it into a word processor as explained in section 7.8 below, there are facilities for editing within SPSS. To insert new material, click the mouse cursor at the point where you want to begin, and start typing. To overwrite the existing text, the procedure is the same except that the Insert mode must be off: press the Ins key on the keyboard, and the cursor will change to a black rectangle. To return to Insert mode, just press the Ins key again.

A block of text can be marked with the click/drag procedure, and the marked block can then be copied or deleted (transferred to the Clipboard), and pasted elsewhere in the document. When you have marked the block of text, select Edit from the menu bar of the Application window. To delete the marked block, click on Cut. To make a copy of the marked block, click on Copy. To insert a copy of the marked block, move the cursor to the point where you want it inserted, and then select Edit and click on Paste.

You can carry out a Search /Replace procedure by selecting Edit /Search or Edit /Replace from the application window.

7.7 Printing output files from SPSS

When you have completed your analysis you may decide to load the output file into a word processor and print it from there: this is a procedure I strongly recommend, and explain in section 7.9 below. But there are bound to be times when you want to print the output from SPSS.

PRINTING THE WHOLE FILE   Check the window to be printed is the active window and from the Application window menu bar select

```
File
     Print . . .
```

The Print dialogue box will appear, with the name of the file to be printed in the title bar. By default, one copy of the whole file will be printed; to print more than one copy, type in the number required in the Copies box. Click on OK

PRINTING PART OF THE FILE   Before selecting the File /Print menu, highlight the area to be printed using the click/drag technique. Then select File /Print from the Application window menu bar. When the Print dialogue box appears, confirm that the Selection radio button is selected: click on OK.

7.8 Loading .lst files into a word processor

Output files are simple text files and can be loaded into a word processor directly. For example, if you are using Microsoft Word, you use the normal File /Open procedure and tell Word to list All Files (*.*) from the List Files of Type drop-down list. Files with the suffix .lst will then be shown in the set of file names and can be selected for opening.

There are two points to remember. First, by default, SPSS output is designed to use a full page width, so you will need to set the margins of the page as narrow as possible. Until you do this many of the lines will run on to the next, and this can produce screens which are very difficult to interpret. Second, you need to ensure that the whole document is formatted with a fixed-width font such as Courier or Roman 10cpi (not Times Roman). Until you do this the columns of figures will not line up and the output will be untidy and potentially misleading. An example of output from SPSS imported into Word before and after making these formatting changes is shown in Figure 7.8 so you can see the difference.

7.9 Printing output files from a word processor

By loading an output file into a word processor, as explained in section 7.8, you gain all the extra facilities of the word processing package for

Before applying a fixed width typeface

Value Label	Value	Frequency	Percent	Valid Percent	Cum Percent
Strongly Agree	I	3	13.6	13.6	13.6
Uncertain	3	7	31.8	31.8	45.5
Disagree	4	9	40.9	40.9	86.4
Strongly Disagree	5	3	13.6	13.6	100.0
Total		22	100.0	100.0	

The output shown above with a fixed width typeface

```
                                            Valid      Cum
Value Label          Value  Frequency  Percent  Percent  Percent
Strongly Agree         1        3        13.6    13.6     13.6
Uncertain              3        7        31.8    31.8     45.5
Disagree               4        9        40.9    40.9     86.4
Strongly Disagree      5        3        13.6    13.6    100.0
                               -------  -------  -------  -------
            Total               22       100.0   100.0
```

Figure 7.8 *Example of output imported into a word processor before and after changing the margins and font*

formatting the output so you can get it exactly as you wish. You can then print the file as you would any other word processor file.

Once the output .LST file has been loaded into a word processor it can be saved in the format of the word processing program. So you can load a file called may5.lst into a program such as Microsoft Word and then save it as may5lst.doc.

7.10 Retrieving an output file from the floppy disk

To retrieve a saved .LST file, it has to be opened in an output window by selecting from the Application window menu bar

```
File
    Open
        SPSS Output
```

The Open Output dialogue box will be presented. If the file you want is on your floppy disk, open the Drives drop-down list and click on the icon for drive a:. All files with the .LST filename extension will be listed in the file list on the left-hand side. If necessary, you can scroll down the list. Click on the name of the file you want, so that its name appears in the File Name text box, and then on the OK button. The file you have retrieved will be displayed in an output window.

7.11 Modifying the source list of variables in dialogue boxes

It is possible to modify the variables shown in the source lists of the dialogue boxes, and the order in which they are listed. Initially, the

variables are shown in the source list of the dialogue boxes in alpha-
betical order. You can ask for them to be listed in the order in which they
occur in the data file if you select Edit /Preferences and click on the File
radio button. Note that if you do alter the display order, the alteration
will not take effect until you open a data file.

When you have a very lengthy set of variables in the data file, it can be
convenient to restrict those which are presented in the source list in the
dialogue boxes. This can be done using Utilities /Define Sets from
the application window menu bar. Give the set a name, specify the
variables to be included in a set, and then click the Add Set button to
create it. To have this newly created set used in the dialogue boxes, select
Utilities /Use Sets, enter the name of the new set in the Sets in Use list
and remove from the list the ALLVARIABLES entry.

You can change the order in which variables are listed in the target lists
by clicking on the name of the variable to be moved and then clicking on
the control box in the top left of the dialogue box menu bar: options to
Move Selection Up and Move Selection Down are offered.

7.12 Changing fonts and type style

The facility for altering screen fonts is available by selecting from the
Application window

```
Utilities
     Fonts
```

The dialogue box allows you to specify the typeface, type size, and
whether you want bold or italic or both. When you have made the
appropriate selections, click on the OK button.

7.13 Adding a title to each page of the output file

SPSS puts a heading at each page of the output file. You can add to or
replace the headings by selecting

```
Utilities
     Output Page Title
```

This produces a box allowing you to type in the page title and page
subtitle you want. You can use a heading which indicates what the
content of the output file is, and this is especially useful if you are
sharing a printer, as you can have your own name put on the pages of
your output. Note that your title and subtitle can contain either inverted
commas or apostrophes, not both.

7.14 Rounding numbers in the output

The output may show more decimal places than you want. You can modify the output display and round the numbers using the Round button. First, choose

```
Edit
    Round
```

from the application window and enter the number of decimal places you want in the text window of the dialogue box revealed. Select that part of the output where you want the figures to be rounded using the click/drag technique and then press Round. This has the effect of rounding the numbers in the selected area. If you click on the Truncate button in the output window, the numbers will be shorn of their decimals but not rounded, so 4.7 would become 4.

7.15 On-screen help on statistical terms

You may come across statistical terms in the output of your analyses which you do not understand or have temporarily forgotten. You can obtain an explanation of them by using the Glossary, which is accessed in two alternative ways. One method is to select Help /Glossary from the Application window menu. The other is to select the Glossary button from the output window. Either procedure will open the Glossary. You can scroll through the file (a tedious process unless you just want to browse), or you click on the Search button in the menu bar and enter the phrase for which you want an explanation.

7.16 Chapter summary

- Before starting any analysis set the output page length and page width. Instruct SPSS to insert commands in the output.
- Most of the analyses can be obtained by selecting from the Statistics menu in the Application window.
- The designated output window has an exclamation mark before the title. Make any output window the designated window by clicking on the ! button.
- Confirm you can save an output file on a floppy disk.
- When printing an output file from a word processor, format it with a fixed width typeface and set the margins as narrow as possible.
- Modify the source list of variables in dialogue boxes to fit your needs.
- Add an appropriate title to each page of the output file.
- Use the Glossary to obtain on-screen help on statistical terms.

8

SYNTAX FILES

If you have followed the exercises in chapter 7, you carried out a simple analysis by selecting commands from the menu and clicking on OK. But I strongly urge you not to do that again! It is far better to store the commands in a syntax window and run them from there.

8.1 What is a syntax file?

A syntax file is a file containing the commands for the analyses you have requested expressed in SPSS's language. There are a number of reasons for always creating a syntax file of the commands you have selected. First, it gives you a record of the analyses you requested. This is especially useful if the output is not what you expected because you made an error in selecting from the menus. Secondly, if you need to run an analysis again you do not have to go through the menus a second time; you can run the commands from the syntax window. Thirdly, by saving the syntax window as a separate file you have a permanent copy to use again whenever you like. A further benefit of syntax files is that when you know the SPSS language for the analyses you want you can write the SPSS commands using a normal word processor, save them in text file form, import them into a syntax window and run them: so one can do the preparatory work even on a machine that does not have SPSS installed.

If you carried out the simple analyses contained in the previous chapter, you may have noticed that the dialogue box for the Frequencies procedure has a button labelled Paste. All the dialogue boxes which are used for selecting an analysis have a Paste button, and you are most strongly urged to use them every time you use SPSS. Pressing the Paste button pastes the SPSS language command for the procedure you have selected into a separate window, the syntax window. When you first start a session with SPSS, there is no syntax window, but the first time you press Paste one is opened and the command you have created from your menu selections is pasted into it. As you make further menu selections and press Paste, the commands are added to the bottom of the set that already exists in the syntax window. Get in the habit of pressing Paste rather than OK!

8.2 Entering commands in a syntax window using Paste

When you have selected items from the on-screen menus, paste the commands into a syntax window by using the Paste button in the dialogue box for the procedure you have selected. If no syntax window is open the first time you use Paste, one is automatically opened to receive the commands you are pasting. Subsequent uses of Paste add the current commands to the syntax window, appending them to the existing contents. If you want to start pasting into a second syntax window, you need to open a new one and make it the designated syntax window by pressing the ! button or icon. The syntax window can be saved as a file and edited.

Exercise 8.1

Repeat Exercise 7.1 from chapter 7 but, instead of pressing OK in the dialogue box, press Paste. The SPSS language for the Frequencies procedure will be pasted into a syntax window. If you are using SPSS version 6, the syntax window is as shown in Figure 8.1. If you are using SPSS version 6.1, the syntax window is as shown in Figure 8.2.

Try running the command. Make sure the cursor is in the line containing the word FREQUENCIES. If you are using SPSS 6, click on the Run button in the syntax window. If you are using SPSS 6.1, click on the Run icon button in the application window icon bar; it has an arrow in the lower right corner. SPSS will carry out the command and produce the output shown in Figure 7.5 in chapter 7.

8.3 Structure of procedure commands

All commands must start on a new line, and must end in a full stop (period). So in Figure 8.2, the command starts with the word FRE-QUENCIES and continues as far as the full stop. Although there are two lines of text, this is one command. Subcommands are used to specify how the procedure (FREQUENCIES in Figure 8.2) should operate. For example, VARIABLES=sales is a subcommand which indicates that the

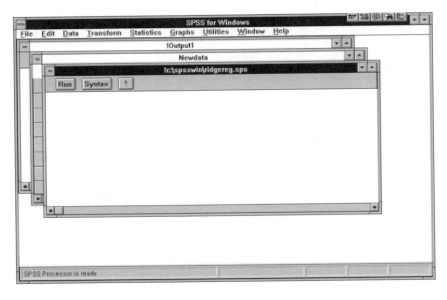

Figure 8.1   *The syntax window for SPSS version 6*

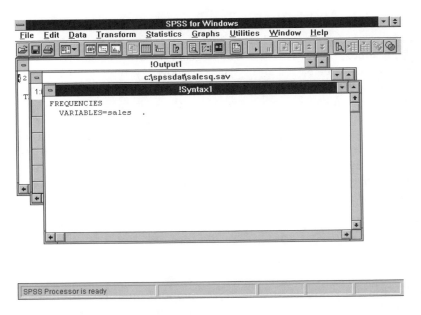

Figure 8.2   *The syntax window for SPSS version 6.1*

procedure should be applied to the variable sales in the data set. Subcommands are separated (usually) by the / character.

8.4 Running the commands from a syntax window

The benefit of a syntax file is that you can run all or some of the commands it contains directly, without having to go through the process of making menu selections again. An example of a syntax window containing a series of commands is shown in Figure 8.3. To identify the commands to run, select them with the click/drag procedure (or from the keyboard by holding down shift and using the up/down arrow keys), so they are highlighted, and then click on the Run button. If you want to run all the commands, the whole file can be selected using the Application window's Edit /Select All option and then clicking the Run button. To run just one command, put the cursor anywhere in the line containing the command and click on Run.

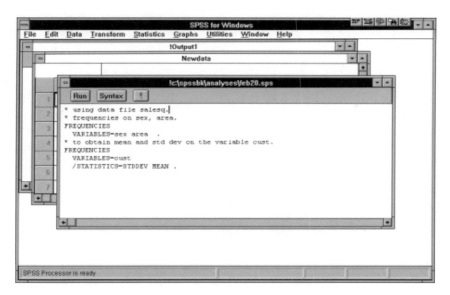

Figure 8.3   *Example of a syntax window containing a series of commands and comment lines*

8.5 Saving the syntax window as a syntax file

SAVING THE SYNTAX FILE FOR THE FIRST TIME   To save the contents of the syntax window as a file on a floppy, check that the window is active and select from the Application window menu bar

```
File
     Save As . . .
```

The dialogue box presented, Save SPSS Syntax as:, is similar to that for saving data or output files. Type the name of the file into the File Name box, ensuring that it has the extension .SPS. Open the Drives drop-down list and click on the icon for the a: drive. Click on the OK button.

SAVING A PREVIOUSLY SAVED SYNTAX FILE AFTER EDITING IT   Any changes you make to a syntax file will be lost unless you save the file. Ensure the window is active and select from the Application window

```
File
```

To save the current version of the file, overwriting previous ones, select

```
Save SPSS Syntax
```

The new version will be saved on the same drive from which it was retrieved.

To save the current version while keeping the previous one, select

```
Save As . . .
```

which will present the Save SPSS Syntax As dialogue box. Type in a new name for the file; remember it must not be more than eight characters and must not contain a blank space. Check that the name has the .SPS extension, or add it by typing it in. Open the Drives drop-down list and click on the icon for the a: drive. Click on the OK button.

8.6 Retrieving a saved syntax file from disk

To retrieve an existing syntax file, select

```
File
    Open
        SPSS Syntax
```

A dialogue box will appear, showing files with the .SPS filename extension. If the file is on a floppy disk, open the Drives drop-down list and click on the icon for the a: drive. The files on the floppy which have the filename extension .sps will appear in the list of files. Click on the name of the file you want to open, check that its name appears in the File Name text box, and click on the OK button.

8.7 Opening another syntax window

The first time you use a Paste button, a syntax window is opened automatically. But you can open a new (empty) one by selecting from the Application window menu

```
File
    New
        SPSS Syntax
```

You can have more than one syntax window open at one time, but, as with output files, only one can be the 'designated' window to which commands are pasted, and from which commands can be run. You know which is the designated window because it has an exclamation mark before the title in the title bar. To make a syntax window the designated window, ensure it is active by clicking in it. If you are using SPSSv6 click on the ! button in the second line of the window; if you are using SPSSv6.1, click on the ! icon button in the icon bar (it is immediately to the left of the run button). Any fresh pastings of syntax will be appended to the bottom of the currently-designated window.

8.8 Transferring syntax files to a word processor

Syntax files are, like output .lst files, simple text files. So a syntax .sps file prepared in SPSS can be loaded into a word processor and reformatted and printed from there. After loading into the word processor, ensure it is in a fixed-width font such as Courier.

8.9 Loading a text file into a syntax window

You can type SPSS syntax using a word processor, and save the file in text format. Such a text file can be imported into SPSS, so that if you are familiar with the exact syntax you can prepare your syntax file on a machine that does not have SPSS installed. When using a word processor, each line of data or commands must be ended with a carriage return, and the file must be saved as an ASCII file.

Assume you have written a text file of SPSS syntax and stored it on a floppy disk with the filename syn.txt. To load it into SPSS, select from the Application window menu bar

```
File
    Open
        SPSS Syntax
```

When the dialogue box appears, open the Drives drop-down list and click on the icon for the a: drive. Type the name of the file (syn.txt) in the File Name text box, and click on OK. The file will then appear in a syntax window.

8.10 Entering commands in a syntax window by typing

You can edit the contents of a syntax window just like any other text file, and type straight into it. This is beneficial to those who are familiar with the command language of SPSS, but if you are not experienced with SPSS be careful when trying to create commands directly. The syntax of commands is not simple, and there are a number of rules you must follow. For example, all command lines must start on a new line, and must end in a full stop (period). Subcommands are separated (usually) by /.

To enter the names of variables in the commands in the syntax window, you can readily type them in. Or you can use the Variables dialogue box which is obtained from the Utilities /Variables menu of the Application window. This displays a dialogue box and you can select a variable from the list in the left-hand side of the box. Information about the variable appears in the right-hand window. If the Paste button at the bottom of the window is clicked, the highlighted variable name is pasted into the syntax window at the point where the cursor was located. This is rather laborious, and most users will probably find this method not worth the effort.

Exercise 8.2

Try editing the contents of the syntax window created in Exercise 8.1 so that you obtain a Frequencies analysis of the data on the variable att1. To do this, make sure the syntax window is the active one, move the cursor (using the mouse) so it is to the right of the words sex area and click the mouse to anchor the insertion point. Use the backspace Delete key to delete these words and type in att1 in their place. Then select the whole file by selecting Edit /Select All from the Application window menus, and click on the Run button. SPSS should then run the commands and give you in the !Output1 window the results of applying the frequencies procedure to the variable att1.

8.11 Typing comments into the syntax window

It is always worthwhile adding comments to the syntax so that later you will be reminded of what a particular procedure achieves. For example, you might want to add the explanatory comment that the command calculates the mean for a certain variable.

Add comments to the syntax by typing them in, but make sure that the line begins with an asterisk * and ends with a full stop. An acceptable comment line would be

```
* This calculates mean on cust.
```

If you omit either the * or the full stop, SPSS will not understand and will give you an error message when you try to run the syntax window's contents.

8.12 Help on syntax: the Syntax button in a syntax window

When you are using a syntax window, pressing the Syntax button will provide help information about the procedure on the current line of the syntax file. The syntax button is included in the syntax window in SPSS version 6.0. In version 6.1, it is in the icon bar just left of centre. The help information can be highly complex, consisting of material from the SPSS technical manuals, and is likely to be meaningful only to those who have a thorough understanding of SPSS commands. Nevertheless, you may find it valuable once you have developed some expertise with the package. So do try using the facility, but do not be depressed if the result is not very helpful.

8.13 Printing syntax files

As a syntax file is a simple text file it can be loaded into a word processor and printed from there. But to print it from SPSS, check the window to be printed is the active window and select from the Application window menu bar

```
File
    Print
```

The Print dialogue box will appear, with the name of the file to be printed in the title bar. By default, one copy of the whole file will be printed. To print more than one copy, type in the number required in the Copies box. Click on OK.

PRINTING PART OF THE FILE Before selecting the File /Print menu, highlight the area to be printed using the click/drag technique. Then select File /Print from the Application window menu bar. When the Print dialogue box appears, check that the Selection radio button is selected and click on OK.

8.14 Altering the page size for printing

To omit page breaks so you get just one continuous printing or to have the output fit A4 paper, change the page size from the dialogue box presented when you choose Edit /Preferences /Output, as explained in section 7.1.

8.15 Chapter summary

- Use the Paste button to paste commands into a syntax window.
- To run commands, select them with the click/drag procedure and click on the Run button.
- Ensure you can save the syntax window as a syntax file and retrieve a syntax file from disk.
- Add comments to the syntax by typing them in, but make sure that the line begins with an asterisk * and ends with a full stop.
- To make a syntax window the designated window, ensure it is active and click the ! button. Any fresh pastings of syntax will be appended to the bottom of the currently-designated window.

TAKING A PRELIMINARY LOOK AT THE DATA

9.1 Checking the data

Before proceeding with detailed statistical investigation, it is always worth having an overview of the data to reveal any peculiarities or possible errors in the data file. If you have coded sex as 1 for male, 2 for female, 3 for missing value (i.e. sex is unknown), then any respondent with a sex score of 8 has obviously been miscoded. It is crucial to make sure the data is correct before analysing it, and so the first step once the data file has been created is to search for possible coding errors. The SPSS procedures EXPLORE and LIST allow you to do this. The most useful is EXPLORE.

9.2 Running the analyses

If you have completed the example exercises described in previous chapters, you will be familiar with the techniques used to get SPSS for Windows to carry out an analysis:

- Select the appropriate menu (e.g. Statistics) from the menu bar to reveal a drop-down menu.
- Select the appropriate entry (Summarize, Compare Means, etc.) from the drop-down menu.
- Select the appropriate entry from the next submenu (e.g. Frequencies, Descriptives, etc.).
- When presented with a dialogue box for the procedure you are requesting, specify the variables to be analysed.
- Click on Paste to have the procedure commands you have selected pasted into a syntax window.
- Click on the Run button or icon button.
- The procedure runs (the name of the procedure appears in the status bar at the bottom of the SPSS window while this is happening), and the output appears in the !Output window.

Once you have learned how to use the various dialogue box options, the procedure should be straightforward. To alter any of the choices you made in the dialogue box, you merely have to get back to it by working through the menu selection process, and then you can change the choices you made and paste the revised commands into the syntax window. Alternatively, you can edit the commands in the syntax file by typing directly into it, as described in chapter 8.

9.3 Exploring the averages and distributions of scores using EXPLORE

NOTE: Although the EXPLORE command is selected from the menu, it is named EXAMINE in the syntax window.

The Explore procedure allows you to find the mean, median, and standard deviation of the scores on any or all of the variables. It provides you with measures of skewness in the distribution, gives box plots and shows the maximum and minimum scores so you can see if there are any aberrant values that might indicate a coding error when the data was keyed in.

The EXPLORE procedure is obtained from

```
Statistics
      Summarize
            Explore ...
```

When presented with the dialogue box illustrated in Figure 9.1, specify the variables to be analysed by adding them to the Dependent List text area and Paste the command into a syntax window. Run the procedure by clicking on the Run button or icon, to obtain a printout as shown in Figure 9.2 which Explored the variable cust in the file salesq.

Figure 9.2 shows a range of statistics including the mean, median, standard error, variance, standard deviation, minimum, maximum, range, interquartile range (IQR), and indices of skew. The 5%Trim figure is the mean of the scores when the most extreme 10% of the scores are omitted from the calculation: the highest 5% of scores and the lowest 5% of scores are both deleted before this mean is calculated. The trimmed mean can be a useful indicator of the 'average', less influenced by one or two extreme, outlying scores than the simple arithmetic mean.

The figure for skewness indicates how non-symmetric the distribution is. A positive value on kurtosis indicates that the distribution of the scores has heavier tails than a normal distribution curve. The values for both skewness and kurtosis will be close to zero if the distribution is normally distributed.

The stem-leaf plot is similar to a histogram, but numbers indicate the actual values plotted. The first column shows the number of scores in the

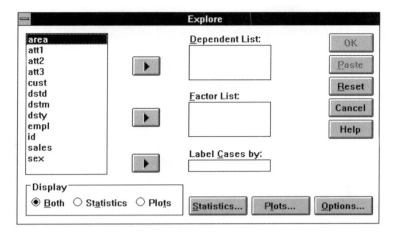

Figure 9.1   *The dialogue box for the EXPLORE procedure*

```
EXAMINE
  VARIABLES=cust
  /PLOT BOXPLOT STEMLEAF
  /COMPARE GROUP
  /STATISTICS DESCRIPTIVES
  /CINTERVAL 95
  /MISSING LISTWISE
  /NOTOTAL.


      CUST
Valid cases: 22.0    Missing cases: .0    Percent missing: .0

Mean     50.818 Std Err      3.6269 Min    28.000  Skewness    .6051
Median   44.500 Variance   289.3939 Max    83.000  S E Skew    .4910
5%Trim   50.308 Std Dev     17.0116 Range  55.000  Kurtosis -1.0005
                                    IQR    30.000  S E Kurt    .9528
-----------------------------------------------------------------
      CUST
Frequency    Stem &  Leaf

     1.00     2  .  8
     6.00     3  .  036899
     7.00     4  .  0123688
     1.00     5  .  8
     2.00     6  .  08
     4.00     7  .  1269
     1.00     8  .  3

Stem width:     10
Each leaf:       1 case(s)


Hi-Res Chart  # 1:Boxplot of cust
```

Figure 9.2   *Output from the command EXPLORE /VARIABLE cust*

band indicated by the stem. For example, the first line of the stem-leaf part of Figure 9.2 shows there was one respondent who scored in the

twenties on customers visited (the stem is 2). The actual score of this
respondent was 28 (the leaf is 8, so the actual score is 2, the stem, and 8
the leaf).

The Explore dialogue box allows you to refine the analysis further.
From the Display area of the box, you can ask for the output to show
statistics, plots (box and stem-leaf plots) or both, which is the default
option.

It is possible to have Explore display the cases with the five largest and
five smallest values on any variables, which is useful for identifying
aberrant, possibly mis-keyed items of data. After pressing the Statistics
button in the Explore dialogue box of Figure 9.1, select Outliers; an
example of the output is shown in Figure 9.3. It shows the five smallest
and five largest scores on the variable, together with the case number of
those scores. The case number is the number assigned to each case by the
system when it reads the data file; the first case is row number 1 in the
data table, the second is row number 2 and so on. The data file salesq
includes ids (identification numbers), which are for this particular set of
data the same as the case number, since they count up from 1 in regular
sequence. But many data files do not do this: the ids may not be in
sequence. Assuming you have a variable labelled id in the data file, you
can tell Explore to print the entries on the variable id by inserting id into
the Label Cases By box of the Explore dialogue box shown in Figure 9.1.

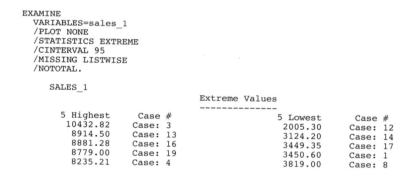

```
EXAMINE
  VARIABLES=sales_1
  /PLOT NONE
  /STATISTICS EXTREME
  /CINTERVAL 95
  /MISSING LISTWISE
  /NOTOTAL.

    SALES_1
                                        Extreme Values
                                        --------------
        5 Highest    Case #                  5 Lowest    Case #
        10432.82     Case: 3                  2005.30     Case: 12
         8914.50     Case: 13                 3124.20     Case: 14
         8881.28     Case: 16                 3449.35     Case: 17
         8779.00     Case: 19                 3450.60     Case: 1
         8235.21     Case: 4                  3819.00     Case: 8
```

Figure 9.3   *Using Explore to list outliers, the extreme scores on a variable*

To obtain further statistics, click on the Statistics button. The box
presented allows you a number of options. You can request maximum-
likelihood estimators of location such as Huber's M-estimator. Percentiles and group frequency tables are also available. Figure 9.4 illustrates
the output obtained from the Frequencies subcommand of Explore; the
subcommand detail FROM (20) BY (10) was typed into the syntax. The
scores on the variable cust have been put into categories as specified by

the subcommand detail and the number of cases in each category is shown.

```
EXAMINE
  VARIABLES=cust
  /PLOT NONE
  /FREQUENCIES FROM (20) BY (10)
  /STATISTICS DESCRIPTIVES
  /CINTERVAL 95
  /MISSING LISTWISE
  /NOTOTAL.
```

       CUST   Number customer visits

   Valid cases: 22.0   Missing cases: .0   Percent missing: .0

                              Frequency Table
                              --------- -----
                   Bin   Valid   Cum
                  Center   Freq   Pct   Pct   Pct
                    25   1.00   4.55   4.55   4.55
                    35   6.00   27.27   27.27   31.82
                    45   7.00   31.82   31.82   63.64
                    55   1.00   4.55   4.55   68.18
                    65   2.00   9.09   9.09   77.27
                    75   4.00   18.18   18.18   95.45
                    85   1.00   4.55   4.55   100.00

Figure 9.4   *Extract of output from the command EXPLORE /VARIABLES cust /FREQUENCIES FROM (20) BY (10)*

Explore will exclude from the analysis any case that has data missing on any of the variables to be explored. You can alter this by selecting the Options button of Figure 9.1; the box revealed lets you choose Exclude cases pairwise, which means that every case that has data for the variable being Explored will be included in the analysis of that variable. So the number of cases Explored for different variables will fluctuate: a case that has missing data on the variable sex will not be included in the analysis of sex, but if the same case does have data for the variable area then it will be included when that variable is Explored.

If you have cases where there is no data on the variables that make up the Factor List, these cases can be made into a separate category or group of respondents by selecting the Report Values option. Their scores on the variables being Explored will then be reported.

You may wish the scores to be analysed separately for subgroups of cases, depending on their scores on one or more of the variables. For example, in salesq, suppose we want to Explore the scores on sales_1 for men and women. Here sex is a factor variable, and we would need to have the name of this variable inserted into the Factor List text box in Figure 9.1. You can have a number of Factor variables; if sex and area are inserted into the Factor List, SPSS would Explore the scores of the variables listed in the Dependent List for each level of sex and then for each level of area. Figure 9.5 shows the output when the command was to Explore sales_1 by sex.

```
EXAMINE
  VARIABLES=sales_1 BY sex
  /PLOT BOXPLOT STEMLEAF
  /COMPARE GROUP
  /STATISTICS DESCRIPTIVES
  /CINTERVAL 95
  /MISSING LISTWISE
  /NOTOTAL.


     SALES_1
 By  SEX       1          male

Percentiles and group frequency tables are also available. Valid cases:
10.0   Missing cases:       .0   Percent missing:    .0

Mean    5950.637  Std Err   876.7274  Min    2005.300  Skewness   .2660
Median  5353.970  Variance 7686509    Max   10432.82   S E Skew   .6870
5% Trim 5920.812  Std Dev 2772.455    Range  8427.520  Kurtosis -1.2330
95% CI for Mean (3967.342, 7933.932) IQR    4678.445  S E Kurt  1.3342

Frequency    Stem &  Leaf
   5.00         0 *   23344
   4.00         0 .   5788
   1.00         1 *   0

Stem width:       10000
Each leaf:        1 case(s)

     SALES_1
 By  SEX       2          female

Valid cases:       11.0   Missing cases:      .0   Percent missing:   .0

Mean    5723.996  Std Err   629.9147  Min    3124.200  Skewness   .3965
Median  5822.680  Variance  4364717   Max    8881.280  S E Skew   .6607
5% Trim 5693.025  Std Dev 2089.191    Range  5757.080  Kurtosis -1.2753
95% CI for Mean (4320.459, 7127.534) IQR    4047.340  S E Kurt  1.2794

Frequency    Stem &  Leaf
   3.00         3 .   148
   2.00         4 .   25
   2.00         5 .   88
   1.00         6 .   4
   1.00         7 .   8
   2.00         8 .   78

Stem width:       1000
Each leaf:        1 case(s)


 Hi-Res Chart  # 4:Boxplot of sales_1 by sex
```

Figure 9.5   *Extracts of output from the command EXPLORE /VARIABLES sales_1 BY sex*

From menus, you cannot ask for separate analyses of subgroups defined by combining scores on separate Factor variables: so you cannot get an analysis broken down into men from one area, men from the second area, women from the first area and women from the second area. To achieve this, you have to paste the command into a syntax file, and then edit it so that it separates the factor variables with the word BY. If we wanted the scores on sales_1 to be analysed for each sex subdivided by area, the syntax file command would have to read:

EXAMINE VARIABLES=sales_1 BY sex BY area.

9.4 Obtaining boxplots of score distributions from EXPLORE

A boxplot such as that shown in Figure 9.6 summarizes the scores on a variable by displaying the median (as a line), the 25th and 75th percentiles as the lower and upper edges of a box surrounding the median. The box length represents the interquartile range of the scores. Outliers are any cases which are between 1.5 and 3 boxlengths from the edge of the box, and Extremes are more than 3 boxlengths away. Lines are drawn from the edge of the box to the largest and smallest values which are not outliers.

A boxplot allows you to make a number of 'eye-ball' judgements about the distribution of the scores. The median is the indicator of the central value, and the length of the box indicates the variability of the scores. If the median is not in the middle of the box, the distribution of scores is skewed.

```
EXAMINE
  VARIABLES=cust BY sex
  /PLOT BOXPLOT STEMLEAF HISTOGRAM
  /COMPARE GROUP
  /STATISTICS DESCRIPTIVES
  /CINTERVAL 95
  /MISSING LISTWISE
  /NOTOTAL.
```

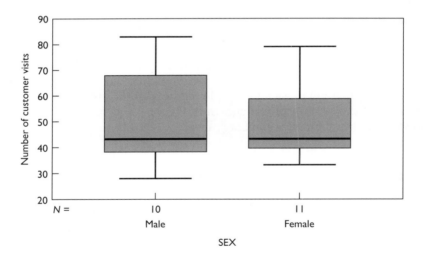

Figure 9.6   *Boxplots for subgroups of respondents (the two sexes) using Explore: Plot Factor Levels Together*

Explore provides boxplots automatically, but pressing the Plots button of Figure 9.1 opens a dialogue box in which you can specify the characteristics of the boxplots or suppress them completely, and ask for a histogram. The boxplot options are Factor Levels Together, which is used for comparing subgroups of respondents (see Figure 9.6 for an example), and Dependents Together, which is used to compare the scores of one set of respondents on a number of variables. When plots are selected, the output is sent to the Chart Carousel, explained in chapter 10. To see the chart, double click on the Chart Carousel icon; a chart window will open and the chart will be drawn in it. Details on saving and printing charts are provided in chapter 10.

9.5 Do subgroups show homogeneity of variance?

If you select the Plots button from the Explore dialogue box (Figure 9.1), the section entitled Spread vs. Level with Levene Test allows you to request plots of the spread of scores against the level of the scores, and to test whether the subsets of scores show homogeneity of variance.

Imagine we wanted to know whether in the data file salesq the variability of the scores of men and women on sales_1 was equal: the Levene test is one method of investigating this. You obtain the test by having at least one Factor List variable and then selecting the Plot button from Explore's dialogue box, and choosing Untransformed. (If sub-groups of respondents show unequal variances on the variables being compared, you may wish to apply a transformation to the raw data. There are options for applying various transformations to the data, or leaving it untransformed.) If the Levene test is significant, reject the null hypothesis that the groups have equal variances.

As well as the Levene test, this procedure gives a boxplot similar to that shown in Figure 9.6 and a graph showing the spread of scores (interquartile range) in each group plotted against the level (median). An example of this type of plot is shown in Figure 9.7. It permits one to see how variability varies with average level.

9.6 Are the scores normally distributed?

If you select the Plots button from the Explore dialogue box (Figure 9.1), the Normality Plots with Tests button provides a graph of the data plotted in such a way that it would be a straight line if the data were normally distributed. This is described as a Normal Q–Q plot, and an example is shown in Figure 9.8. If the data is not normally distributed, the points will differ from the straight line, and the amount by which they differ is itself plotted as a detrended normal plot: to see this plot, select it from the drop-down list in the upper left of the Chart Carousel window. If the data were normally distributed, the detrended plot would be a horizontal line passing through 0. These plots allow you to judge visually whether the data is normally distributed.

```
EXAMINE
  VARIABLES=sales_1 BY sex
  /PLOT BOXPLOT STEMLEAF SPREADLEVEL (1)
  /COMPARE GROUP
  /STATISTICS DESCRIPTIVES
  /CINTERVAL 95
  /MISSING LISTWISE
  /NOTOTAL.
```

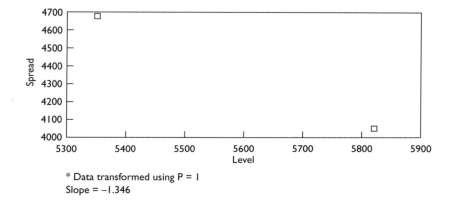

* Data transformed using P = 1
Slope = −1.346

Figure 9.7   *Example of output from Explore: Plot Spread vs. Level*

```
EXAMINE
  VARIABLES=sales_1
  /PLOT BOXPLOT NPPLOT
  /COMPARE GROUP
  /STATISTICS DESCRIPTIVES
  /CINTERVAL 95
  /MISSING LISTWISE
  /NOTOTAL.
```

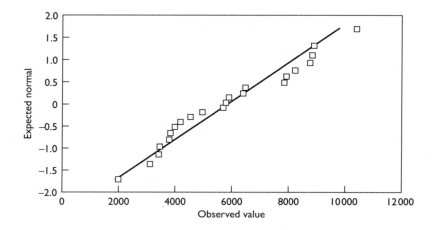

Figure 9.8   *Example of normal plot output from Explore: Plot Npplot*

Tests of whether a set of data is normally distributed are the Lilliefors test and the Shapiro–Wilks test (when the number of scores is less than 50), and these are calculated and the probability values shown when you ask for Normality Plots with Tests. A low significance value means that the scores are not normally distributed; but with large sets of data, non-perfect normal distribution is almost certain to occur, and so the interpretation of these tests should be treated cautiously: the visual displays indicate how non-normal the distribution is.

9.7 Obtaining a simple listing of the data, using LIST

A listing of the data merely reproduces the lines from the data file, and is probably less helpful than printing the data file itself. To obtain a simple listing of the data, select

```
Statistics
     Summarize
          List Cases ...
```

The dialogue box requires you to specify which variables should be listed. The box area entitled Cases to List lets you indicate whether you want all the cases listed (this is the default) or the first 10, 20, etc. by selecting First Through and then typing a number into the box. (If you ask for the first 20, these will be the first 20 rows of the data file.) You can have the case number included in the listing by selecting Number Cases from the bottom of the dialogue box; remember this is the number of the row in the Data Editor table, not any identification number which you may have added as a variable (such as id in the salesq data file).

When SPSS generates the output, it will try to provide a table such as Figure 9.9. But if you have lengthy rows of data for each case, the scores will be given in a set of lines for each case. You can ask for just the first line to be shown, by making the appropriate choice in the Display area of the dialogue box.

You can have every 5th, 20th, etc. row listed as shown in Figure 9.10 if you enter the appropriate number in the Interval text box.

It is not possible, from the Menu system, to have the listing of cases starting anywhere except with case number 1. If you want to list cases starting with a higher number, such as listing cases 100 to 150, you have to paste the LIST command into a syntax file and then edit it so that it reads as follows:

```
LIST VARIABLES=ALL /CASES=FROM 100 TO 150.
```

```
LIST
  VARIABLES=id sex cust
  /CASES= BY 1
  /FORMAT=  WRAP   UNNUMBERED .

ID SEX CUST
  1   2     43
  2   1     46
  3   1     48
  4   1     83
  5   3     71
  6   2     72
  7   2     42
  8   1     28
  9   1     41
 10   1     76
 11   2     39
 12   1     30
 13   1     68
 14   2     33
 15   2     36
 16   2     79
 17   1     38
 18   2     48
 19   2     58
 20   2     60
 21   1     39
 22   2     40

Number of cases read:  22    Number of cases listed:  22
```

Figure 9.9 *Example of output from LIST for all cases and some variables*

```
LIST
  VARIABLES=id sex cust
  /CASES= BY 5
  /FORMAT=  WRAP   UNNUMBERED .

ID SEX CUST
  1   2     43
  6   2     72
 11   2     39
 16   2     79
 21   1     39

Number of cases read:  22    Number of cases listed:   5
```

Figure 9.10 *Example of output from LIST for every fifth case*

You can specify the variables to be shown in the listing by naming them after VARIABLES=. So to have only sex and cust listed for cases 100 to 150, the command would be:

```
LIST VARIABLES=sex cust /CASES=FROM 100 TO 150.
```

9.8 Chapter summary

- Always get an overview of the data before doing any analyses, to discover any possible errors in the data file.
- Although the EXPLORE command is selected from the menu, it is named EXAMINE in the syntax window.

- Explore provides a range of statistics for the scores on the variables, including the mean, median, standard error, variance, standard deviation, minimum, maximum, range, interquartile range (IQR), and indices of skew.
- Explore can display the cases with the five largest and five smallest values on any variables, and give stem-leaf plot and boxplots.
- Explore can demonstrate whether subgroups show homogeneity of variance and whether the scores are normally distributed.
- A listing of the data using LIST reproduces the lines from the data file.

GRAPHS

10.1 Histograms and barcharts from FREQUENCIES

Histograms and barcharts, stem-and-leaf plots and boxplots showing the distribution of scores on a variable are obtained from the Statistics /Summarize menu. Scattergrams and all other types of chart, including more complex barcharts and histograms, are obtained by using the Graphs menu of the SPSS window menu bar, which is covered in later sections of this chapter.

Histograms and barcharts have a superficial similarity in that they both represent data as the length of a bar on a chart. A histogram is used to show a frequency distribution when the variable being plotted is continuous, such as the scores on att1 or sales_1 in the data file salesq. Figure 10.1 illustrates a histogram. With large sets of data, it may be necessary to group the scores into intervals before plotting a histogram. For example, if you have data on people's age you might group them into intervals of 0–20 years old, 21–40 years old, etc. as explained in section 12.6.

Barcharts are used to show a distribution of scores on a non-continuous or categorical variable. For example, Figure 10.2 is a barchart of scores on the variable sex; the categories of sex are not continuous and the bars are separated rather than being adjacent to each other as they are in the histogram of Figure 10.1. In SPSS, a histogram shows an empty space for a value having no cases, whereas a barchart does not: any category having no entries will be omitted from the graph.

Histograms and barcharts of the distribution of the scores on variables in the data file can be obtained from

```
Statistics
     Summarize
          Frequencies
```

Click on the Charts button of the dialogue box to reveal another. You can ask for either type of display (but not both), ask for a normal curve to be superimposed on a histogram, have the axis labelled as actual frequencies or as percentages. Click on Continue and then on the Paste button in the Frequencies dialogue box.

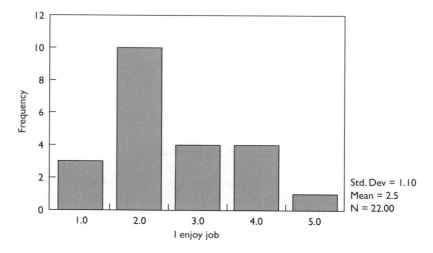

Figure 10.1   *Example of histogram showing distribution of scores on att1*

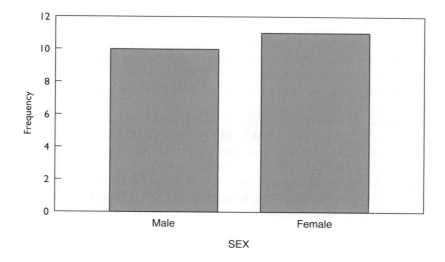

Figure 10.2   *Example of barchart showing frequency of scores on the variable sex*

When the Frequencies /Charts has run, click on the Chart icon in the !Output1 window's icon bar or on the Chart Carousel icon. The Chart Carousel window will be opened, showing the chart of the results. Click on the Edit button of the Chart Carousel icon bar, and the chart will be shown in a window headed !Chart. The facilities available in the !Chart window are described in section 10.10 below. You can save the chart with File /Save As or File /Chart (section 10.11), and print it with File /Print (section 10.14).

10.2 Boxplots and stem-and-leaf plots from EXPLORE

A boxplot summarizes the scores on a variable by displaying the median (as a line), and the 25th and 75th percentiles as the lower and upper edges of a box surrounding the median. The box length represents the interquartile range of the scores. Outliers are cases which are between 1.5 and 3 boxlengths from the edge of the box, and Extremes are more than 3 boxlengths away. Lines are drawn from the edge of the box to the largest and smallest values which are not outliers. An example is given in Figure 10.4, but for these scores there are no Outliers or Extremes.

The boxplot allows you to make a number of 'eye-ball' judgements about the distribution of the scores. The median is the indicator of the central value, and the length of the box indicates the variability of the scores. If the median is not in the middle of the box, the distribution of scores is skewed.

A stem-and-leaf plot is similar to a histogram, but numbers indicate the actual values plotted. Figure 10.5 shows a stem-and-leaf plot. The first column shows the number of scores in the band indicated by the stem. For example, the first line of Figure 10.5 shows there was one respondent who scored in the twenties on customers visited (the stem is 2). The actual score of this respondent was 28 (the leaf is 8, so the actual score is 2, the stem, and 8 the leaf).

Stem-and-leaf plots, histograms, boxplots and spread-by-level plots can be obtained from

```
Statistics
    Summarize
        Explore
```

Identify the variable(s) to be plotted by entering them into the Dependent List. If data from subgroups of cases are to be plotted separately, enter the variable for separating the subgroups into the Factor List box. In Figure 10.4, scores on cust are plotted for each sex separately, so sex was entered into the Factor List. Click the Plots button, which opens the dialogue box shown in Figure 10.3. Select Stem-and-leaf or Histogram or both and then click the Continue button, and Paste.

When the Explore /Plots procedure has run, click on the Chart icon in the !Output1 window's icon bar or the Chart Carousel icon. The Chart Carousel window will be opened, showing the chart of the results. Click on the Edit button of the Chart Carousel icon bar, and the chart will be shown in a window headed !Chart. The facilities available in the !Chart window are described in section 10.10 below. You can save the chart with File /Save As or File /Chart (section 10.11), and print it with File /Print (section 10.14).

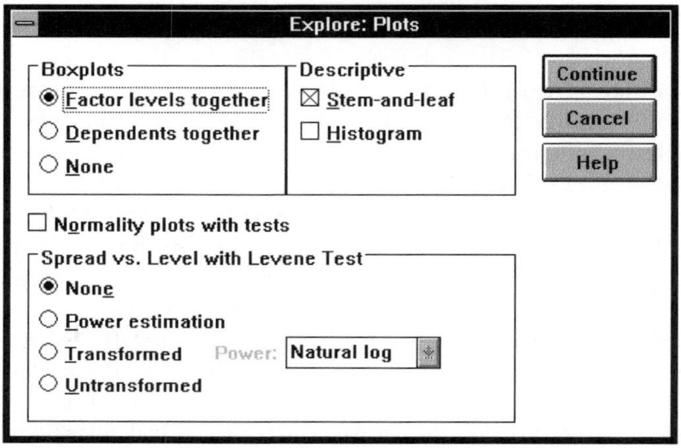

Figure 10.3   *The Explore: Plots dialogue box*

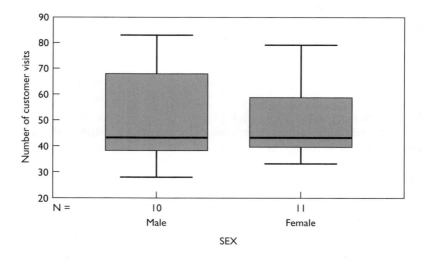

Figure 10.4   *Boxplot of scores on cust for each sex*

```
EXAMINE
  VARIABLES=cust
  /PLOT BOXPLOT STEMLEAF
  /COMPARE GROUP
  /STATISTICS NONE
  /CINTERVAL 95
  /MISSING LISTWISE
  /NOTOTAL.

  Frequency      Stem &  Leaf

       1.00        2  .  8
       6.00        3  .  036899
       7.00        4  .  0123688
       1.00        5  .  8
       2.00        6  .  08
       4.00        7  .  1269
       1.00        8  .  3

  Stem width:     10
  Each leaf:          1 case(s)
```

Figure 10.5   *Stem-and-leaf plot from the command EXAMINE /VARIABLES cust*

10.3 Obtaining graphs, charts and scattergrams from GRAPHS

The basic steps in creating a chart from the Graphs menu are straightforward, but there are numerous alternatives in format. It would be tedious and unnecessary to describe them all here. Once the user is familiar with the basic steps, there should be little difficulty in investigating the other features available.

To create a chart via the Graphs menu, you must have a data file open in an active !Data Editor window. (To make the window active, click on its title bar.) Then click on Graphs in the SPSS window menu bar. You can select from the drop-down menu the type of chart you want to create. It offers a barchart, line graph, area chart, pie chart, boxplot, scattergram, histogram and others. The system will guide you through a series of dialogue boxes in which you can specify how you want the chart drawn, the titles and legends to be put on it, the scales for the axes, etc. The particular boxes presented to you depend on the choices you have made previously, so I shall only describe the general structure of the system here. Once you have understood the basic techniques, you will undoubtedly enjoy some hours investigating the many other options.

When you have indicated which type of chart you want, the first dialogue box has a Define button which takes you further into the system. (Figure 10.6 illustrates the dialogue box when a bar graph has been requested.) But it also has an area entitled Data in Chart Are, with three alternatives. The headings offered are rather unclear, and the following explanation may be helpful.

If you want a chart showing the average score of subgroups of your respondents on one of the variables you measured, or if you want to

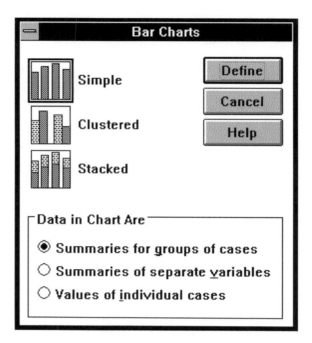

Figure 10.6   *Dialogue box from the Graphs /Bar . . . menu*

show how many people obtained each score on one or more of the variables, ask for Summaries for Groups of Cases. This option can plot, for example, a barchart showing the number of males and females in the data set, or the average on sales_2 of the respondents from different employers. This is the default option – the one that is active unless you select one of the others. Figure 10.7 provides an example.

If you want to summarize more than one variable, such as the mean score on sales_1 and sales_2, select the Summaries of Separate Variables option. The charts produced can be quite complex, as you can obtain summaries of a number of variables for subgroups of respondents. So you could have the average of sales_1 and of sales_2 for men and women from the data file salesq plotted on one chart, as in Figure 10.8.

The third option is Values of Individual Cases. This means that the data on the selected variables is plotted for each case (row of data). Respondent (case) is plotted along the horizontal axis with this option. An example is shown in Figure 10.9, which displays the values on the att1 variable of salesq for each case. It is worth emphasizing that this type of display is rarely useful (although they are popular with many beginners).

If the Summaries for Groups of Cases option has been selected from the Define chart dialogue box (Figure 10.6) and the Define button is pressed, you are presented with another dialogue box allowing you to

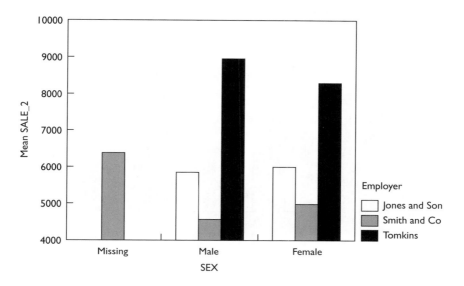

Figure 10.7 *Example of barchart showing mean on sales_2 subdivided by sex for each employer. Note: This graph was obtained with the Summaries for Groups of Cases option*

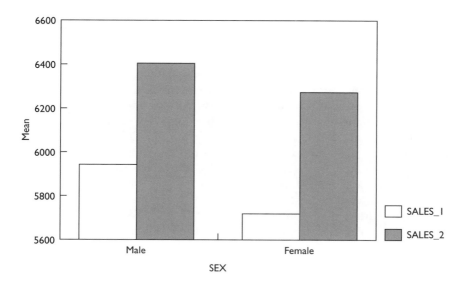

Figure 10.8 *Example of barchart of scores on sales_1 and sales_2 for each sex. Note: This graph was obtained by selecting the Summaries of Separate Variables option*

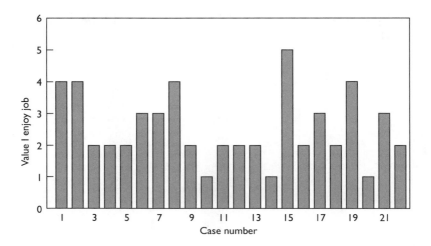

Figure 10.9   *Example of barchart of scores on att I for each respondent. Note:*
This graph was obtained by selecting the Values of Individual Cases option

specify what the lines/bars represent. The options vary according to the type of chart you have chosen. The box presented after selecting Graphs /Bar . . . and Summaries for Groups of Cases is shown in Figure 10.10. By default, the chart shows the number of cases having a particular value on the variable being plotted, but you can ask instead for a plot which shows the percent of cases, cumulative number or cumulative percentages. The Other Summary Function allows you to make further choices: Other is usually the mean of the data for the variable, but for stacked bar, stacked area and pie charts it is the sum.

It is possible to have different summary statistics, by selecting the variable and entering it in the Variable box of the Bars Represent section, then clicking on the Change Summary button. From the Summary Function dialogue box you can specify the summary statistics you want from the list of alternatives offered, which includes median, mode, number of cases, standard deviation and others. You can also ask for a plot of the number or percentage falling above or below a particular value (which you enter into the Value text box), percentiles, even the percent or number of cases with values between and including a Low and High value which you enter into text boxes. The range of possibilities is enormous, and experimentation is the best way to discover what they all do!

If the data set to be plotted has any missing values (such as a value of 3 on the variable sex in the data file salesq), and you do not want the missing values to appear on the graph, section 10.17 explains how to suppress them: select the Options button from the Define Chart dialogue box and click on the button entitled Display Groups Defined by Missing

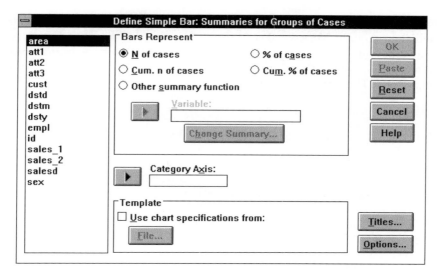

Figure 10.10   *The dialogue box for choosing which summary of data for groups of cases is required*

Values, so the cross in the box is removed. Missing value cases will not then be plotted.

10.4 Creating a bar chart

Suppose we want a barchart showing the means on sales_2 of respondents subdivided by sex and employer (Figure 10.7). To obtain this graph, select

```
Graphs
        Bar . . .
```

which opens the Bar Charts window. You can choose a Simple, Clustered, or Stacked barchart by selecting the appropriate icon. A Simple barchart represents each value on the variable being plotted as a bar, and the bars are equally spaced along the axis. In Clustered charts, some bars are clustered together as in Figure 10.7. A stacked barchart shows two or more variables in each bar.

To create Figure 10.7, select the Clustered barchart option, check that Summaries for Groups of Cases is selected in the area headed Data in Chart Are, and click on Define. This reveals the Define Clustered Bar dialogue box.

You must identify the variables to be plotted: in this example it is sales_2. Click in the list on the left of the box the variable to be plotted, on the button marked Other Summary Function, and on the arrow button to insert the variable name in the text box headed Variable which will then contain MEAN(sales_2). Enter the variable sex into Category Axis and empl into Define Clusters by. Click on the Options button and deselect Display Groups Defined by Missing Values. Click Continue and then Paste. The syntax should read:

```
GRAPH /BAR(GROUPED)=MEAN(sales_2) BY sex BY empl.
```

Run the syntax; after a few seconds the chart will be presented in the Chart Carousel.

10.5 Creating a scattergram from GRAPHS

To create a scattergram select

```
Graphs
     Scatter
```

Indicate whether you want a simple scatterplot, an overlay in which multiple scatterplots are put into the same frame, a scatterplot matrix, or a 3-dimensional plot. Initially, the Simple option is likely to be most useful. An example is shown in Figure 17.2. You may wonder what a scatterplot matrix is. Suppose you selected three variables and asked for this option, then you would obtain scatterplots for variable1 versus variable2, variable2 v variable3, and variable1 v variable3 . . . and the same plots with the axes swapped so you also get variable2 versus variable1, variable3 v variable2, and variable 3 v variable1!

Having selected the type of scatterplot required, click on Define and this will produce a window in which you specify the variables to be plotted on each axis by selecting them from the list on the left and clicking the right-pointing arrow for the Y (vertical) axis and then repeat the procedure for the X (horizontal) axis.

You can separate the plots for subgroups of respondents: for example, one could plot cust versus sales_1 for all the respondents in salesq, but have the data for females indicated by a different marker from those used to plot males' data. This is achieved by entering sex as the variable in the Set Markers By text box. Click on Paste, run the syntax and then click on the Chart icon to see the graph on screen.

Individual points can be labelled if you enter a variable in Label Cases By in the dialogue box revealed when you select Graphs /Scatter. In SPSS version 6.1, clicking on a point in the scatterplot will make the Data Editor active, with the row corresponding to that point highlighted.

You can swap the axes of the scatterplot if you select

```
Chart
     Series
          Displayed
```

Scatterplots in three dimensions require you to specify the three variables to be used as the axes. When the plot is presented, and put into a !Chart window, you can enjoy playing with it by rotating it around various axes if you select from the menus

```
Attributes
     3-D Rotation
```

10.6 Obtaining the regression line on a scattergram

If you want the regression line shown in the scatterplot, while the graph is shown click the Edit button and then Chart /Options from the menu. Click on the Fit Options button to reveal the dialogue box shown in Figure 17.3. The linear regression line is the default, although quadratic and cubic can be selected instead. Click on Continue to return to the Scatterplot Options box, and then on OK. The regression line will be added to the plot.

10.7 Creating a line graph of means of subgroups

It is often helpful when trying to interpret the results of an analysis to plot the means of subgroups of respondents. This is particularly true if analysis of variance with more than one independent variable has been performed, as it demonstrates the effects of any interaction between the variables. Although a line graph is not the most appropriate way of plotting means when the subgroups are divided on a non-continuous scale, it can be a useful aid to understanding the pattern of results.

Suppose we wished to plot the means of the data on the variable sales_2 for males and females from each of the two areas, North and South as in Figure 10.11. Select Graphs /Line from the menu, to reveal a dialogue box in which you select the Multiple option icon and the Summarize for Groups of Cases alternative. Click on Define to open another dialogue box; click on sales_2 then on Other Summary Function and finally on the right-pointing arrow button next to the Variable text box. MEAN(sales_2) will appear in the text box. Insert the variable area as the Category axis and insert sex as Define Lines By. Use the Options button to allow access to the method for suppressing the displaying of missing value cases. Click on Continue and then on Paste. The syntax should read:

```
GRAPH
   /LINE(MULTIPLE)MEAN(sales_2) BY area BY sex.
```

When the syntax is run and the chart made visible on the screen by pressing the Chart icon in the output window, the graph should look like Figure 10.11.

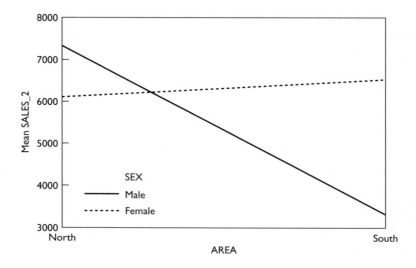

Figure 10.11   *Line graph of means of sales_2 for each area for each sex*

10.8 Displaying the chart

When the chart is first created, it is displayed in the Chart Carousel window. Click on the Edit button of the Chart Carousel icon bar, not the Edit menu of the SPSS window, and the chart will be shown in a window headed !Chart.

You will find that with the Chart Carousel window open, the menu bar of the SPSS window alters, and the entries become

```
File Edit Carousel Window Help
```

File allows you to save and print the charts in the carousel. To alter the typeface used in the charts and to have grid lines displayed, use Edit /Preferences from the menu bar. Carousel allows you to move between the charts in the carousel and to have a chart put into a chart editing window. These functions can also be accessed from the icons in the icon bar of the Chart Carousel window itself.

10.9 The Chart Carousel window

The chart carousel is like a magazine of slides for a slide projector. The magazine may be empty, or it may contain a set of charts stored singly as slides. The Chart Carousel window's menu bar has a number of entries. On the left-hand side is a drop-down list of the charts that are available at the present time: those which are currently in the magazine. If you click on the down-pointing arrow with the line underneath it, a list of the available charts will be revealed. You can click on any of the entries, and the name will then be pasted into the text window. Clicking on it will then put the named chart into the Carousel window.

If the carousel contains a number of charts, the menu bar's down arrow icon selects the next chart in the carousel and puts it into the window; the up arrow icon selects the previous chart in the carousel. If the carousel has only one chart in its magazine, these two buttons will be dimmed to indicate they are not available.

The Edit button in the carousel window menu bar is clicked if you want to alter the chart shown in the carousel window (as you almost certainly will). This puts the chart shown in the Chart Carousel into a Chart window, entitled !Chart. Only when a chart is in a !Chart window can it be edited.

The Discard button in the carousel window, as the name suggests, deletes the current chart.

The 'typed page' icon switches you to the output window, where the text output of the analyses are situated. If you inadvertently click on this icon, and want to return to the Chart Carousel, click on the chart icon in the text output window.

10.10   The !Chart window

Charts are inserted into a !Chart window by selecting the Edit button from the Chart Carousel menu bar. When the !Chart window is open, the SPSS window menu alters again and has the entries:

```
File Edit Gallery Chart Series Attributes Window Help
```

These menus allow you to make numerous alterations to the chart in the !Chart window.

The icon bar of the !Chart window duplicates the commands available from the Attributes menu. By clicking on the icons you can, reading from left to right, set the pattern for filling enclosed areas, set the colours, specify the marker used to plot a point, set the thickness and style of lines, specify whether bars have a shadow or 3-d appearance, determine whether bars are labelled, decide how interpolated lines are drawn, vary the font and size of text used in the chart, apply 3-d rotation for a 3-d plot, swap axes, explode the slice of a pie chart, spin a 3-d plot and, with the right-hand icon, switch to the output text window.

The facilities for editing charts are so numerous that it is best to learn by experimentation. How to achieve some of the effects you are most likely to need is described in section 10.15.

10.11   Saving a chart

You can save a chart either from the Chart Carousel or from the !Chart window. Charts are saved with the filename extension .CHT.

If you are in a !Chart window, select from the menu bar

```
File
     Save As
```

The name of the file may appear in the Files box, and you can then click on it so it appears in the Name box. The directory in which it will be saved is shown, and you can alter this by clicking on the required alternative in the Directories box: to save the file to the floppy disk, you need to click on [-A-].

If the chart is in the Chart Carousel, it can be saved by selecting from the SPSS window menu bar the File /Save As options or the File /Save Chart option. When you have either clicked on a name from the list offered or entered a new name and indicated the directory or drive to save the file on, click on the Save Chart button at the bottom of the dialogue box to save the file.

The Save As: Chart Carousel dialogue box contains a Save All button. This allows you to save all the charts in the Chart Carousel: type in a name of no more than five characters. If you typed in name, all the charts will be saved as name1.cht, name2.cht, etc.

10.12 Transferring a chart to another application

When you are looking at a chart, it can be copied into other Windows applications, such as Word for Windows. Copy the chart to the windows clipboard using Edit /Copy Chart, then open a document in Word and select Edit /Paste Special. A dialogue box is presented: select the Picture option and click OK. The chart will be pasted into the document as a picture and can be edited using Microsoft Draw.

In SPSS version 6.1, charts can be saved in a variety of formats such as .bmp, .wmf, .tif for importing into other applications. To save the chart in one of these formats, use File /Export Chart. This is not included in SPSS version 6.0.

10.13 Retrieving charts

To retrieve a previously saved chart, use

```
File
     Open
```

from the menu bar of the SPSS window. A drop-down menu asks you to indicate which type of file you want to open, and if you click on the chart file option a list of .cht files will be offered. If your file is on your floppy disk, you will have to click on [-A-] in the Directories list to have the .cht files from the floppy disk presented in the list of files available to be opened. Just click on the name of the file you want and then click on OK: the file will then be presented in a !Chart window. The title of the window will show the drive from which the file came and the file name, such as !A:\PLOT1.CHT.

10.14 Printing charts

If the chart is in the Chart Carousel or in a !Chart window, it can be printed by selecting from the SPSS window menu bar

```
File
     Print
```

The Print Chart dialogue box is presented. By default, the Redraw image for printer facility is operative. This has the effect of redrawing the chart image so that it corresponds to the fonts available in the printer.

10.15 Editing charts

There are numerous editing possibilities, once the chart is in an active chart window, and only some of them will be explained here: once the basics are understood, the user will learn most, and most enjoyably, by experimenting with the host of alternatives.

To use the editing facilities, you need to appreciate that a chart contains two kinds of object. 'Series objects' are the bars, lines and markers that represent the data. 'Chart objects' are the layout and labelling features. To modify an object, you either use the Series and Chart menus of the SPSS window, or you can double click on the object you wish to modify. With either procedure, an appropriate dialogue box is then presented allowing you to specify the attributes of the object. For example, to change the way the bar in a barchart is filled with a pattern, double click on one of the bars. To change the label for the vertical axis, double click on the existing label.

With a chart window active, the menu bar of the SPSS window contains the menu titles:

```
File Edit Gallery Chart Series Attributes Window Help
```

To alter the title of the chart, select Chart /Title from the SPSS window menu, and type text into the Title 1 and/or Title 2 text boxes; then click on OK.

To alter the title or labels of the horizontal axis, double click on the existing ones. This reveals the Category Axis box, and you can enter a different title. To alter the labels of the categories, click on the Labels button. In the Category Axis: Labels dialogue box you can click on the existing label, shown in a list in the label text area, and it will appear in the text box. You can then edit it and click on the Change button. When the labels have been altered, a click on the Continue button returns you to the Category Axis box and you click on OK.

To alter the title, scale or labels of the vertical axis, double click on the existing vertical axis title, and the Scale Axis box is exposed. It functions in a similar way to the Category Axis box used to modify the horizontal axis.

That part of the chart which indicates which variables are shown is known as the legend. Double clicking on the existing legend will reveal a Legend box allowing you to add a title to the legend, alter the labels of the legend, vary its position or suppress it completely.

To add a short text message to the chart, select

```
Chart
      Annotation
```

The resulting box allows you to type in the message and locate it at a set point defined by position on the vertical and horizontal axes.

To alter the layout or change the scales of the chart axes select Chart /Options and further dialogue boxes appropriate to the type of chart you are editing allow you specify how you want the chart to be constructed. The options offered depend on the type of chart you are editing, but this menu gives great flexibility in chart design.

To have a normal curve added to a histogram or add a regression line to a scatterplot, use the menu

```
Charts
      Options
```

You can swap axes, so that histograms, for example, are oriented horizontally rather than vertically, by selecting Series /Displayed or Attributes /Swap Axes, or by clicking on the icon in the icon bar which portrays a movement of the axes.

To alter the patterns used to fill areas of the chart, and similar features of the chart, select Attributes.

To alter the text fonts and sizes, select Attributes /Text.

To suppress the display of some of the variables you have previously selected for inclusion in the chart, select Series /Displayed.

To alter the sequence in which variables are grouped in a clustered barchart or a stacked chart, select Series /Displayed and alter the order in which variables are listed in the Display text box of the Displayed Data dialogue box. (Click on the variable name, then click on the control box in the top left of the title bar. This opens a list containing the options to move the selected item up or down in the list.)

You can replace the current chart with another of a different type, using the same data, by selecting Gallery.

Line graphs, area charts and pie charts can be requested at the first stage of creating a chart. But more complex charts such as mixed bars and lines, exploded pie charts and dropped line charts are available once you have created a chart, put it into a !Chart window, and selected Gallery from the menu bar. Experimenting with the possibilities is perhaps the best way to learn how to control these displays. As usual, the system provides appropriate dialogue boxes at every point.

10.16 Chart templates

A chart template allows you to save the style of a chart so that it can be applied to other charts, so you do not have to go through the process of designing a chart every time. Essentially, when you save a chart, the features of that chart can be applied when you create a new chart or can be applied to a chart already in the chart window.

USING A TEMPLATE WHEN CREATING A CHART   When you access the Define chart dialogue box, it contains an area titled Template, with the option Use Chart Specifications From:. If you select this and then click on the File button in the template area, a list of chart files, with the filename extension .cht is shown. Select the one you want from the list so its name appears in the Chart Template File text box and click on OK. The chart you are creating will be assigned the attributes of the chart you are using as a template.

ASSIGNING A TEMPLATE TO AN EXISTING CHART   If you have a chart in a chart window, and want to apply a template to it, select from the menu File / Apply Chart Template . . . This has an option for Apply title and footnote text. If this is active, the titles and footnotes of the template will be added to the chart to which the template is being applied, over-riding any previous titles or footnotes.

10.17 Dealing with missing data when creating charts

When you are charting data that has some data missing, SPSS will omit any case that has data missing on the variables being plotted. This cannot be altered when you are plotting data for individual cases, nor if you are plotting a histogram. But for other charts, you do have a choice. To over-ride the default setting, you must select the Options button from

the chart definition box. Exclude Cases Listwise means, although the
name is rather confusing, that any row of data which has a missing data
point for any of the variables selected for plotting will be omitted from
the graph. This is the default condition. The alternative is Exclude Cases
Variable by Variable, which means that when a particular variable is
plotted, any case with missing data is omitted, but the case is included
when you analyse another variable if the case has a score on that
variable.

For some charts, missing values are plotted as a separate category. For
example, a barchart of the frequency of sex for the data from salesq has a
bar for the case where the sex is unknown (sex had a value of 3 which
was defined as a missing value). If any cases had the system-missing
value, there would be a separate bar for them. You may wish to suppress
the plotting of these missing-value cases. To do so, select the Options
button from the Define Chart dialogue box and click on the button
entitled Display Groups Defined by Missing Values, so the cross in the
box is removed. Missing-value cases will not then be plotted.

10.18 Adding grid lines to charts

You can ask for horizontal or vertical grid lines to be added to charts by
selecting from the menu Edit /Preferences /Graphics. The dialogue box
which will appear has one section headed Grid Lines, and you use the
check boxes to request horizontal lines (Scale axis) and/or vertical lines
(Category axis).

10.19 Chapter summary

- Histograms and barcharts, stem-and-leaf plots and boxplots showing
  the distribution of scores on a variable are obtained from the Statistics
  /Summarize /Frequencies or /Explore menu.
- Scattergrams and all other types of chart, including more complex
  barcharts and histograms, are obtained by using the Graphs menu of
  the SPSS window menu bar.
- Using the Graphs menu, when you have indicated which type of
  chart you want, the dialogue box has an area entitled Data in Chart
  Are, with three alternatives. Ensure you understand what the alternatives mean.
- If the data set to be plotted has any missing values, suppress them by
  selecting the Options button from the Define Chart dialogue box and
  click on the button entitled Display Groups Defined by Missing
  Values, so the cross in the box is removed.
- When the chart is first created, it is displayed in the Chart Carousel
  window. Click on the Edit button of the Chart Carousel icon bar and
  the chart will be shown in a window headed !Chart.

- The SPSS window menu alters and has the entries:

  `File Edit Gallery Chart Series Attributes Window Help`

  These menus allow you to make numerous alterations to the chart in
  the !Chart window.
- Ensure you can save, retrieve, print charts and transfer them to other
  applications.

RANKING AND SORTING THE DATA

11.1 Ranking scores

If you want to convert a set of scores into rank values, select from the menu

```
Transform
    Rank Cases
```

The dialogue box shown in Figure 11.1 will be presented. Enter into the Variable(s) box the variables to be ranked. Turn on the option Display Summary Tables, by clicking in the check box; this has the effect of putting a message in the output window to tell you what the procedure has done. An example of the message is shown in Figure 11.2.

To have rank values assigned in ascending order, so the lowest score has a rank value of 1, you need do nothing, but if you want the scores ranked in descending order so the largest value has the rank of 1 then

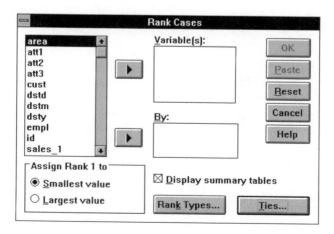

Figure 11.1   *The Rank Cases dialogue box*

you select Largest Value in the Assign Rank 1 To section of the dialogue box. Paste the command into the syntax window and run it.

The Rank procedure creates a new variable, which by default has the name of the variable being ranked preceded by the letter R. So when sales_1 are ranked, you obtain a new variable called rsales_1. When you have run Rank you will see the message illustrated in Figure 11.2 in the output window; switch to the Data Editor window and you will find that the new variable has been added to the data in the table. The name of the new variable must be used if you wish to list or analyse the ranked values.

```
RANK
  VARIABLES=sales_1  (A) /RANK /PRINT=YES
  /TIES=MEAN  .

From       New
variable   variable  Label
--------   --------  -----
SALES_1    RSALES_1  RANK of SALES_1
```

Figure 11.2   *The output from the Rank procedure. (Switch to the Data window to see the new variable rsales_1.)*

There are a number of options on how to assign ranks to tied values. Unless you specify otherwise, via the Ties button, tied values will be given the mean rank value of the scores. Alternative methods of ranking, unlikely to be used by the beginner, are available from the Rank Types button.

11.2 Ranking within subgroups

The basic Rank command ranks the whole set of scores on the variables specified. You frequently need the ranking of scores within subgroups; for example, one may require the data for males and females to be ranked separately. This is achieved by entering a variable name into the By box of the Rank Cases dialogue box. So to have the scores of the males and females on sales_1 ranked separately, you insert sales_1 into the Variables box, sex into the By box and click on Paste. The syntax is shown in Figure 11.3.

11.3 Rank correlation

Rank correlations are provided by the CORRELATIONS procedure, described in section 17.3. If the data is on an interval or ratio scale, you

```
RANK
   VARIABLES=sales_1  (A) BY sex  /RANK /PRINT=YES
   /TIES=MEAN .

From       New
variable   variable  Label
--------   --------  -----
SALES_1    RSALES_1  RANK of SALES_1 by SEX
```

Figure 11.3   *The output from ranking within subgroups of sex. (Switch to the Data window to see the new variable rsales_1.)*

do not have to use the rank procedure before finding the rank correlation, as the ranking is done automatically.

11.4 Putting the cases in a different order: SORT

There are occasions when you may wish to sort the cases into a new order. For example, if you were analysing just the first 50 cases in a large data file, you might want those first 50 cases to be all males, or all of a given level of income or having some other feature. You can have the cases sorted into a specified order using the SORT procedure. The procedure is obtained from the menu

Data
     Sort Cases

Enter the variable(s) to be used for sorting the data into the Sort By box, and select ascending or descending Sort Order.

If you enter two variables in the Sort By box, the cases will be sorted first of all by the first one in the list and then by the second one in the list and so on. So if you wanted the data in salesq to be sorted so that all the males (sex = 1) from the North (area = 1) came first, followed by all the men from the South (area = 2), then all the women from the North and finally all the women from the South, you would put sex and area into the Sort By box. When the cases have been sorted, they are shown in the new order in the Data Editor window.

11.5 Restoring the original order after using SORT

If the cases were originally ordered by some other variable such as id, the original order can be restored by running the Sort procedure again with id as the defining variable. (This is one reason why it is always worth having an identifying variable such as the variable id in salesq; you can restore the original order.) If, however, you do not have a variable with which you can sort to regain the original order, you can only get back to the original by reloading the data file from the disk. This makes it important that if you have sorted the data you should save the data file under a new filename so that the original order is preserved in the original data file on the disk.

11.6 Chapter summary

- To convert a set of scores into rank values, use Rank Cases.
- When a variable ve is ranked, you obtain a new variable called rve. Switch to the Data Editor window to see the scores on rve, the ranked variable.
- To rank within subgroups, enter the variable name for forming subgroups into the By box of the Rank Cases dialogue box.
- To obtain rank correlations refer to section 17.3
- To sort the cases into a new order, use SORT.

CHANGING THE WAY DATA IS CODED AND GROUPED

12.1 Why you might want to modify the data

In analysing data you may want to calculate a new variable from the original data. For example, from respondents' sales and the number of customers visited, you may want to create a new variable which is the average sales per customer visit or you may want to know the average of respondents' scores on a number of measures such as finding the mean for each person of their responses to att1, att2 and att3. This is achieved using the COMPUTE procedure.

Sometimes you may want to code the data in a different way from that used when the data file was initially created. For example, the salesq file includes data on the number of customers visited. You may want to divide the respondents into just two groups: those who visited more than 40 customers, and those who visited less than 40. The RECODE procedure will do this for you.

Another common situation is when you want to reverse the scoring of one of the variables. For example, in the Sales Personnel Questionnaire, there were three questions asking respondents about their attitude to their job. Questions 5 and 6 (named as att1 and att2) have the responses coded so that 1 indicates the respondent is very satisfied and 5 indicates dissatisfaction. But for question 7 (att3), 1 indicates dissatisfaction and 5 indicates satisfaction. Suppose you wanted the scores on att3 to be scored in the opposite direction, so they are consistent with att1 and att2, with a low score meaning very satisfied and a high score (5) meaning very dissatisfied. This kind of alteration is easily made using the RECODE command.

12.2 Calculating 'new' scores and transforming scores: COMPUTE

Compute is found from the menu under

Transform
    Compute

It opens the dialogue box entitled Compute Variable shown in Figure 12.1. Type a name for the variable you are computing into the Target Variable text box: the name must not be more than eight characters long, must not contain a space, must not end in a full stop. You can assign a label to the new variable name by pressing the Type&Label button from the dialogue box and responding to the box revealed.

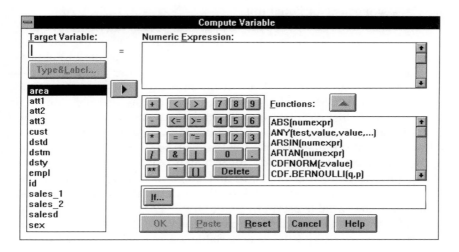

Figure 12.1   *The Compute Variable dialogue box*

The new variable will be calculated from some combination of the existing variables, linked by mathematical operators. For example, you might want to calculate a new variable, totatt, which is the total of the scores on att1, att2 and att3. The box headed Numeric Expression is where you indicate the formula that is used to calculate the new variable, and you select existing variables to enter into the formula by the usual process of clicking on their names in the left-hand list and then on the right-pointing arrow. Mathematical operators (the plus sign, multiplication sign, etc.) are entered into the formula by clicking on the appropriate button in the area which looks like a calculator keypad. So the formula for calculating totatt is att1 + att2 + att3, and you enter this into the Numeric Expression box by clicking on att1 in the left-hand list and on the arrow, then on the + sign in the on-screen keypad, then on att2 in the variable list and the right arrow, etc.

When you have created the formula you want, click on the Paste button at the bottom of the screen and the syntax window will contain these lines:

```
COMPUTE totatt = att1 + att2 + att3.
EXECUTE.
```

When you run these two commands, switch to the data window to see the new variable (totatt in this example) which has been added in the first empty column to the right of the original data.

The keypad area allows you to use not only arithmetic operators in your formula, but also relational operators such as < and > as well as logical operators: the keypad has an & key to represent AND, a key with a vertical line to represent OR, and a ~ key which represents NOT. (So the ~= key means Not Equal to.)

You will notice that a list appears under the label Functions, and this allows access to a set of transformations and mathematical functions which can be used in the formula. For example, if you wanted to obtain the log of the scores on variable cust, you would enter a new variable name, logcust, and then scroll down the Functions list until the LG10 function was exposed. Click on that and then on the upward-pointing arrow above the list of Functions. The function you selected will appear in the Numeric Expression list, with question marks to show that you still have to enter the arguments for the expression (i.e. the variables to be used when calculating the log, mean, square root or whatever you are asking for). Click on the first question mark in the expression in the Numeric Expression list, then click on the appropriate variable (cust, for example) in the variable list on the left of the dialogue box. The Numeric Expression will then read LG10[cust]. Click on Paste and run the Compute procedure, and the new variable logcust will be added to the Data Editor. It is important to realize that the Functions facility deals with missing values in a way that can be misleading. See section 12.4 below for an explanation and details on how to avoid being misled.

The Functions list allows you to select a number of transformations and statistics expressions. You can obtain the absolute value of scores with ABS, the SQRT provides square roots, arcsines are provided by ARSIN, and there are many others. The statistical functions allow you to obtain the mean, sum, standard deviation, variance, minimum or maximum of a set of scores, but remember this refers to a set of scores obtained by each respondent. Suppose you want to obtain the average score on att1, att2 and att3 for each respondent: you would put a name for the new variable in the Target variable box and then from the Functions list select MEAN (numexpr, numexpr, . . .). It appears in the Numeric Expression window, and you then click on the names of the variables for which you want the mean by clicking on them in the variable list and then clicking on the right arrow. In this example, you would select att1, att2 and att3 so that the formula in the Numeric Expressions text box read MEAN (att1, att2, att3).

Clicking on the Paste button at the bottom of the screen will present the syntax window containing these lines:

```
COMPUTE Meanatt = MEAN (att1, att2, att3).
EXECUTE.
```

When these two commands have been run, switch to the data window to see the new variable (Meanatt in this example) which has been added in the first empty column to the right of the original data.

The earlier example of calculating the total of scores att1, att2 and att3 could be obtained more simply by using the function SUM (att1, att2, att3), but do see section 12.4 below regarding the treatment of missing values when functions are used.

The Functions list contains an entry ANY(test,value,value . . .), one of the Logical Functions. What this does is to check whether the scores for each respondent on a named variable (the one referred to as test) match a specified value. For example, ANY(year,90,91) will examine the data for each respondent to see whether the score on the variable year matches the values given: 90 or 91. If there is a match, the new variable is added to the Data Editor and a score of 1 is given.

Exercise 12.1

Use Compute to calculate a new score called avsales1 which is the average sales_1 per customer visited for each respondent in the data file salesq. The formula for avsales1 is sales_1/cust.

12.3 Using Compute with certain cases only: COMPUTE IF

You may want to compute a new variable for just some cases in your data file, cases that meet certain criteria. For example, you might want to calculate the sum of att1, att2 and att3 only for people from the North area. To do this, you click on the If . . . button in the Compute Variable dialogue box shown in Figure 12.1, and this opens another box entitled Compute Variable: If Cases. The structure of this box resembles the previous Compute Variable one, but you can specify the conditions to apply before the Compute procedure takes place. For example, suppose you want to calculate a new variable called Northtot which is the total of att1, att2 and att3 but is only calculated for those respondents who had a score of 1 on the variable area (these are the respondents who worked in the North). To do this, you need the box in Compute Variable: If Cases to contain the expression area = 1.

The expression is created very much as the Numeric Expression in Compute Variable was obtained, by selecting variable names from the list, entering them into the box by clicking on the arrow button, and using the calculator keypad to obtain arithmetic or logical expressions and functions. Before the formula is entered in the box, click on the Include if Cases Satisfies Condition: button. After the formula has been entered, click on the Continue button at the bottom of the box. Once the Compute box has been completed, clicking on Paste will insert into the syntax window the lines:

```
IF (area = 1) Northtot = att1 + att2 + att3.
EXECUTE.
```

When these commands are run, the variable Northtot will be added to the data window and the values inserted just for those respondents who have an entry of 1 on the variable area.

12.4 Missing values in COMPUTE

If you are using compute with an arithmetic expression, such as att1+att2+att3, then any case which has a missing value on any of the variables included in the formula (in this example att1, att2, att3) will be classified as having a missing value on the new variable you are computing.

Statistical functions work differently: if you compute a new variable using the function MEAN (att1, att2, att3), then the new variable will have a missing value if the respondent has missing data on *all* of the variables in the expression. This could be misleading: you might ask for the mean of att1, att2 and att3 for a respondent who only has scores on att1 and att2. The mean that is given will be the mean of the two scores the respondent has, and you may be unaware that for this respondent the mean calculated is not the mean of three variables but only of two. To prevent this happening use MEAN.3(att1, att2, att3). Before the opening bracket, put a decimal point and follow this with a number equal to the number of variables listed in the function. With this formulation, any case that has a missing value on any one of the variables named between the brackets will have a missing value assigned on the computed variable.

12.5 Obtaining z-scores

When a series of parametric data is transformed so that it has a mean of zero and a standard deviation of 1.00, the scores are known as z-scores. To obtain z-scores for any variable, use the Descriptives procedure and select the Save Standardized Values as Variables option in the Descriptives dialogue box. Details are given in section 15.4.

12.6 Changing the way data is coded: RECODE

RECODE is obtained from the menu by selecting

```
Transform
      Recode
            Into Different Variables
```

which yields the dialogue box shown in Figure 12.2. It is always wise to choose Recode /Into Different Variables. The recoded values make a new variable, which you have to name as described below, and the original variable and the scores on it are retained in the data file. If you choose Recode /Into Same Variables, the recoded values will replace the old values in the Data Editor. This is a dangerous thing to do, as you run the risk of losing the original values which you may need later. It is always possible to reload the original data file from disk so that you get the original scores back, but it is easy to make mistakes and save a version of the data which overwrites the original file. If this happens you can have lost the original scores for good.

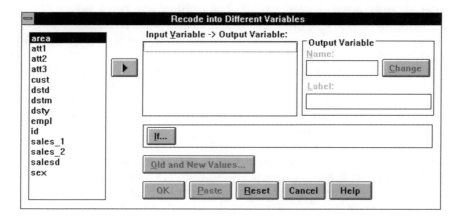

Figure 12.2   *The dialogue box for RECODE*

Specify the variables to be recoded by entering them in the Variables list and provide a name for the variable when it has been recoded by typing in the new name in the Output Variable Name box and clicking on Change. The new name will be inserted next to the old name in the Input Variable → Output Variable list. Next select the Old and New Values button to obtain the display shown in Figure 12.3. Specify the old value and the new value; for example, if you want a score of 5 to be recoded as a 1, 5 goes into the Old Value's Value box, and 1 into the New Value's Value box. You then click on the Add button.

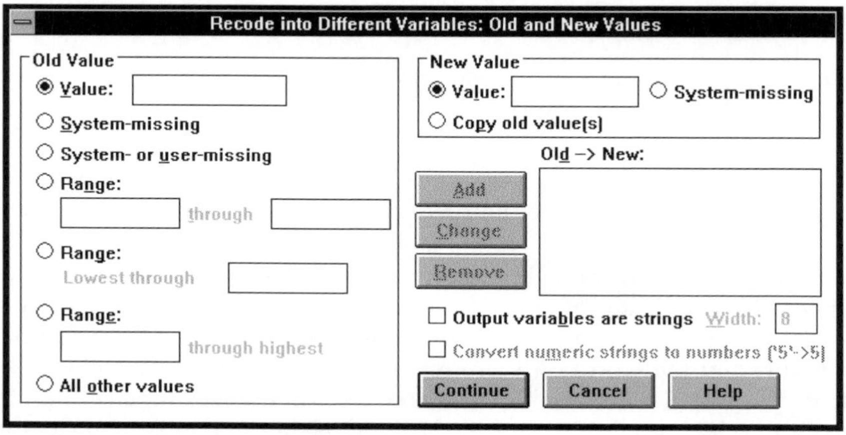

Figure 12.3   *The dialogue box for assigning new values in RECODE*

As the lower left part of Figure 12.3 implies, you can specify a range of values to be recoded as a single value. Suppose we wanted to recode the data so that two groups are formed according to their standing on the cust variable, with all cases where cust is 40 or less being given a new, recoded score of 1 and all those with a cust score of 41 or more having a recoded score of 2. You could define one range as 0 through 40 and assign it the new value of 1, click on Add, and then define the second range as 41 through highest, assign it a new value of 2 and click on Add. Note that you can specify one category for recoding as lowest score to a specified value and another as from a specified value to the highest score, which is useful for forming two groups such as those scoring below and above the median.

When you have specified the old values to be recoded, it is necessary to decide how any unspecified values are to be treated. If you do nothing, they will all be given the system-missing value, which is rarely what is needed. To ensure that any old values you do not want recoded are carried over into the new variable with the same values as before, make sure you select All Other Values in the Old and New Values dialogue box, and then select Copy Old Values in the New Value area of the box and finally press the Add button. The entry ELSE → COPY appears in the list to show that all unspecified values will be carried over into the new variable.

You can ask for only certain cases to be recoded: if you wanted only the men's scores (sex = 1 in salesq) recoded, for example, click on the If . . . button. This opens the If dialogue box which is explained in section 12.3.

When all selections have been made from the dialogue boxes, Paste the syntax into a syntax window. An example of the recode syntax is shown in Figure 12.4.

```
RECODE
   cust
   (Lowest thru 40=1) (41 thru 60=2) (61 thru Highest=3) INTO custrc.
EXECUTE  .
```

Figure 12.4 *Examples of the syntax for RECODE*

When the commands are run, switch to the data window to see the new recoded variables which have been added to the data. To save the new variables, save the contents of the data editor as a data file.

Recode /Into Same Variables operates in a similar way to Recode /Into Different Variables, except that as noted above it runs unnecessary dangers.

RECODE only applies to the data in the active file. The original data file is not affected by running the RECODE command, so there is no risk of making permanent (and non-reversible) changes to the entries in the data file. To store a copy of the data to which the RECODE has been applied, carry out the recode, and then save the data file. It is a wise precaution to save it under a different name from the original data file (use File /Save As . . .) just in case there are any catastrophes later.

Exercise 12.2

Recode the scores on the variable sales_I in the data file salesq so that values of 8000 or over are coded as 3, values of 4000 or less are coded as I and values between 4000 and 8000 are coded as 2.

12.7 Automatic Recode

This procedure automatically recodes all the scores on a variable into consecutive integers. For example, the customers visited scores in salesq include a 28, a 29, a 30, a 33, and the largest figure is 83. If you use

```
Transform
      Automatic Recode
```

the scores will be modified so that the lowest score is changed to 1, the second-lowest to 2, the third-lowest to 3 and so on. The procedure creates a new variable for the recoded scores, which must be given a new name by highlighting the variable entered in the Variable → New Name list, typing the new name in the text box to the right of the New Name button, then clicking on that button. When automatic recode runs, switch to the data window to see the new variable. The values on the new variable are automatically given value labels corresponding to the original values on the variable which has been recoded. Figure 12.5 illustrates the effect of using Automatic Recode.

```
AUTORECODE
  VARIABLES=cust   /INTO custautr
  /PRINT.
```

```
                    CUST        CUSTAUTR  Number customer visits
                Old Value       New Value  Value Label
                       28              1   28
                       30              2   30
                       33              3   33
                       36              4   36
                       38              5   38
                       39              6   39
                       40              7   40
                       41              8   41
                       42              9   42
                       43             10   43
                       46             11   46
                       48             12   48
                       58             13   58
                       60             14   60
                       68             15   68
                       71             16   71
                       72             17   72
                       76             18   76
                       79             19   79
                       83             20   83
```

Figure 12.5   *Example of the effects of Automatic Recode*

12.8 Multiple responses

Surveys often use questions with non-exclusive responses: suppose that instead of asking the people who completed the sales questionnaire described in chapter 4 which employer they worked for now, we asked them to indicate which of the employers they had ever worked for. We might find individuals who had worked for employer 1 (Jones) only, others who had worked for 1 (Jones) and 2 (Smith), others who had worked for 2 (Smith) and 3 (Tomkins), and so on. There are alternative ways of dealing with such data. One method would be to have a variable for each employer and use a score of 1 to indicate 'yes' and 2 to indicate 'no'. This is referred to as the multiple dichotomy method.

The alternative method is known as the multiple category method. Here one would have three variables, and the score on each one would indicate which employer had been mentioned. In our example, a score of 1 would represent Jones, 2 Smith and 3 Tomkins. So a respondent who had been employed by Jones and by Tomkins would score 1 on variable1, 3 on variable2 and have a missing value on variable3.

Whichever method one chose, the responses on the variables need to be combined either into a multiple dichotomy set or into a multiple category set. This is achieved by selecting from the menu

Statistics
     Multiple Response
          Define Sets

The dialogue box allows you to specify the variables to be entered into a set. You have to indicate for each variable whether the scores are dichotomies (the scores represent yes or no) or whether the scores have more than 2 alternatives. The former is used for the multiple dichotomy method, the latter for the multiple category method. You have to enter a name for the set and Add it to the list, where the name you gave will be preceded with a $ sign.

The analysis of multiple response sets is achieved by selecting either

```
Statistics
     Multiple Response
          Frequencies
```

or

```
Statistics
     Multiple Response
          Tables
```

Frequencies produces tables which show the number of respondents giving each possible response (i.e. each employer, in our example) collapsed across the variables in the set. The Tables subcommand is used to produce cross-tabulations, in which the responses are collapsed across the variables in the defined set and then tabulated against scores on another variable.

12.9 Collapsing data across cases: AGGREGATE

You may wish to collapse data across a set of cases, and form a new 'case' which has scores which are derived from the collapsed data. As an example, you could collapse the scores for each of the sexes and have one case representing 'men' and a second case representing 'women'. (This procedure should be used only rarely and after some thought about whether it is justified. This example is merely to allow me to explain what Aggregate achieves.)

To obtain an aggregation, select

```
Data
     Aggregate
```

Specify in the Break Variable(s) box the variable to be used to identify the groups to be formed. In the example I am using, this would be sex. In the Aggregate Variable(s) box you enter the variables to be aggregated; SPSS will create a new variable. You have to indicate the function to be used in making the aggregation: do you want the aggregate score to be the mean of the individual cases, or their sum, or the percentage of cases falling between certain limits, or some other function? The mean is used by default; if you want any other function, you have to select the Functions button and fill in the dialogue box.

The Aggregate procedure creates a new data file, aggr.sav, in the current directory. If you want a different name or the file to be saved elsewhere, click on the File button and complete the dialogue box.

12.10 Chapter summary

- To calculate a new variable from the original data use the COMPUTE procedure.
- To code the data in a different way from that used when the data file was initially created use the RECODE procedure. It is always wise to choose Recode /Into Different Variables.
- To obtain z-scores use the Descriptives procedure as explained in section 15.4.
- To collapse data across a set of cases and form a new 'case' which has scores derived from the collapsed data use AGGREGATE.

SELECTING SUBGROUPS FOR ANALYSIS

13.1 When analysing subgroups is needed

In the data file salesq we have a record of the number of sales (sales_1) by male and female respondents from the North and the South. Imagine you want to analyse separately the sales_1 scores for people from the North and then analyse the scores for people from the South. Split File allows you to do so and you can then return to analysing all the cases by turning Split File off.

13.2 Selecting temporary subgroups: SPLIT FILE

From the menu select

```
Data
    Split File
```

In the dialogue box revealed (Figure 13.1) select the Repeat Analysis for Each Group button. Then select the variable to be used to divide the cases into subgroups and enter it in the Groups Based On text box. Suppose that we want to use a *t*-test to compare males and females from the North on the variable sales_1 and then compare the scores of the males and females from the South on sales_1. We want to select people from the North and then those from the South, so the variable area would need to be entered in this box. When Pasted, the syntax window contains these lines:

```
SORT CASES BY area.
SPLIT FILE
  BY area.
```

To carry out a *t*-test on sales_1 data, one then selects the necessary commands from the menu and pastes them into the syntax window, and then turns Split File off by returning to the Split File dialogue box,

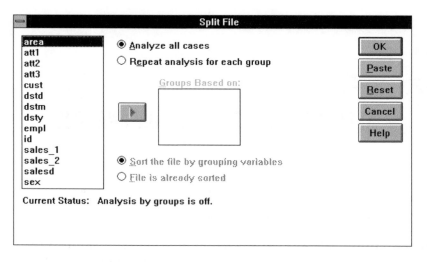

Figure 13.1   *The dialogue box for Split File*

selecting Analyze All Cases and pressing Paste. The complete syntax is included in Figure 13.2.

The output from running this syntax is shown in Figure 13.2. Two separate *t*-tests have been performed, one on respondents from the North and one on respondents from the South.

Once invoked the Split File command continues to be operative throughout an SPSS run of commands unless you turn it off by going back to the Split File box and selecting the Analyze All Cases button.

When it is operating, Split File sorts the data in the data file so that it has all cases with the same value on the grouping variables in the correct sequence. (This is done automatically, but if the data is already sorted in the appropriate order, the sorting can be omitted by selecting the button marked File is Already Sorted.)

13.3 Selecting permanent subgroups: SELECT CASES

Select Cases resembles Split File except that it continues to operate for the rest of the SPSS run. So if we select just the females from the data file using Select Cases, and do some analysis on the female's scores, we cannot return to analysing the male's scores in the same run. In practice it is usually simpler to use Split File rather than Select Cases.

If you do choose from the menu

```
Data
     Select Cases
```

it opens a dialogue box shown in Figure 13.3, which has a number of paths through it. Suppose you want to compare (using a *t*-test) the sales_1

```
SORT CASES BY area .
SPLIT FILE
  BY area .
T-TEST
  GROUPS=sex(1 2)
  /MISSING=ANALYSIS
  /VARIABLES=sales_1
  /CRITERIA=CIN(.95) .
SPLIT FILE
  OFF.
```

AREA: 1   North
t-tests for independent samples of SEX

Variable	Number of Cases	Mean	SD	SE of Mean
SALES_1				
male	3	5321.3433	3134.367	1809.627
female	6	6577.0533	2284.411	932.607

Mean Difference = -1255.7100

Levene's Test for Equality of Variances: F= .122   P= .737

t-test for Equality of Means Variances	t-value	df	2-Tail Sig	SE of Diff	95% CI for Diff
Equal	-.69	7	.510	1807.547	(-5531.12, 3019.698)
Unequal	-.62	3.12	.580	2035.806	(-7734.56, 5223.140)

AREA: 2   South
t-tests for independent samples of SEX

Variable	Number of Cases	Mean	SD	SE of Mean
SALES_1				
male	7	6220.3343	2823.499	1067.182
female	5	4700.3280	1409.678	630.427

Mean Difference = 1520.0063

Levene's Test for Equality of Variances: F= 7.577 P= .020

t-test for Equality of Means Variances	t-value	df	2-Tail Sig	SE of Diff	95% CI for Diff
Equal	1.10	10	.297	1382.937	(-1562.19, 4602.203)
Unequal	1.23	9.23	.250	1239.483	(-1284.66, 4324.675)

Figure 13.2 *Example of using SPLIT FILE to analyse males and females separately*

scores of men and women but only for those respondents who worked in the North of the country (area = 1). To select respondents from the North, i.e. who have an area score of 1, click on the If . . . button, which opens another box, entitled Select Cases: If. This requires you to enter the variables to be used for selecting cases and mathematical or logical expressions and is described in section 12.3. So for the example of selecting the cases where area = 1, you need to have this formula in the main text box of this dialogue box. Click on Continue to return to the Select Cases box and then press Paste to insert the syntax into a syntax window.

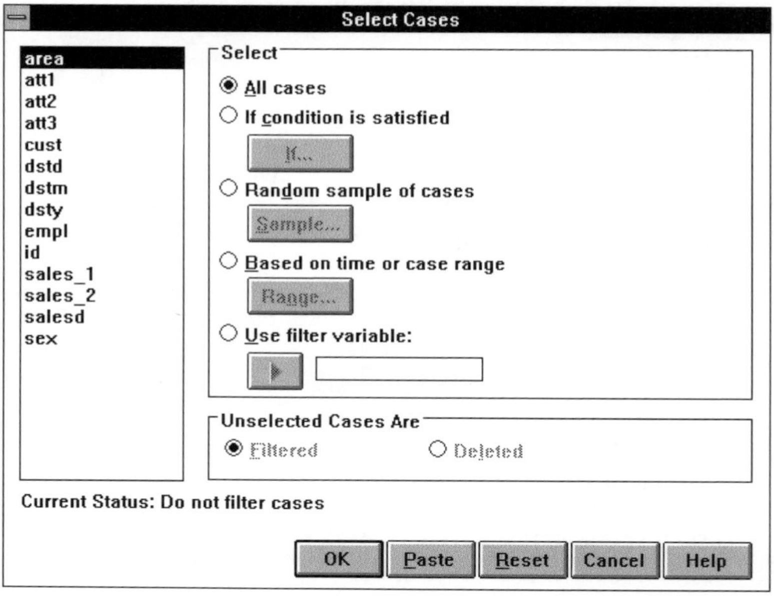

Figure 13.3　*The dialogue box for Select Cases*

13.4 Selecting a random sample of cases

With a very large data file, you may wish to select a sample of cases for analysis. To select a 10% random sample, use from the menu

```
Data
     Select Cases
```

In the Select Cases dialogue box select Random Sample of Cases and click on the Sample button. Another box is revealed and allows you to specify a percentage of the cases or an exact number of cases selected randomly from the data file.

13.5 Selecting the first *n* cases

To analyse just the first *n* cases in the data file, you have to type the command into a Syntax file. To select the first 10 cases, the syntax line would read:

```
N 10.
```

This operates for the remainder of the SPSS run, so only the first *n* cases can be analysed by any subsequent procedures.

If you have entered an identification number as a variable (as has been done with the variable id in the data file salesq), you can achieve the same effect from the menus using the Select Cases technique, described above in section 13.3. To analyse only the 10 cases with identification numbers below 11, select

```
Data
     Select Cases
```

and then use

```
If id<11.
```

13.6 Chapter summary

- Analysing subgroups is needed to carry out an analysis on a subset of cases such as just the males. To select temporary subgroups use SPLIT FILE and turn it off afterwards using the Split File box and the Analyze All Cases button.
- To select a random sample of cases of data use Data /Select Cases.

HOW MANY RESPONDENTS GAVE A PARTICULAR ANSWER? FREQUENCY DATA

14.1 Obtaining tables showing how many people gave each response: FREQUENCIES

Probably the first question you ask of your data is: how many people gave each alternative response to a particular question? The answer is obtained using the FREQUENCIES command. If you want cross-tabulations, showing how many people with a particular score on one variable obtained a particular score on another variable, the procedure needed is CROSSTABS described in section 14.4.

Obtain the frequencies procedure by selecting

```
Statistics
     Summarize
          Frequencies
```

The dialogue box shown in Figure 14.1 is presented. Select each variable to be analysed by clicking on its name, which will then be highlighted. Then click in the button marked with a right-pointing arrow, and the variable will appear in the right-hand box, the one headed Variable(s).

The result of running Frequencies on the variable sex in salesq is shown in Figure 14.2. The table shows the frequency of each score on the variable sex. In the data file salesq, the scores are 1 for male, 2 for female and 3 which was defined as a missing value and represents sex unknown. The frequencies are shown as percentages in the Percent column. Valid Percent gives the percentages when missing values are excluded, so for males there are 10 cases, which is 45.5% of 22 (the total number of cases in the data file) but 47.6% of 21 (the number of cases where sex is known). The Cum Percent column shows the cumulative percentages of the valid percent column.

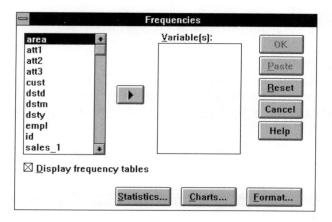

Figure 14.1   *The dialogue box for Frequencies*

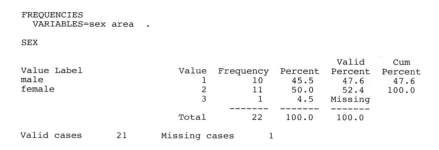

```
FREQUENCIES
  VARIABLES=sex area   .

SEX
                                                    Valid     Cum
Value Label                    Value  Frequency  Percent  Percent  Percent
male                             1        10       45.5     47.6     47.6
female                           2        11       50.0     52.4    100.0
                                 3         1        4.5    Missing
                                        -------   -------  -------
                               Total      22      100.0    100.0

Valid cases        21    Missing cases      1
```

Figure 14.2   *Output from the Frequencies procedure*

To obtain the means or other statistics using Frequencies, request them by clicking on the button labelled Statistics . . . at the bottom left of the dialogue box shown in Figure 14.1, which reveals another dialogue box illustrated in Figure 7.6.

14.2 Histograms and bar charts showing distributions of scores

The Frequencies procedure provides histograms and bar charts showing the distribution of the scores on any variable. These are useful for seeing whether the distribution approximates a normal one, or whether it is likely that some of the data has been miskeyed. Details on how to obtain these types of data plot and their interpretation are given in section 10.1.

14.3 How many times did a respondent give a particular answer? COUNT

You may wish to know how often a respondent used a particular response category. For example, in salesq, how often did the respondents use the response 3 on the attitude questions? This kind of question can be answered by using the Count procedure, obtained from the menu by selecting

```
Transform
     Count
```

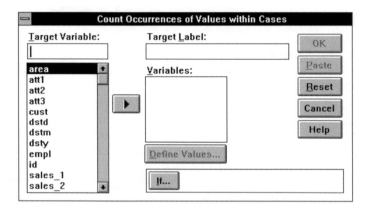

Figure 14.3   *The dialogue box for Count*

COUNT creates a new variable, and the dialogue box shown in Figure 14.3 asks you to enter a name for this in the Target Variable text box. You then specify the variables to be analysed, and click on the Define Values button which opens another box in which you indicate the value or range of values to be counted. To count how many times the response 3 was given to att1, att2 and att3 in salesq, you would enter these variables into the Variables list, enter a name such as num3 for the new variable, and put a label such as 'Number of 3 responses on att questions' in the Target Label text box. Click on Define Values, and in the Value text box you would enter 3, click on the Add button, and then on Continue which takes you back to the Count Occurrences box. Clicking on Paste puts the syntax illustrated in Figure 14.4 into a syntax window. When the procedure is run, the new variable is added to the data in the Data Editor. Switch to the data window to see the new variable.

It is possible to perform COUNT on specified cases, such as only those which have a score of 1 on sex. This is achieved by selecting the If . . . button, and entering requirements in the Count Occurrences: If Cases dialogue box. Click on Include if Cases Satisfy Conditions:, specify the

```
COUNT
    num3 = att1 att2 att3  (3)  .
VARIABLE LABELS num3 'Number of 3 responses on att questions' .
EXECUTE .
```

Figure 14.4   *Example of the syntax for the Count procedure*

variable to be used to identify the cases (e.g. sex) and then indicate how the cases are to be identified by inserting the appropriate conditions (e.g. sex = 1). The way the If function operates is described in section 12.3.

14.4 Obtaining cross-tabulations

You often want to examine how scores on two (or more) variable are related; for example, in salesq, what is the relationship between sex and employer? This requires a two-dimensional table showing the number of people of each sex who are employed by each employer. Tables like this are obtained using CROSSTABS, which is obtained by selecting

```
Statistics
      Summarize
            Crosstabs
```

The dialogue box shown in Figure 14.5 asks you to enter a variable to form the rows of the table and a variable to form the columns from the variable list. If you insert more than one variable into the Row(s) or Column(s) boxes, you will obtain a set of cross-tabulations. An example of the output when a cross-tabulation of sex by employer was requested is shown in Figure 14.6.

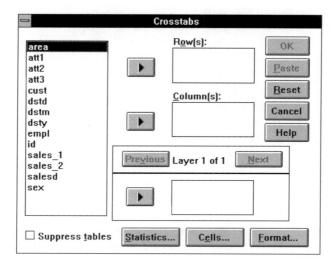

Figure 14.5   *The dialogue box for Crosstabs*

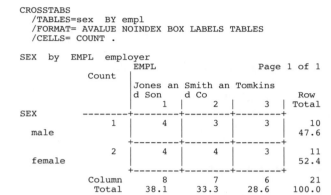

```
CROSSTABS
  /TABLES=sex  BY empl
  /FORMAT= AVALUE NOINDEX BOX LABELS TABLES
  /CELLS= COUNT .

SEX  by  EMPL  employer
                       EMPL                      Page 1 of 1
             Count
                   |Jones an Smith an Tomkins
                   |d Son    d Co
                   |      1 |      2 |      3 | Row
SEX         -------+--------+--------+--------+   Total
                 1 |      4 |      3 |      3 |    10
         male      |        |        |        |    47.6
                   +--------+--------+--------+
                 2 |      4 |      4 |      3 |    11
         female    |        |        |        |    52.4
                   +--------+--------+--------+
             Column       8        7        6       21
             Total     38.1     33.3     28.6    100.0

Number of Missing Observations:  1
```

Figure 14.6   *Output from the command CROSSTABS /TABLES sex BY empl*

Note that in Figure 14.6, the total is 21 and one missing observation is indicated; this is because the original data had one case where sex was coded as 3, which had been defined as a missing value indicating the sex of that respondent was unknown. Consequently there are only 21 cases that can be used in the sex by employer table.

The contents of the CROSSTABS table are set by clicking on the Cells button, which opens a box in which you can ask for Expected frequencies, and for the observed frequencies to be expressed as percentages of the row, column, and/or total number of cases in the table. Figure 14.7 shows in the top left cell of the table a list which identifies each of the figures in the cells in the main body of the table. In Figure 14.7 there are the actual frequency of cases in each cell, the expected value if there were no relationship between the two variables tabulated, the frequencies as a percentage of the total in the row, as a percentage of the total in the column, and as percentage of the overall total. There are also figures for residual, std res and adj res which are associated with the chi-square test and are unlikely to be needed. (Residual is the difference between the observed frequency and the expected frequency.)

You may want a further breakdown of the figures, with separate tables of variable1 by variable2 for each level of variable3; for example, suppose we want a sex by employer table, like that shown in Figure 14.6 but for each area group separately. The variable area is referred to as control variable, and you have to enter it in the box under the heading Layer 1 of 1 in the dialogue box shown in Figure 14.5. You can have further control variables by clicking on the Next button.

If you wish to have the table organized in descending order of variable scores, or to obtain an index of the tables you are requesting, these can be set by using the Format button in the Crosstabs dialogue box.

```
CROSSTABS
  /TABLES=sex  BY empl
  /FORMAT= AVALUE NOINDEX BOX LABELS TABLES
  /CELLS= COUNT EXPECTED ROW COLUMN TOTAL RESID SRESID ASRESID .
```

SEX   by   EMPL   employer

	EMPL			Page 1 of 1
Count Exp Val Row Pct Col Pct Tot Pct Residual Std Res Adj Res	Jones an d Son 1	Smith an d Co 2	Tomkins 3	 Row Total
SEX				
1 male	4 3.8 40.0% 50.0% 19.0% .2 .1 .2	3 3.3 30.0% 42.9% 14.3% -.3 -.2 -.3	3 2.9 30.0% 50.0% 14.3% .1 .1 .1	10 47.6%
2 female	4 4.2 36.4% 50.0% 19.0% -.2 -.1 -.2	4 3.7 36.4% 57.1% 19.0% .3 .2 .3	3 3.1 27.3% 50.0% 14.3% -.1 -.1 -.1	11 52.4%
Column Total	8 38.1%	7 33.3%	6 28.6%	21 100.0%

Number of Missing Observations: 1

Figure 14.7 *Extract of output from the command CROSSTABS /TABLES sex BY empl with additional cell contents*

14.5 Obtaining the two-sample chi-square test

The chi-square test is used when respondents have been allocated to categories on two variables (e.g. sex, area). The test compares the number of cases falling into each cell of the table with the frequency that would be expected if there were no association between the two variables that form the table. (The expected frequencies are calculated for each cell in the table by multiplying the appropriate row and column totals and dividing by *N*.)

Chi-square and other tests of association such as the contingency coefficient, and also correlations are available from the Statistics button of the Crosstabs dialogue box (Figure 14.5).

The output from the chi-square test for two samples is shown in Figure 14.8. The frequency table showing the number of cases in each cell of the table is followed by the value of chi-square (labelled Pearson), the degrees of freedom (D.F.), and the probability (Significance). If the Significance value is equal to or less than 0.05, you can conclude that the

```
CROSSTABS
  /TABLES=sex  BY area
  /FORMAT= AVALUE NOINDEX BOX LABELS TABLES
  /STATISTIC=CHISQ
  /CELLS= COUNT TOTAL .
```

SEX   by   AREA

```
                    AREA          Page 1 of 1
            Count
            Tot Pct |North   South
                                       Row
                    |    1 |     2 | Total
  SEX       --------+--------+--------+
              1     |    3 |     7 |   10
  male              | 14.3 |  33.3 | 47.6
                    +--------+--------+
              2     |    6 |     5 |   11
  female            | 28.6 |  23.8 | 52.4
                    +--------+--------+
            Column       9      12      21
            Total     42.9    57.1   100.0
```

Chi-Square	Value	DF	Significance
Pearson	1.28864	1	.25630
Continuity Correction	.48125	1	.48786
Likelihood Ratio	1.30665	1	.25300
Mantel-Haenszel test for linear association	1.22727	1	.26794
Fisher's Exact Test:			
One-Tail			.24494
Two-Tail			.38700

Minimum Expected Frequency -   4.286
Cells with Expected Frequency < 5 -   2 OF   4 (50.0%)

Number of Missing Observations: 1

Figure 14.8   Output from CROSSTABS /TABLES sex BY area /STATISTICS CHISQ

chi-square test indicates that there is a significant association between the two variables. The output also gives you the figures for Likelihood Ratio chi-square and the Mantel–Haenszel chi-square test, which tests whether there is a linear relationship between the row and column variables. It is only applicable to ordinal data, and should not be used if the data is nominal.

The chi-square test is only valid if three conditions are met. First, the data must be independent: no respondent can appear in more than one cell of the table. Secondly, no cell should have an expected frequency of less than 1. The output from SPSS tells you the minimum expected frequency, so it is simple to check whether this condition has been met. If the test is not valid, you must either alter the data table by amalgamating categories (using the Recode procedure explained in section 12.6) to remove cells with small expected frequencies, or collect more data.

The third requirement is that no more than 20% of the Expected Frequencies in the table can be less than 5. So if you have a 2 × 5 table which has 10 cells, the test will be invalid if 3 expected frequencies are below 5. If your data fails to meet this criterion, you have to collect more data or it may be possible to change the table; for example you could merge groups together. As Figure 14.8 shows, the output tells you the number of cells with an expected frequency less than 5 (Cells with E.F.<5) if this requirement is violated. (It is not printed if the requirement is met.) So the chi-square test is not valid on this table, as more than 20% of cells have an expected frequency smaller than 5; since it would not be meaningful to amalgamate groups, it would be necessary to collect more data in order to test the hypothesis that there is a tendency for sex to be related to area of work.

With 2×2 tables, a different formula for chi-square is used which incorporates a correction for continuity. Figure 14.8 shows the chi-square values with and without this correction: the values in the row labelled Continuity Correction are the ones to use if you have a 2×2 table as is the case in Figure 14.8.

If N is less than 20 in a 2×2 table, the Fisher Exact test should be used, rather than chi-square: SPSS will provide this for you automatically if any cell has an expected value less than 5. In Figure 14.8, the minimum expected frequency is shown to be 4.286, and so the result of the Fisher test is printed out.

14.6 Loglinear analysis

Loglinear analysis is a technique for analysing multiway contingency tables of frequency counts (cross tabulations) which are more complex than the two-dimensional tables shown in Figures 14.6, 14.7 and 14.8. It involves transforming the frequency values into their natural logs, and has the benefit of allowing tests for interactions in the classifications. Accounts can be found in texts on multivariate statistics such as Stevens (1996). It is not a procedure likely to be needed by the beginner, but is available from the Statistics /Loglinear entry of the Application window.

14.7 Chapter summary

- To obtain tables and histograms or barcharts showing how many people gave each response use FREQUENCIES.
- To find out how often a respondent used a particular response category use COUNT.
- Obtain cross-tabulations from Summarize /Crosstabs.
- The two-sample chi-square is made available from the Statistics button of the Summarize /Crosstabs dialogue box. Do not confuse this two-sample chi-square with the one obtained from the chi-square option of the Nonparametric Tests menu entry, which gives the one-sample chi-square.

WHAT IS THE AVERAGE SCORE? MEASURES OF CENTRAL TENDENCY AND DISPERSION

15.1 Finding the mean and standard deviation

Note that when you require the means of subgroups of respondents, such as the mean of males and then separately the means of females you need the MEANS procedure (see section 15.3) which also provides the mean score of all the respondents on any of the variables. But the simple way to obtain the mean, sum, and standard deviation of all respondents on any of the variables in the data file, is to use the EXPLORE, FREQUENCIES, or DESCRIPTIVES procedures which are accessed by selecting

```
Statistics
     Summarize
```

Specify the variables to be analysed, by clicking on their names in the list and then on the button with the right-pointing arrow. The mean and standard deviation are provided automatically. To obtain the sum, variance, range, standard error, and indices of kurtosis or skew, select the Options button and then specify the statistics required. You can have the means listed in alphabetic order of the variable names if you use Descriptives, select Options and in the dialogue box which is then presented select Name Display Order.

When carrying out parametrical statistical tests, such as the *t*-test, the output will give the means and variances of the data, so there is no need to obtain them using a separate procedure.

15.2 Finding median or mode

The median and mode are obtained if you use

```
Statistics
     Summarize
          Frequencies
```

When presented with the dialogue box, click on the Statistics button, and check the appropriate boxes.

The median is also provided by the Explore procedure, described in chapter 9.

15.3 Finding the means of subgroups of respondents

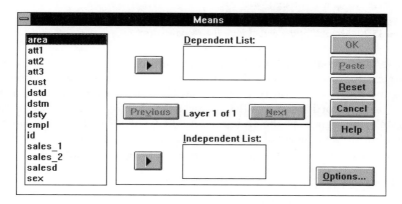

Figure 15.1   *The MEANS dialogue box*

To obtain the means of subgroups of respondents, use the Means procedure, which is obtained by selecting

```
Statistics
     Compare Means
          Means
```

and reveals the dialogue box shown in Figure 15.1. Suppose you want the means scores of males and females on the sales_1 variable in the salesq data file. Having selected Statistics /Compare Means /Means from the Application window menu, insert the dependent variable (sales_1) in the Dependent List text box of the Means dialogue box, and then insert sex into the Independent List text box, and click on Paste. The output is shown in Figure 15.2. It shows the mean and standard deviation on sales_1 for each of the two sex groups from the data file salesq. Observe that the respondent whose sex is unknown, who was given a sex score of 3 (missing value), is not included in the table and is shown as the missing case at the end of the printout.

```
MEANS
  TABLES=sales_1  BY sex
  /CELLS MEAN STDDEV COUNT
  /FORMAT= LABELS .

                  - - Description of Subpopulations - -

Summaries of          SALES_1
By levels of          SEX

Variable        Value  Label             Mean      Std Dev      Cases

For Entire Population                  5831.9205   2377.9699       21

SEX                 1    male           5950.6370   2772.4555       10
SEX                 2    female         5723.9964   2089.1906       11

    Total Cases = 22
  Missing Cases = 1 or    4.5 Pct
```

Figure 15.2   *Example of the output from the Means procedure*

The Means dialogue box allows you to subdivide the respondents into further subgroups by using the unhelpfully-titled Layer 1 of 1 option. To find the mean scores on the sales_1 variable of males and females from each area (North and South), enter sales_1 as the Dependent List variable, enter sex as the Independent List variable, then click on the Next button and insert area in the Independent List box. The output is shown in Figure 15.3 and gives the means of the subgroups.

```
MEANS
  TABLES=sales_1  BY sex  BY area
  /CELLS MEAN STDDEV COUNT
  /FORMAT= LABELS .

                  - - Description of Subpopulations - -

Summaries of          SALES_1
By levels of          SEX
                      AREA

Variable        Value  Label             Mean      Std Dev      Cases

For Entire Population                  5831.9205   2377.9699       21

SEX                 1    male           5950.6370   2772.4555       10
   AREA             1    North          5321.3433   3134.3666        3
   AREA             2    South          6220.3343   2823.4992        7

SEX                 2    female         5723.9964   2089.1906       11
   AREA             1    North          6577.0533   2284.4114        6
   AREA             2    South          4700.3280   1409.6785        5

    Total Cases = 22
  Missing Cases = 1 or    4.5 Pct
```

Figure 15.3   *Output from requesting means of subgroups using MEANS*

If you want the mean scores on sales_1 for the separate sex groups and then for the separate area groups, edit the syntax in the syntax window to read

MEANS /TABLES sales_1 BY sex area.

```
MEANS
   TABLES=sales_1  BY sex
   /CELLS MEAN STDDEV COUNT
   /FORMAT= LABELS
   /STATISTICS ANOVA .
```

- - Analysis of Variance - -

```
Dependent Variable    SALES_1
     By levels of     SEX

     Value  Label           Mean    Std Dev  Sum of Sq    Cases
       1    male       5950.6370  2772.4555 69178584.1       10
       2    female     5723.9964  2089.1906 43647171.8       11
                      ---------------------------------------------
Within Groups Total    5831.9205  2436.8417  112825756       21
```

```
                      Sum of                  Mean
Source                Squares    d.f.       Square     F      Sig.
Between Groups 269059.8850          1   269059.8850  .0453    .8337
Within Groups 112825755.86         19  5938197.6767                   Eta
   =   .0488     Eta Squared =    .0024
```

Figure 15.4 *Output of analysis of variance obtained from the MEANS procedure*

One-way analysis of variance (described more fully in chapter 16) to compare the means of the subgroups is obtained by selecting the Options button and checking the box labelled ANOVA table and eta. (Eta is appropriate if the dependent variable is measured on an interval scale, and the independent variable is nominal or ordinal. Eta squared can be interpreted as the proportion of the total variability in the dependent variable that can be accounted for by knowing the values of the independent variable.) So if you have used sales_1 as the dependent variable and sex as the independent variable, selecting the Options button and requesting the ANOVA table and eta will give a one-way analysis of variance on the sales_1 scores of the subgroups of the sex variable (i.e. males and females). An excerpt of the output is provided in Figure 15.4. It shows the mean and standard deviation for each sex group and then an analysis of variance summary table. Here F is a mere 0.0453, which is not significant ($p = 0.8337$), so there is no significant difference between the groups on the sales_1 scores.

15.4 Obtaining z-scores

The Descriptives procedure is used to obtain z-scores for any variable, by selecting the Save Standardized Values as Variables option in the Descriptives dialogue box. This option creates a new variable which is added to the data file, and is named as z+the first 7 letters of the variable name so that the z-scores of sales_1 are labelled zsales_1. When the syntax is run, the output window's contents are as illustrated in Figure 15.5. Switch to the data window to see the new column of z-scores.

This z-score facility will exclude any cases that have a missing value score on the variable being analysed. If you want to exclude from the

```
DESCRIPTIVES
  VARIABLES=sales_1  /SAVE
  /FORMAT=LABELS NOINDEX
  /STATISTICS=MEAN STDDEV MIN MAX
  /SORT=MEAN (A) .

Number of valid observations (listwise) =        22.00

                                                 Valid
  Variable      Mean    Std Dev   Minimum   Maximum       N   Label
  SALES_1    5859.62    2324.30   2005.30  10432.82      22

The following Z-Score variables have been saved on your working file:

  From        To
  Variable    Z-Score    Label                          Valid N
  --------    -------    -----                          -------
  SALES_1     ZSALES_1   Zscore(SALES_1)                     22
```

Figure 15.5   *Output when obtaining z-scores on a variable. Switch to the Data Editor window to see the zsales_1 scores*

analysis any case that had a missing value on any of the variables for which you are obtaining z-scores, you have to paste the command into a syntax file and then insert into the command line a /MISSING LISTWISE subcommand.

15.5 Chapter summary

- To obtain the mean, sum and standard deviation of all respondents on any of the variables use the EXAMINE, FREQUENCIES, or DESCRIPTIVES procedures.
- To obtain the means of subgroups of respondents use the MEANS procedure.
- To obtain the median or mode use FREQUENCIES.
- Obtain z-scores using DESCRIPTIVES.

PARAMETRIC STATISTICAL TESTS COMPARING MEANS

16.1 Basic preliminaries about the parametric tests

This chapter describes the commands needed to obtain the commoner parametric statistical tests used to compare the means of sets of scores. Guidance on selecting which test to use is provided in section 2.9. To compare the means of two sets of scores, use the *t*-test. If you are comparing the scores of the same respondents on two variables, use the within-subjects (paired-samples) *t*-test. To compare the scores of two groups of different subjects on one variable, use the between-subjects or independent-samples *t*-test. To compare the mean of a sample with a specified test value, use the one-sample *t*-test if you have SPSS version 6.1. (It is not included in SPSS version 6.0). If you wish to compare more than two sets of scores, you need the analysis of variance and should refer to section 16.5.

The printouts for the parametric tests show two-tailed significance (probability) levels which are appropriate for testing non-directional hypotheses. If you have a directional hypothesis you can halve the probability values which SPSS prints out.

Except for section 16.12, the examples shown in this chapter use the names of the variables in the salesq file; if you are applying the commands to a set of data with different variable names, you must of course use those variable names.

DEALING WITH CASES THAT HAVE MISSING DATA   The *t*-test procedures will exclude any case which has missing data on either the variable used to create the groups being compared or on the variable which is being subjected to the *t*-test. This is referred to as Exclude Cases Analysis-by-analysis. If you are requesting a number of *t*-tests on a series of variables, the package will omit those cases which have missing data on the variable being analysed and do this separately for each test. You can ask the program to omit from all *t*-tests, any cases which have missing values on either the grouping variable or on any of the variables being *t*-tested.

This is obtained by clicking on the Options button in the T Test dialogue box and then selecting the Exclude Cases Listwise alternative.

One-way analysis of variance obtained from the Statistics /Compare Means menu will exclude any case which has a missing value on the dependent or on the factor variables, or has a score on the factor variable which is outside the range specified with Define Range. If you are requesting a number of analyses, you can ask for any case that has missing values on any of the variables involved to be excluded from all analyses. This is done by clicking on the Options button of the dialogue box and selecting the Exclude Cases Listwise option.

16.2 Within-subjects (paired-samples) t-test

The dialogue box for the paired-samples *t*-test, shown in Figure 16.1, is obtained by selecting

```
Statistics
     Compare Means
          Paired-Samples T Test
```

Indicate the two variables to be compared by clicking on each of them; the first one will appear in the Current Selection Variable 1: area, and the second one will appear as Variable 2. To insert these into the Paired Variables list, click on the right-pointing arrow button: the two variables will then be shown as a linked pair. You can create further pairs in the same way.

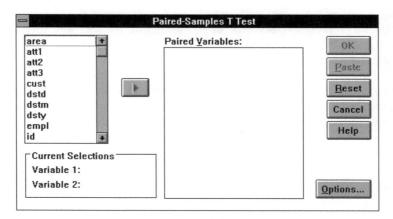

Figure 16.1   *The dialogue box for the paired-samples* t-test

Clicking on Paste will put into the Syntax window the procedure commands shown in Figure 16.2, where the scores on att1 and att2 have been selected for comparison. When the procedure is run, the output shown in Figure 16.2 appears in the output window. The top part of the output shows the means, standard deviations and standard errors of the scores on the two variables and the correlation between them (0.700 in this example). The significance of the correlation is provided: the value of .000 in Figure 16.2 indicates that the correlation is significant beyond the 0.001 level.

The paired t-test involves taking the difference between the two scores for each respondent and finding the mean of these difference scores. The bottom part of the output gives this mean difference, its standard deviation and standard error. The value of the t statistic is then shown, with its degrees of freedom (df) and its probability level (2-tail Sig): if the probability is less than 0.05 (in Figure 16.2 it is .004), you can conclude there was a statistically significant difference between the means of the two sets of scores. In Figure 16.2, the mean on att2 at 3.0909 is significantly different from the mean on att1, which is 2.5455. The final line of the output shows the 95% confidence interval of the mean difference.

```
T-TEST
  PAIRS= att1  WITH att2 (PAIRED)
  /CRITERIA=CIN(.95)
  /FORMAT=LABELS
  /MISSING=ANALYSIS.

                    - - - t-tests for paired samples - - -

               Number of        2-tail
  Variable       pairs    Corr   Sig      Mean      SD     SE of Mean
  ------------------------------------------------------------------
  ATT1                                   2.5455    1.101      .235
                   22      .700   .000
  ATT2                                   3.0909     .921      .196
  ------------------------------------------------------------------

        Paired Differences
  Mean      SD       SE of Mean        t-value    df   2-tail Sig
  ------------------------------------------------------------------
  -.5455   .800         .171           -3.20      21      .004
  95% CI (-.900, -.190)
```

Figure 16.2   *Output from a paired-sample t-test*

The Options button of the T Test box allows you to suppress the printing of the variable labels, and alter the confidence intervals shown by entering a number (such as 99 for the 99% interval) in the text box.

16.3 Between-subjects (independent-samples) t-test

The Dialogue box for the independent-samples t-test, shown in Figure 16.3, is obtained by selecting

```
Statistics
    Compare Means
        Independent Samples T Test
```

The variables to be compared have to be inserted into the Tests Variable(s) text window. The variable used to divide the respondents into the two groups to be compared has to be inserted into the text window Grouping Variable, and you then have to click the Define Groups button, which opens a dialogue box. The normal procedure is to enter into the Group 1 and Group 2 text boxes the values on the grouping variable which define the two groups to be compared. So, for example, to compare the scores on sales_1 for respondents of employer 2 with those for respondents on employer 3, you insert the variable (empl) in the Grouping Variable box of the Independent Samples T Test dialogue box (Figure 16.3), click on the Define Groups button and when presented with the Define Groups dialogue box enter 2 into the Group 1 text box and 3 into the Group 2 text box. Click on Continue to return to the T Test box, and click on Paste.

The Options button of the T Test box allows you to suppress the printing of the variable labels.

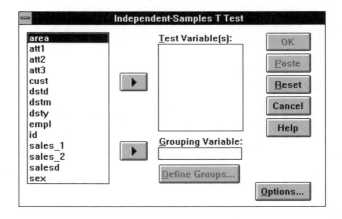

Figure 16.3   *The dialogue box for the independent-samples t-test*

An example of the syntax for the independent groups *t*-test and the output provided is shown in Figure 16.4. The first section shows that the variable being tested was sales_1, and that the groups of scores being compared were those for the two employers Smith and Co and Tomkins. (The variable labels which were assigned earlier are printed.) The mean score on sales_1 for each group is shown, with the standard deviations and standard errors. The mean difference and the outcome of Levene's test for equality of variances are provided, and then *t* values, degrees of freedom, probability of *t*, standard errors for the difference and 95%

confidence intervals (CI) for the difference are given. If the Levene test shows a probability value less than 0.05, the populations from which the two groups are samples had unequal variances and you should use the t value for unequal variances (the final line of Figure 16.4). If the Levene test had a probability value greater than 0.05 (as here), you are entitled to use the t value for equal variances. Remember that it is the absolute value of t which is taken: ignore the negative sign. You do not need a table of t values, as the printout shows the significance value. In Figure 16.4 the significance is shown as .000 indicating that the means differ at less than the 0.001 level.

```
T-TEST
  GROUPS=empl(2 3)
  /MISSING=ANALYSIS
  /VARIABLES=sales_1
  /CRITERIA=CIN(.95) .

t-tests for independent samples of  EMPL   employer


                          Number
          Variable        of Cases    Mean        SD       SE of Mean
        ------------------------------------------------------------------
          SALES_1
          Smith and Co       8     4625.1713   1089.784    385.297
          Tomkins            6     8207.4150    925.178    377.702
        ------------------------------------------------------------------

        Mean Difference = -3582.2437

        Levene's Test for Equality of Variances: F= .322   P= .581

        t-test for Equality of Means                  95%
   Variances  t-value   df   2-Tail Sig   SE of Diff    CI for Diff
   -----------------------------------------------------------------------
   Equal      -6.47     12      .000        553.249   (-4787.98, -2376.51)
   Unequal    -6.64     11.74   .000        539.549   (-4758.12, -2406.36)
   -----------------------------------------------------------------------
```

Figure 16.4 *Output for an independent t-test*

When the Define Groups button in Figure 16.3 is pressed, the Define Groups dialogue box has an option Cut point, and a text box into which a value can be entered. This has the effect of dividing the cases into two groups, one which has scores below the value entered as the Cut point and the other having scores equal to or above the Cut point. This can be useful if, for example, you wanted to compare the means of two groups formed by dividing them into those scoring below and above a certain value on one of the variables.

An example of the syntax and printout is shown in Figure 16.5, where two groups were formed according to whether they scored below 3 or above or equal to 3 on the variable att2 and their scores on the variable cust were compared. The Levene test was not significant ($p = 0.266$), so the t value for equal variances is the one to consider. In Figure 16.5

```
T-TEST
  GROUPS=att2(3)
  /MISSING=ANALYSIS
  /VARIABLES=cust
  /CRITERIA=CIN(.95) .

t-tests for independent samples of  ATT2
```

Variable	Number of Cases	Mean	SD	SE of Mean
CUST Number customer visits				
ATT2 >= 3	16	46.8125	14.820	3.705
ATT2 < 3	6	61.5000	19.191	7.835

```
Mean Difference = -14.6875

Levene's Test for Equality of Variances: F= 1.307  P= .266
```

	t-test for Equality of Means				95%
Variances	t-value	df	2-Tail Sig	SE of Diff	CI for Diff
Equal	-1.91	20	.070	7.671	(-30.693, 1.318)
Unequal	-1.69	7.36	.132	8.667	(-35.187, 5.812)

Figure 16.5   *Example of use of Cutpoint in the independent t-test*

$t = -1.91$ and $p = .070$, so there is no significant difference between the two means.

16.4 One-sample t-test

The one-sample *t*-test is available in SPSS version 6.1 but not in version 6.0. It is used to compare the mean of a sample with a specified test value. For example, it could be used to see whether the mean of the scores on the variable att1 is significantly different from 3, the neutral point of the scale for att1 which ran from 1 to 5.

Obtain the one-sample *t*-test by selecting it from the Statistics /Compare Means menu. Select the variable to be tested and type into the text box the test value with which the mean is to be compared. An example of the syntax and output is illustrated in Figure 16.6. The test value is shown and the *t* value and significance (probability) are printed. Here, $t = -1.94$, $p = .066$. As .066 is larger than 0.05, the mean on att1 is not significantly different from 3.

16.5 Basic principles of the analysis of variance

When you have three or more sets of parametric data, you may want to test the hypothesis that the means of the sets differ. You cannot use the *t*-test, as that only compares two sets, so the parametric analysis of variance is the technique to employ.

```
T-TEST
  /TESTVAL=3
  /MISSING=ANALYSIS
  /VARIABLES=att1
  /CRITERIA=CIN (.95) .

One Sample t-tests
```

Variable	Number of Cases	Mean	SD	SE of Mean
ATT1	22	2.5455	1.101	.235

Test Value = 3

Mean Difference	95% CI Lower	Upper	:	t-value	df	2-Tail Sig
−.45	−.943	.034	:	−1.94	21	.066

Figure 16.6 *Syntax and output for the one-sample t-test*

As the name implies, analysis of variance examines the variance within the whole sets of scores. Imagine we have sets of data from three separate groups of subjects, and want to know whether there is a difference between the three groups. If there were no difference between the groups (the null hypothesis is true) their data would all come from the same population, and the three sets of data would all have the same means and the same variances. The variance of each group would be an estimate of the population variance (variance due to random fluctuations between respondents, known as error variance because it arises due to chance alterations in the data). Our best estimate of the population variance is given by calculating the mean of the variances of the three groups. So by looking at the average variance of the three groups, we can get an estimate of the error variance.

Again, if the null hypothesis is true, the means of the three groups will be the same, and the variance of the means (i.e. how much the means differ from each other) will be very small. (We would expect it to be the same as the population variance.) The variance of the means of the three groups is known as the treatment variance. So if the null hypothesis were true, and the three groups did not differ from each other, the variance between the means (the treatment variance) would equal the error variance; if we divided the treatment variance by the error variance, the answer would be 1.00. The result of dividing the treatment variance by the error variance is denoted as *F*.

If the null hypothesis is not true, there is a difference between the three groups. The variance of the means will be larger than the error variance. If we divide the variance of the means (the treatment variance) by the error variance, we shall get a number (*F*) bigger than 1.00.

In the analysis of variance, we compare the treatment variance with the error variance to test the hypothesis that there is a significant difference between the means. There are different types of analysis of variance, and you need to ensure you apply the procedure which is appropriate for the situation you are analysing. When you want to compare three or more levels of one between-subjects variable, use a one-way analysis of variance. But analysis of variance can be extended to situations in which there are two or more independent variables. Imagine we have measured the performance of young (under 30) and old (over 50) subjects at two different times of day (2 am and 2 pm), and used different subjects in each group so there were four separate groups altogether. We might be interested in knowing whether performance differed according to the subject's age, differed according to time of day, and whether there was an interaction between these variables. Interaction means that the effect of one variable was influenced by the other; for example, we might find that the difference between performance at 2 pm and 2 am was less for the younger subjects than for the older ones. If this were so, the analysis of variance would show a significant interaction term.

In the example just given, both variables are between-subjects, as different people were used in each of the four groups. But analysis of variance can be applied to within-subjects (repeated measures) studies, where the same subjects are used in different conditions. For example, we would have a repeated measures study if we had carried out our time-of-day/age of subjects experiment, and tested the same respondents at 2 am and 2 pm.

16.6 Which anova do you require?

Which analysis of variance you need is determined by the design of your study. There are two points you need to know: (1) how many independent variables were there (one or more than one)? (2) taking each independent variable in turn, was it a between-subjects (independent samples) variable or a within-subjects (repeated measures) one? If you have more than one independent variable and all variables are between-subjects, you need the two-way analysis of variance for independent groups. If all variables are within-subjects (repeated measures), you need the repeated measures anova. If there are both between-subject and within-subject variables, you need the mixed anova. Table 16.1 will help you decide which type of anova you need.

16.7 Obtaining the anova

The following sections describe how to obtain the anova for each of the situations described in Table 16.1, and explain how to interpret the printout. SPSS has three separate procedures for calculating the analysis of variance: ONEWAY, ANOVA and MANOVA. If you have one inde-

Table 16.1   *Deciding between the various types of analysis of variance*

How many independent variables?	Between or within subjects?	SSPS procedure required	See section
I	Between	ONEWAY or ANOVA	16.8.1 16.8.2
I	Within	MANOVA	16.9
2 or more	All between	ANOVA	16.10
2 or more	One or more between and one or more within	MANOVA	16.11
2 or more	All within	MANOVA	16.12

pendent between-subjects variable, ONEWAY or ANOVA can be used. If you have two or more independent between-subjects variables, use ANOVA. If any of the variables is within-subjects, you need MANOVA. For each procedure, dialogue boxes are used to tell the program which are the dependent variables and how any subgroups of respondents are identified. When necessary the system will present dialogue boxes so you can tell it which variables are within subjects and which are between subjects.

Note that in the analysis of variance summary tables which appear in the output, the column headed F Prob shows the probability of getting the observed F value by chance. If the entry is .0000, this means the finding is significant beyond the 0.0001 (0.01%) level, and the variable being tested had a significant effect.

One-way analysis of variance can be obtained from the Statistics /Compare Means menu entry, but all other forms of the analysis of variance are accessed by selecting

```
Statistics
     ANOVA Models
```

The drop-down menu has four entries: Simple Factorial, General Factorial, Multivariate, Repeated Measures. Simple Factorial is used for one-way analysis of variance. Unlike ONEWAY, Simple Factorial allows you to have more than one independent variable. Multivariate is used when you have more than one *dependent* variable, and Repeated Measures is used when you have at least one repeated-measures (within-subjects) independent variable.

16.8 One independent variable, between-subjects: One-way analysis of variance

This form of analysis of variance can be obtained in three ways. If you use the MEANS procedure described in section 15.3, one-way analysis of variance (ANOVA) can be requested via the Options button. Alternatively, you can request ONEWAY from the Statistics /Compare Means menu entry (section 16.8.1) or choose ANOVA by selecting the Simple Factorial option from Anova Models (section 16.8.2). ONEWAY and ANOVA are basically the same and give similar output.

16.8.1 Using ONEWAY

Select from the menu system

```
Statistics
    Compare Means
        One-way ANOVA
```

The dialogue box shown in Figure 16.7 will be presented.

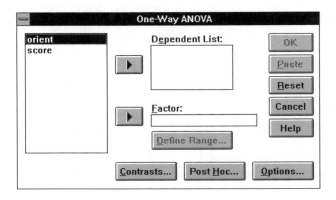

Figure 16.7 *The dialogue box for ONEWAY*

Suppose you want to compare the scores on sales_1 for respondents from the three different employers in the file salesq. This involves the one-way analysis of variance and can be achieved by following the stages listed here:

1 Identify the dependent variable. In this example, the variable sales_1 is the dependent variable. Click on its name and then on the right-pointing arrow button so that sales_1 appears in the box headed Dependent List.

2 Identify the variable (Factor) which distinguishes the subgroups of respondents. In the example, this is the variable empl, the variable name for employer. Click on its name in the variable list and then click on the right-arrow button next to the box headed Factor. The variable name will then appear as the Factor.

You must specify the maximum and minimum values on this variable, which in this example are 1 and 3. Click on the button marked Define

Range, and another dialogue box (Figure 16.8) is presented. Type the minimum and maximum values in the appropriate boxes, then click on Continue and you will be returned to Figure 16.7. If you had a variable that had five values and wanted to compare the five levels, you would enter the values 1 and 5 as the minimum and maximum values in the boxes of the Define Range dialogue box.

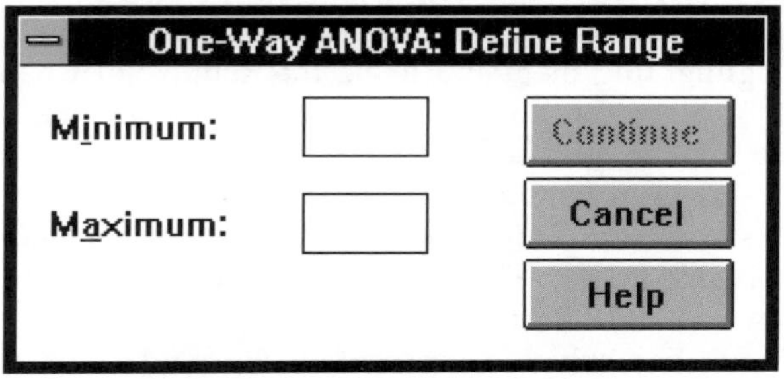

Figure 16.8   *The dialogue box in which you identify the maximum and minimum values of the independent variable (factor)*

If you want the output to show you the means on the dependent variable (sales_1 in this example) for the various levels of the independent variable, click on the Options button; yet another dialogue box is revealed, and you select Descriptive. To test whether the groups being compared have equal variance, you can ask for the Levene statistic from the One-Way Options button. When you have finished with this box, click on Continue, to be returned to Figure 16.7 and click on Paste.

Analysis of variance can tell you that there is a difference between the means of the three or more groups of respondents, but it does not tell you just where the differences occur: is group 1 different from both group 2 and group 3, does group 2 differ from both group 1 and group 3? Questions like this are answered by comparing the means of the subgroups, and there are two types of procedure. One is referred to as *a priori* comparisons, and these are ones that were planned before the data was collected: you might, for example, have predicted that group 3 differs significantly from group 1 but not from group 2. *Post hoc* tests, on the other hand, are comparisons suggested after you have examined the data.

A priori contrasts, including orthogonal contrasts, can be obtained in One-Way by clicking the Contrasts . . . button. How to use this is best explained with an example. Suppose we are comparing the scores on sales_1 for the three employers in salesq, and had predicted that there would be a significant difference between the scores for employer 1 and the combined scores for employers 2 and 3. To test this prediction we would use linear contrasts: the coefficient for employer 1's data can be set at −1 and the coefficients for employers 2 and 3 each set to 0.5. The coefficient of −1 for group 1 is entered in the box marked Coefficient, and the Add button used to insert it into the list. The coefficient of 0.5 for group 2 is then entered in the Coefficient box and Add used to insert it in the list, and finally the coefficient for group 3 is inserted in the list by using the Add button. The order of the coefficients is crucial, as they are applied in sequence to the ascending order of values on the factor variable: the first coefficient is assigned to the lowest value, the second to the next-to-lowest value and so on. Coefficients can be removed or altered by highlighting them and using the Remove or Change buttons. Further sets of contrasts can be entered if you click on the Next button. An example of the output obtained when *a priori* contrasts were requested is shown in Figure 16.10.

Post hoc tests such as Duncan's test, Tukey's test, Scheffe's test (and others) are obtained if you click on the Post Hoc . . . button in the One-Way ANOVA box and select the tests you require from the list provided in the dialogue box which is presented. Figure 16.9 shows how the output of the Scheffe test is presented.

Figure 16.9 shows the output of the ONEWAY procedure, in which the scores on the variable sales_1 were compared for the three employers, descriptive statistics were requested and a Scheffe *post hoc* test was specified. The first section is a conventional anova summary table, showing the degrees of freedom, Sum of Squares, Mean Square, F ratio and probability of F for the between-groups variable. The F ratio is the between-groups mean square divided by the within-groups mean square. The probability associated with F is given in the final column: if it is less than 0.05 (in Figure 16.9 it is .0058), this shows there is a significant difference between the groups being compared. In our example, it indicates that there was a significant difference between the employers in the sales_1 scores. Remember that if the entry is .0000, this means the finding is significant beyond the 0.0001 (0.01%) level.

The second section of Figure 16.9 was produced by incorporating /STATISTICS DESCRIPTIVES in the procedure command. It provides summary statistics for the groups being compared; as can be seen, rounding the numbers to two decimal places, the mean for group 1 (those respondents employed by employer 1) is 5333.23, the standard deviation is 2761.36, the standard error is 976.29. The 95% confidence limits for the mean are followed by the minimum and maximum scores on sales for this group of respondents.

The additional output obtained by including the subcommand /RANGES SCHEFFE is illustrated in Figure 16.9. This section of the output indicates, with the asterisks, that group 3 (i.e. employer 3) is significantly different from both group 1 and group 2. The absence of asterisks shows that groups 1 and 2 do not differ from each other.

In Figure 16.10, ONEWAY was run with *a priori* contrasts requested. The Contrast Coefficient Matrix shows that coefficients were set at −1,

```
ONEWAY
  sales_1 BY empl(1 3)
  /RANGES=SCHEFFE
  /HARMONIC NONE
  /STATISTICS DESCRIPTIVES
  /FORMAT NOLABELS
  /MISSING ANALYSIS .
```

```
              - - - - - O N E W A Y - - - - -
        Variable  SALES_1
     By Variable  EMPL      employer

                    Analysis of Variance

                       Sum of        Mean         F      F
          Source   D.F.   Squares       Squares     Ratio  Prob.
Between Groups     2   47480438.83   23740219.42   6.8375  .0058
Within Groups     19   65968934.14    3472049.165
Total             21  113449373.0

                        Standard   Standard
Group   Count    Mean   Deviation    Error   95 Pct Conf Int for Mean
Grp 1      8  5333.2313  2761.3599  976.2882 3024.6817  TO   7641.7808
Grp 2      8  4625.1713  1089.7836  385.2967 3714.0913  TO   5536.2512
Grp 3      6  8207.4150   925.1783  377.7025 7236.5146  TO   9178.3154

Total     22  5859.6232  2324.2958  495.5415 4829.0881  TO   6890.1582


GROUP        MINIMUM      MAXIMUM
Grp 1      2005.3000   10432.8200
Grp 2      3124.2000    6441.3800
Grp 3      6497.0500    8914.5000
TOTAL      2005.3000   10432.8200
...........................................................

              - - - - - O N E W A Y - - - - -

        Variable  SALES_1
     By Variable  EMPL      employer

Multiple Range Tests:  Scheffe test with significance level .05

The difference between two means is significant if
  MEAN(J)-MEAN(I)  >= 1317.5829 * RANGE * SQRT(1/N(I) + 1/N(J))
  with the following value(s) for RANGE: 3.75

  (*) Indicates significant differences which are shown in the lower
triangle
                           G G G
                           r r r
                           p p p
                           2 1 3
       Mean       EMPL
    4625.1713     Grp 2
    5333.2313     Grp 1
    8207.4150     Grp 3     * *
```

Figure 16.9 *Output from the ONEWAY analysis of variance with Scheffe test*

0.5 and 0.5. The printout shows that the T probability was greater than 0.05, so you would conclude that group 1 is not significantly different from the pooled value of groups 2 and 3. (T in the SPSS output represents the value, known as Student's t, which is usually shown in statistics textbooks as t.) If you look at the means of the three subgroups included in Figure 16.9, you will see that a more sensible comparison would be to compare group 3 (mean = 8207.415) with the pooled mean

```
ONEWAY
  sales_1 BY empl(1 3)
  /CONTRAST= -1 .5 .5
  /HARMONIC NONE
  /FORMAT NOLABELS
  /MISSING ANALYSIS .
```

```
            - - - - - O N E W A Y - - - - -
     Variable  SALES_1
  By Variable  EMPL        employer
```

Analysis of Variance

Source	D.F.	Sum of Squares	Mean Squares	F Ratio	F Prob.
Between Groups	2	47480438.83	23740219.42	6.8375	.0058
Within Groups	19	65968934.14	3472049.165		
Total	21	113449373.0			

```
            - - - - - O N E W A Y - - - - -
     Variable  SALES_1
  By Variable  EMPL        employer
```

Contrast Coefficient Matrix

```
            Grp 1        Grp 3
                  Grp 2

Contrast  1  -1.0    .5    .5
```

Pooled Variance Estimate

	Value	S. Error	T Value	D.F.	T Prob.
Contrast 1	1083.0619	828.9610	1.307	19.0	.207

Separate Variance Estimate

	Value	S. Error	T Value	D.F.	T Prob.
Contrast 1	1083.0619	1012.8755	1.069	8.1	.316

Figure 16.10   *Excerpt of output from ONEWAY with a priori contrasts requested*

of groups 1 and 2 (means = 5333.2313 and 4625.1713). You might like to carry out this analysis to confirm that you understand how it is done.

16.8.2 One-way analysis of variance using the ANOVA Models menu entry

Select from the menu system

```
Statistics
     ANOVA Models
          Simple Factorial
```

A dialogue box will appear (Figure 16.11). Suppose you want to compare the scores on sales_1 for respondents from the three different employers in the file salesq. This involves the one-way analysis of variance and can be achieved by following the stages listed here:

1   Identify the dependent variable. You have to tell SPSS which is the dependent variable by clicking on its name (sales_1 in this example) and then on the right-arrow button so that it appears in the box headed Dependent.
2   Identify the variable that distinguishes the groups you are comparing, known as a Factor. In this example, this is called empl, for

employer. Click on empl and then on the right-arrow next to the box headed Factor(s), and it will appear in the box as empl(??). The (??) informs you that you have to tell SPSS the maximum and minimum scores on the Factor variable: in this example they are 1 and 3. Click on the Define Range button, type the minimum and maximum values in the appropriate boxes of the dialogue box which is revealed (similar to Figure 16.8), then click on Continue to return to Figure 16.11.

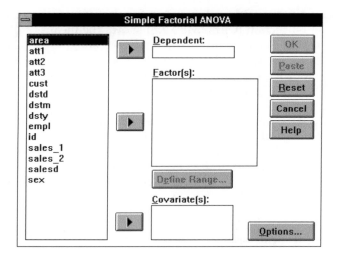

Figure 16.11   The dialogue box from Anova Models /Simple Factorial

You may want the printout to show the mean scores of each of the subgroups of respondents (each level on the Factor). If you click on Options in Figure 16.11, another box is shown. To obtain the means, you must first change the Method from Unique to Hierarchical or Experimental by clicking on the appropriate radio button. Then the check box which allows you to request the Means and Counts will become available: click it, then on Continue to return to Figure 16.11. Click on Paste to insert the syntax in a syntax window.

The three methods (Unique, Hierarchical and Experimental) mentioned in the previous paragraph control how the effects are assessed. The Unique method assesses all effects simultaneously, Hierarchical adjusts main effects for factors that precede them in the factor list, and Experimental assesses any covariate effects before main effects and interactions. If the number of cases in each cell of the table is the same, the different methods produce the same result.

An alternative way of obtaining the means is to run the Means procedure by selecting

```
Statistics
     Compare Means
          Means
```

When faced with the dialogue box for this procedure, you would add the dependent variable (sales_1, in this example) to the Dependent List box and the name of the factor (empl, in this example) to the Independent List.

The syntax and output for this Simple Factorial command is shown in Figure 16.12. As the command included the subcommand /STATISTICS MEAN, the first section (CELL MEANS) shows the means and n for the total set of scores. Then the mean and n for each subgroup (1, 2 and 3 on the Factor empl) are given. The figures in brackets below the means are the n values for each subgroup. (The mean on score of those respondents from level 2 on the factor empl was 4625.17, and there were 8 people in this group.)

The analysis of variance table is then given. Here, F for the empl variable is 6.838, and the significance is shown as .006.

Figure 16.9 and Figure 16.12 show the outputs for analyses of the same set of data. There are slight differences in their layout and in the figures: using ONEWAY (Figure 16.9), more significant figures are shown than when ANOVA is used (Figure 16.12).

16.9 One independent variable, within-subjects

When you have one independent within-subjects variable with more than two levels and want to compare the scores on the levels, the MANOVA procedure is needed. In salesq, each respondent gave a score on three attitude questions, and we might wish to compare these three sets of scores.

To obtain the repeated-measures anova select from the menu system

```
Statistics
     ANOVA Models
          Repeated Measures
```

This presents the dialogue box shown in Figure 16.13.

1 Name the within-subject factor. The within-subject factor is initially labelled factor1, and you need to enter a more meaningful title for it. In our example, the factor is made up from the three scores on measures of attitude (att1, att2 and att3), so we can label the within-subjects variable attitude by typing the name attitude to replace the name factor1.

2 Identify the number of levels of the within-subjects factor. You need to type the appropriate number into the Number of Levels box: here

```
ANOVA
  VARIABLES=sales_1
  BY empl(1 3)
  /MAXORDERS ALL
  /STATISTICS MEAN
  /METHOD HIERARCHICAL
  /FORMAT LABELS .

                       * * *  C E L L   M E A N S  * * *
                    SALES_1
                by EMPL        employer

Total Population
  5859.62
  (    22)

EMPL
     1          2          3
  5333.23    4625.17    8207.41
  (    8)  (    8)  (    6)

              * * *  A N A L Y S I S   O F   V A R I A N C E  * * *
                    SALES_1
                by    EMPL       employer

                     HIERARCHICAL sums of squares
                     Covariates entered FIRST

                          Sum of                  Mean              Sig
Source of Variation       Squares       DF       Square        F    of F

Main Effects             47480439       2    23740219.416    6.838  .006
    EMPL                 47480439       2    23740219.416    6.838  .006

Explained                47480439       2    23740219.416    6.838  .006
Residual                 65968934      19     3472049.165
Total                   113449373      21     5402351.094

22 cases were processed.
0 cases (.0 pct) were missing.
```

Figure 16.12   Syntax and output for the Simple Factorial Anova. Note: The Hierarchical method has been selected and the means of the subgroups requested

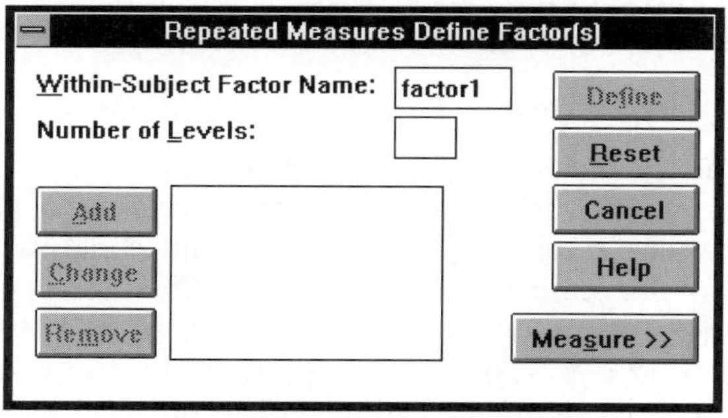

Figure 16.13   The dialogue box for Anova Models /Repeated Measures

there are three levels. Only when you have inserted the number of levels can you click on the Add button, and the untitled box will have inserted into it the factor name and number of levels; here it is attitude(3).

3   Identify the variables which make up the within-subject factor. You
    still have to tell SPSS which are the variables in the data which make
    up the factor. To do this, click on the Define button and the Repeated
    Measures Anova dialogue box shown in Figure 16.14 will be revealed.
    Select the data variables (in this example they are att1, att2 and att3)
    by clicking on them and then on the right-arrow button. They will
    then be added to the box headed Within-Subjects Variables.

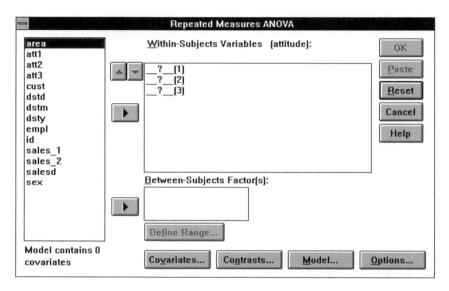

Figure 16.14   *The dialogue box for Repeated Measures Anova, to identify the
variables making up the within-subjects factor. Note: The variable names shown in
the variable list box will be whatever names you have used for the variables in the
data. If you follow the example in the text, the list will be: att1, att2, att3*

The syntax and output for this analysis is shown in Figure 16.15. If you
have an independent variable with just two levels rather than the three
used in this example, the output is shorter and contains only the two
analysis of variance summary tables for between-subjects effects and for
the within-subject effect.

   The first section of the output in Figure 16.15, the test of between-
subjects effects can be ignored. The second section includes the Mauchly
sphericity test, which tests to see whether there is heterogeneity of
covariance. Non-experts can take comfort from Stevens (1996): 'There are
various tests of sphericity . . . we don't recommend using these tests'
(p. 460). The value of the Greenhouse–Geisser epsilon and the Huynh–
Feldt epsilon are indications of whether the data shows sphericity: if
sphericity is met, the Greenhouse–Geisser epsilon equals 1. The worst
possible violation gives epsilon = $1/(k-1)$ which in this example is

$1/(3-1) = 0.5$. Advanced textbooks on statistics such as Howell (1992) or Stevens (1996) discuss the meaning of sphericity and how to use the Greenhouse–Geisser epsilon to modify the degrees of freedom. Stevens (1996) says that one should adjust the degrees of freedom from $(k-1)$ and $(k-1)(n-1)$ by multiplying each of these by epsilon, which will reduce the degrees of freedom and mean that a higher value of F is needed before it is taken as statistically significant. In the printout shown in Figure 16.15, the epsilon values are such that one would need to adjust the degrees of freedom when looking up the significance of F, but as this is not a serious piece of data analysis I shall not consider the matter any further here. The output shows the results of multivariate tests (Pillais, Hotellings, etc.), but these can be ignored as they are only relevant when there are a number of dependent variables.

The main part of the output is at the end, and is a conventional anova table. In Figure 16.15 it shows the mean square (MS) for the variable attitude was 4.20, F was 2.83, and the probability (sig) was .070. As the significance here is larger than 0.05, there was no significant difference between the scores for the different levels of the variable, i.e. the scores on att1, att2 and att3 do not differ significantly.

16.10 Two-way analysis of variance with two (or more) independent variables, all between-subjects

When you have more than one independent variable and they are all between-subjects factors, you can analyse the effects of each variable and the interaction between them using the ANOVA procedure. Suppose that for the data in salesq we wanted to see whether there is a difference on sales_2 for people from different areas and of different sexes, and whether there is an interaction between these two factors. Is it the case, for example, that men sold more than women in the North but women sold more than men in the South?

To apply the analysis of variance for two (or more) between subjects variables, select from the menu system

```
Statistics
     ANOVA Models
          Simple Factorial
```

The dialogue box shown in Figure 16.11 is presented.

1 Identify the dependent variable. Click on its name (sales_2 in this example) in the variable list and insert it in the Dependent variable text box by clicking on the arrow button next to that box.
2 Define each of the Factors (independent variables). The Factors are what divide the respondents into subgroups, and in this example

```
MANOVA
   att1  att2  att3
   /WSFACTORS attitude(3)
   /METHOD UNIQUE
   /ERROR WITHIN+RESIDUAL
   /PRINT
     SIGNIF( MULT AVERF )
   /NOPRINT PARAM(ESTIM) .
```

- -
* * * * * * A n a l y s i s   o f   V a r i a n c e * * * * * *

        22 cases accepted.
         0 cases rejected because of out-of-range factor values.
         0 cases rejected because of missing data.
         1 non-empty cell.

         1 design will be processed.

- -
* * * * * * A n a l y s i s   o f   V a r i a n c e -- design   1 * * *

Tests of Between-Subjects Effects.

   Tests of Significance for T1 using UNIQUE sums of squares
   Source of Variation   SS   DF   MS   F Sig of F
   WITHIN+RESIDUAL   10.32   21   .49
   CONSTANT   600.02   1   600.02   1221.18   .000

- -
* * * * * * A n a l y s i s   o f   V a r i a n c e -- design   1 * * *

Tests involving 'ATTITUDE' Within-Subject Effect.

Mauchly sphericity test, W =   .35167
Chi-square approx. =   20.90096 with 2 D. F.
Significance =   .000

Greenhouse-Geisser Epsilon =   .60668
Huynh-Feldt Epsilon =   .62400
Lower-bound Epsilon =   .50000

AVERAGED Tests of Significance that follow multivariate tests are
equivalent to univariate or split-plot or mixed-model approach to repeated
measures.
Epsilons may be used to adjust d.f. for the AVERAGED results.

- -
* * * * * * A n a l y s i s   o f   V a r i a n c e -- design   1 * * *

EFFECT .. ATTITUDE
Multivariate Tests of Significance (S = 1, M = 0, N = 9)

Test Name   Value   Exact F Hypoth. DF   Error DF Sig. of F
Pillais   .33193   4.96845   2.00   20.00   .018
Hotellings   .49684   4.96845   2.00   20.00   .018
Wilks   .66807   4.96845   2.00   20.00   .018
Roys   .33193
Note.. F statistics are exact.

- -
* * * * A n a l y s i s   o f   V a r i a n c e -- design   1 * * *

Tests involving 'ATTITUDE' Within-Subject Effect.

AVERAGED Tests of Significance for ATT using UNIQUE sums of squares
Source of Variation   SS   DF   MS   F Sig of F
WITHIN+RESIDUAL   62.27   42   1.48
ATTITUDE   8.39   2   4.20   2.83   .070

- -

Figure 16.15   Syntax and output for MANOVA with one within-subjects variable

they are area and sex. When faced with Figure 16.11, click on an appropriate variable (such as area) in the variable list and then on the right arrow next to the box entitled Factor(s): the variable name will appear in that box. Then click on Define Range and type in the minimum and maximum values on this variable. (In this example they are 1 and 2, since the two levels of the area factor were encoded as 1 or 2.) When you have entered these values, Continue will return you to Figure 16.11. Repeat the procedure for any more independent variables. So here you click on sex, insert it into the Factor list, then Define its Range.

Most beginners will use the default method of assessing the effects in the analysis of variance, referred to as the Unique method. There are alternatives, known as Hierarchical and Experimental methods, which can be specified through the Options button. Options also allows you to specify how Covariates are entered, but again this is a facility unlikely to be needed by the beginner.

If you want the printout to show the mean scores of each of the subgroups of respondents (each level on the Factor), click on Options in Figure 16.11; another box is shown. To obtain the means, you must change the Method from Unique to Hierarchical or Experimental by clicking on the appropriate radio button. Then the check box which allows you to request the Means and counts will become available: click it, then on Continue to return to Figure 16.11.

The syntax and output for this two-way analysis of variance with independent groups is shown in Figure 16.16. The first section, the result of including /STATISTICS MEAN in the command, gives the mean scores on the dependent variable for all respondents and then for those respondents scoring 1 and 2 on area and then for those scoring 1 and 2 on sex. The means for all the subgroups created by crossing each level of the area factor with the sex factor are also shown. In all cases, the figures in brackets are the number of respondents in each subgroup.

The second section of Figure 16.16 shows the anova table listing the sources of variation, divided into main effects and interactions, and for each one there is the sum of squares, the degrees of freedom, the mean square (the sum of squares divided by the degrees of freedom), the value of F and the probability of F (Sig of F). If any value in this final column is smaller than 0.05, there is an effect significant at the 0.05 (5%) level. F for the area factor is 3.070 and the probability is .098, which means there was no overall difference between the two areas. The F value for sex is 1.911 and the probability is .185, so there is no overall difference between the two sexes. The interaction between the two factors has $F = 4.612$ and a probability of .046. So the area $\times$ sex interaction is significant at the 0.05 level. To see what this means, look at the mean scores of the four area/ sex subgroups. For area 1, males (sex = 1) sold less (6115.15) than

```
ANOVA
  VARIABLES=sales_2
  BY area(1 2) sex(1 2)
  /MAXORDERS ALL
  /STATISTICS MEAN
  /METHOD HIERARCHICAL
  /FORMAT LABELS .
```

```
                        * * * C E L L   M E A N S * * *
                    SALES_2
                by AREA
                   SEX

    Total Population
      5938.41
    (     21)

    AREA
         1            2
      6946.66    5182.22
    (     9)  (     12)

    SEX
         1            2
      6411.53    5508.29
    (    10)  (     11)


              SEX
               1            2
    AREA
         1   6115.15    7362.41
           (     3)  (      6)

         2   6538.56    3283.35
           (     7)  (      5)
    * * * A N A L Y S I S   O F   V A R I A N C E  * * *
                    SALES_2
                by AREA
                   SEX

              HIERARCHICAL sums of squares
              Covariates entered FIRST
```

Source of Variation	Sum of Squares	DF	Mean Square	F	Sig of F
Main Effects	25976610	2	12988304.994	2.490	.113
AREA	16010992	1	16010992.356	3.070	.098
SEX	9965618	1	9965617.633	1.911	.185
2-Way Interactions	24051760	1	24051759.756	4.612	.046
AREA SEX	24051760	1	24051759.756	4.612	.046
Explained	50028370	3	16676123.248	3.197	.050
Residual	88662741	17	5215455.350		
Total	138691111	20	6934555.535		

```
22 cases were processed.
1 cases (4.5 pct) were missing.
```

Figure 16.16 *Syntax and output for Simple Factorial anova with two between-subjects independent variables*

females (sex = 2), who sold 7362.41. But for area 2, the men sold 6538.56 and the women sold 3283.35. So the difference between the sexes differs according to which area one examines.

When there are two or more variables being analysed, it often helps one to gain an understanding of the data if the means of the subsets of scores are plotted on a graph. The way to obtain such a graph is explained in section 10.7.

16.11 Two (or more) independent variables, with at least one between-subjects and at least one within-subjects (mixed design)

In the data set salesq, we have two figures (sales_1 and sales_2) showing amount sold by each respondent, and data on the respondents' sex. So there is one within-subjects variable (amount sold) which has two levels (sales_1 and sales_2), and one between-subjects variable (sex). Suppose we want to know whether there is a difference between sales_1 and sales_2 and whether any difference that there is varies according to the respondent's sex. To answer the question, we need to use the MANOVA procedure.

To obtain the mixed anova, from the menu system select

```
Statistics
     ANOVA Models
          Repeated Measures
```

You will be presented with the Repeated Measures ANOVA /Define Factors dialogue box (Figure 16.13).

1 Define the within-subjects factor. The within-subjects factor is initially labelled factor1 (as shown in Figure 16.13), and you need to enter a more meaningful title for it. In our example we are taking the two scores (sales_1 and sales_2) of each respondent on the sales questions as the within-subjects variable, and we can call it amsold, standing for 'amount sold'. Type in the name amsold so that it replaces the name factor1. You then need to type the appropriate number into the Number of Levels box: here it is 2, as there were two items of data per respondent. Then click on the Add button, and the untitled box will have inserted into it the factor name and number of levels; here it is amsold(2).

2 Identify the variables which make up the within-subjects factor. You still have to tell SPSS which are the variables in the data which make up the factor. To do this, click on the Define button of the dialogue box shown in Figure 16.13, which will lead to the screen showing the Repeated Measures ANOVA dialogue box illustrated in Figure 16.14. Select the data variables (sales_1, sales_2) by clicking on them and then on the right-arrow button. These variable names will be inserted into the Within-Subjects Variables list as the different levels of the within-subjects factor. Do *not* press Paste yet: you still have to define the between-subjects factor!

3 Define the between-subjects factor. While you are faced with the Repeated Measures ANOVA dialogue box (Figure 16.14), click on

the name of the between-subjects variable (in the example we are describing it will be sex), and then on the right-pointing arrow next to the box headed Between-Subjects Factor(s). The variable will be inserted into that list. You have to define the range of scores on this variable: click on the Define Range button of Figure 16.14, and another box is shown with spaces for you to type in the minimum and maximum values on the variable. (In this example they are 1 and 2.) Then click on Continue to return to Figure 16.14.

OBTAINING MEANS OF SUBGROUPS   Note that if you want the printout to show the means for the different levels of the between-subjects factor, you have to click on the Options button of the Repeated Measures ANOVA box (Figure 16.14). Click on the names of the variable or variables listed under Between-Subjects Factors(s): and then on the arrow button so the variable names appear in the Display Means For list. Pressing the Continue button returns you to the Repeated Measures

```
MANOVA
  sales_1  sales_2  BY sex(1 2)
  /WSFACTORS amsold(2)
  /METHOD UNIQUE
  /ERROR WITHIN+RESIDUAL
  /OMEANS TABLES(sex )
  /PMEANS TABLES(sex )
  /PRINT
    SIGNIF( MULT AVERF )
  /NOPRINT PARAM(ESTIM) .

Note: there are 2 levels for the AMSOLD effect.  Average tests are
identical to the univariate tests of significance.

- - - - - - - - - - - - - - - - - - - - - - - - - - - - - - - - - -
* * * * * * A n a l y s i s   o f   V a r i a n c e * * * * * *
     21 cases accepted.
      0 cases rejected because of out-of-range factor values.
      1 case rejected because of missing data.
      2 non-empty cells.

      1 design will be processed.
- - - - - - - - - - - - - - - - - - - - - - - - - - - - - - - - - -
* * * * A n a l y s i s   o f   V a r i a n c e -- design   1 * * * *

Combined Observed Means for SEX
Variable .. SALES_1
          SEX
          male          WGT.    5950.63700
                        UNWGT.  5950.63700
          female        WGT.    5723.99636
                        UNWGT.  5723.99636
- - - - - - - - - - - - - - - - - - - - - - - - - - - - - - - - - -
  Variable .. SALES_2
          SEX
          male          WGT.    6411.53500
                        UNWGT.  6411.53500
          female        WGT.    5508.29364
                        UNWGT.  5508.29364
- - - - - - - - - - - - - - - - - - - - - - - - - - - - - - - - - -
```

Continued on facing page

```
* * * * A n a l y s i s   o f   V a r i a n c e -- design  1 * * * * *

Tests of Between-Subjects Effects.

Tests of Significance for T1 using UNIQUE sums of squares
Source of Variation         SS        DF       MS         F   Sig of F
WITHIN+RESIDUAL      237856316.5      19  12518753
SEX                    3343563.49      1  3343563.5       .27     .611

- - - - - - - - - - - - - - - - - - - - - - - - - - - - - - - - - - -
Adjusted and Estimated Means
Variable .. T1
  CELL        Obs. Mean   Adj. Mean    Est. Mean   Raw Resid. Std. Resid.
   1          8741.376    8741.376     8741.376       .000       .000
   2          7942.428    7942.428     7942.428       .000       .000

- - - - - - - - - - - - - - - - - - - - - - - - - - - - - - - - - - -
* * * * A n a l y s i s   o f   V a r i a n c e -- design  1 * * * * *

Combined Adjusted Means for SEX
Variable .. T1
         SEX
       male      UNWGT.  8741.37565
       female    UNWGT.  7942.42843

- - - - - - - - - - - - - - - - - - - - - - - - - - - - - - - - - - -
* * * * A n a l y s i s   o f   V a r i a n c e -- design  1 * * * * *

Tests involving 'AMSOLD' Within-Subject Effect.

Tests of Significance for T2 using UNIQUE sums of squares
Source of Variation         SS        DF       MS         F   Sig of F
WITHIN+RESIDUAL        9387076.48      19  494056.66
AMSOLD                  157459.03      1  157459.03       .32     .579
SEX BY AMSOLD          1198970.00      1  1198970.0      2.43     .136
- - - - - - - - - - - - - - - - - - - - - - - - - - - - - - - - - - -
Adjusted and Estimated Means
Variable .. T2
  CELL        Obs. Mean   Adj. Mean    Est. Mean   Raw Resid. Std. Resid.
   1          325.904     325.904      325.904        .000       .000
   2         -152.525    -152.525     -152.525        .000       .000
- - - - - - - - - - - - - - - - - - - - - - - - - - - - - - - - - - -
* * * * A n a l y s i s   o f   V a r i a n c e -- design    * * * * * *

Combined Adjusted Means for SEX
Variable .. T2
         SEX
       male      UNWGT.   325.90410
       female    UNWGT.  -152.52486
- - - - - - - - - - - - - - - - - - - - - - - - - - - - - - - - - - -
```

Figure 16.17 *Syntax and output for analysis of variance with one within-subjects variable and one between-subjects variable. Note: In this example the within-subjects variable, amsold, has two levels: sales_1 and sales_2. The between-subjects variable is sex and has been coded as 1 or 2, so there are two levels*

ANOVA box, and then you can Paste the syntax into the syntax window.

If you ask for the means, the syntax will include the subcommands

```
/OMEANS TABLES(sex )
/PMEANS TABLES(sex )
```

where sex is the name of the between-subjects variable. The printout will show the means of the subgroups before the anova summary tables, as shown in Figure 16.17. The printout will also include after the anova summary tables sets of Adjusted Means, the result of the /PMEANS subcommand. These are described in the SPSS manuals as 'predicted and adjusted (for covariates) means, which are displayed for each error term in each design'. They can be ignored unless you understand what they are for, but do not confuse them with the subgroup means of the original data. (You can suppress these tables of adjusted means by editing the syntax file to remove the /PMEANS subcommand.)

The syntax and output for this mixed anova analysis with the request for the means of the subgroups is shown in Figure 16.17. Note that the subcommand /WSFACTORS is included when a within-subjects variable has been identified. The analysis of variance output is in separate sections. The first (Tests of Between-Subjects Effects) compares the means for the different levels on the between-subjects (sex) variable: here $F = 0.27$, $p = .611$, so there is no overall difference between the sexes on the amount sold. The section headed Tests involving Within-Subject Effect shows that comparing the levels of amsold (the within-subjects variable) gave $F = 0.32$, $p = .579$, showing no significant difference between the levels of amsold, i.e. between sales_1 and sales_2. The interaction between the two variables gave $F = 2.43$, $p = .136$. So for this data there is also no significant interaction between the two variables of amount sold and sex.

When there are two or more variables being analysed and any significant F is obtained, it often helps to gain an understanding of the data if the means of the subsets of scores are plotted on a graph. The way to obtain such a graph is explained in section 10.7.

16.12 Two (or more) independent variables, all within-subjects (repeated measures)

To explain this analysis, we shall have a rest from the salesq data file and use a separate example. An investigator studied people's ability to recognize faces in upright and inverted orientation, and when the faces were shown in black-and-white (b/w) or colour. There were two independent variables, orientation and colour, both with two levels (upright or inverted; b/w or colour) so there were four conditions: upright b/w, inverted b/w, upright colour, inverted colour. The researcher used one group of respondents; everyone took part in all of the four conditions. Both independent variables are within-subjects, as each person saw both levels of every variable. So the two-way analysis of variance for repeated measures is needed.

The data, and the order in which it should be entered into SPSS, is shown in Table 16.2.

When entering the data into SPSS for a within-subjects factorial design, it is vital that the order of columns is correct: all the subconditions at one level of one variable occur before the subconditions at the second level of

Table 16.2   *Data from an experiment on facial recognition*

Subject	INVBW	INVCOL	UPBW	UPCOL
I	1.25	2.33	1.67	2.18
2	1.82	2.56	1.48	2.04
3	1.59	2.69	1.58	2.58
4	1.73	3.01	1.63	2.21
5	1.72	2.87	1.88	2.73
6	1.49	3.23	1.22	3.20
7	1.03	3.78	0.94	3.71
8	1.35	3.22	1.21	3.15
9	1.47	3.21	1.20	3.40
10	1.02	3.26	1.02	3.11

that variable. In Table 16.2, the first two columns both refer to the Inverted condition, one with black-and-white faces and the other with colour. Then the data for the Upright condition is given, again with two columns since there has to be one for each black-and-white and one for colour. You will also see that the order of the two levels of the colour condition is consistent: for both Inverted and Upright faces, they are in the same order (BW followed by COL).

To obtain the repeated-measures anova, select from the menu system

```
Statistics
      ANOVA Models
            Repeated Measures
```

This presents a dialogue box shown in Figure 16.13.

1   Identify the within-subjects factors. The within-subject factor is initially labelled factor1, and you need to enter a more meaningful title for it. In the faces experiment, the variables were position (upright or inverted) and colour (b/w or colour). You need to give these variables names, which should be different from those used as variable names (column headings) in the data file. We shall call them downup and colour. So when presented with Figure 16.13, type in the name downup so that it replaces factor1 in the box and enter the appropriate number in the Number of Levels box. In the experiment, there were two levels of downup, so enter 2. Then click on the Add button, and the untitled box will have inserted into it the factor name and number of levels; here it is downup(2).

The second within-subjects factor is defined in a similar way. Type the name (in this example it is colour) into the box where factor names appear, the number of levels into the appropriate box, and then click on Add. The Factor list then reads:

```
downup(2)
colour(2)
```

2   Identify the variables which make up the within-subjects factors. You
    still have to tell SPSS which are the variables (columns) in the data
    which make up the factors. Click on one of the factor names
    (downup(2)) and then on the Define button. You will be presented
    with the Repeated Measures ANOVA dialogue box shown in Figure
    16.18. The variables from the data are listed on the left-hand side. You
    have to select the data variables so that they are matched correctly
    with the names and levels of the within-subject variables.

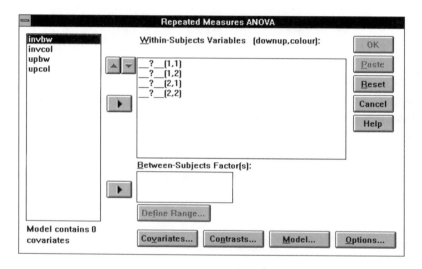

Figure 16.18   The dialogue box for Repeated Measures ANOVA for the two
within-subjects variables (downup, colour)

In this example, the first factor, which appears in the brackets after the
Within-Subjects Variables title is downup; the second factor is colour. You
will see that there are entries in the central box: __?__[1,1] etc. The first of
these has to be paired with the first level on downup and the first level
on colour, i.e. the variable INVBW: click on this name in the variable list
and then on the right-pointing arrow. The second entry in the within-
subjects variable list, __?__[1,2], has to be paired with the data variable
corresponding to the first level on the first factor (downup) and the
second level on the second factor (colour): the INVCOL data. The third
entry is paired with second level on the first factor (downup is the factor and the second level is UP) and the first level on the second factor
(colour is the factor and the level is BW), so the variable needed is
UPBW. The fourth entry is paired with the second level of the first factor
and the second level of the second factor: the variable UPCOL.
    This is a little confusing, but it is vital to appreciate that the first level
of the first factor is entered first, with the levels of the second factor

entered sequentially. Then the second level of the first factor is entered, with the levels of the second factor entered sequentially. So if you have two factors, A and B, with three levels of A (A1, A2 and A3) and two levels of B (B1 and B2), the final sequence which has to appear in the Within-Subjects Variables list is: A1 B1; A1 B2; A2 B1; A2 B2; A3 B1; A3 B2.

```
MANOVA
  invbw  invcol  upbw  upcol
  /WSFACTORS downup(2) colour(2)
  /METHOD UNIQUE
  /ERROR WITHIN+RESIDUAL
  /PRINT
    SIGNIF( MULT AVERF )
  /NOPRINT PARAM(ESTIM) .
DESCRIPTIVES
  VARIABLES=invbw invcol upbw upcol
  /FORMAT=LABELS NOINDEX
  /STATISTICS=MEAN SUM STDDEV MIN MAX
  /SORT=MEAN (A) .


Note: there are 2 levels for the DOWNUP effect.  Average tests are
identical to the univariate tests of significance.

Note: there are 2 levels for the COLOUR effect.  Average tests are
identical to the univariate tests of significance.
- - - - - - - - - - - - - - - - - - - - - - -
* * * A n a l y s i s   o f   V a r i a n c e -- design   1 * *

Tests of Between-Subjects Effects.

Tests of Significance for T1 using UNIQUE sums of squares
Source of Variation          SS        DF        MS         F  Sig of F
WITHIN+RESIDUAL             .96         9       .11
CONSTANT                 188.23         1    188.23   1771.90    .000


- - - - - - - - - - - - - - - - - - - - - - - - - - - - - -
* * *A n a l y s i s   o f   V a r i a n c e -- design   1 * *

Tests involving 'DOWNUP' Within-Subject Effect.

Tests of Significance for T2 using UNIQUE sums of squares
Source of Variation          SS        DF        MS         F  Sig of F
WITHIN+RESIDUAL             .30         9       .03
DOWNUP                      .16         1       .16      4.63    .060


- - - - - - - - - - - - - - - - - - - - - - - - - - - - -
* * *A n a l y s i s   o f   V a r i a n c e -- design   1 * *

Tests involving 'COLOUR' Within-Subject Effect.

Tests of Significance for T3 using UNIQUE sums of squares
Source of Variation          SS        DF        MS         F  Sig of F
WITHIN+RESIDUAL            4.54         9       .50
COLOUR                    22.76         1     22.76     45.10    .000


- - - - - - - - - - - - - - - - - - - - - - - - - - - - - -
* * * A n a l y s i s   o f   V a r i a n c e -- design   1 * *

Tests involving 'DOWNUP BY COLOUR' Within-Subject Effect.

Tests of Significance for T4 using UNIQUE sums of squares
Source of Variation          SS        DF        MS         F  Sig of F
WITHIN+RESIDUAL             .27         9       .03
DOWNUP BY COLOUR           .04         1       .04      1.20    .302


- - - - - - - - - - - - - - - - - - - - - - - - - - - - - -
```

Figure 16.19 *Syntax and output for analysis of variance with two repeated-measures independent variables (MANOVA) and syntax for obtaining the means of the various conditions (DESCRIPTIVES)*

Click on Paste to have the syntax inserted in a syntax window.

To obtain the means etc. for each subset of data, you can use the Descriptives procedure, obtained by selecting from the menu

```
Statistics
     Summarize
          Descriptives
```

The appropriate syntax is included in Figure 16.19, but the printout for the Descriptives command is not shown, as it should be self-explanatory. It gives the means etc. for each column of the data set of Table 16.2. It is worth running this procedure, if only to check that you have completed Figure 16.18 correctly!

The syntax and output for this analysis is shown in Figure 16.19. The first section of the output, Tests of Between-Subjects Effects, can be ignored. The test of the DOWNUP effect has $F = 4.63$, $p = .060$; the COLOUR effect has $F = 45.10$ and p is .000, while the interaction of the two variables has $F = 1.20$ and p is .302. So in this set of data, only colour has a significant effect. The effect of orientation is not significant ($p = .06 > 0.05$).

When there are two or more variables being analysed and a significant F value has been obtained, it often helps to gain an understanding of the data if the means of the subsets of scores are plotted on a graph. The way to obtain such a graph is explained in section 10.7.

16.13 Chapter summary

- When using parametric tests, to compare the scores of two groups of different subjects on one variable, use the between-subjects or independent-samples t-test. Remember that it is the absolute value of t which is important: ignore any minus sign.
- To compare the mean of a sample with a specified test value, use the one-sample t-test which is available in SPSS version 6.1 but not version 6.0.
- To compare the mean scores of three or sets of data use the analysis of variance. Table 16.1 will help you decide which type of anova you need.

CORRELATIONS AND MULTIPLE REGRESSION

17.1 The concept of correlation

A correlation expresses the extent to which two variables vary together. A positive correlation means that as one variable increases so does the other. For example, there is a strong positive correlation between size of foot and height, and a weak positive correlation between how much one is paid and one's job satisfaction. A negative correlation is when one variable increases as the other decreases; for example, there is a negative correlation between job satisfaction and absenteeism: the more satisfied people are with their job, the lower the amount of absenteeism they show.

Correlations vary between −1.00 and +1.00; a correlation of 0.00 means there is no relationship between the two variables. For example, one would expect the correlation between size of foot and job satisfaction to be about 0.00 (although I have never seen any data on this relationship!).

If two variables have both been measured on an interval scale, use the Pearson product moment correlation coefficient. When data is ordinal, use the Spearman Rank (rho) correlation coefficient.

Whichever coefficient is chosen, you should always plot a scattergram of the relationship between the two variables to check that the relationship can reasonably be assumed to be linear. Simple correlations indicate how far there is a linear relationship between the two variables. In a curvilinear relationship, low scores on x are associated with low scores on y, medium scores on x are associated with high scores on y, and high scores on x are associated with low scores on y. This relationship would not appear in a correlation coefficient, which would have a low value (about 0), but will be revealed if the two sets of data are plotted graphically.

When you have a scattergram it is possible to draw in the best-fitting straight line that represents the relationship between x and y. The best-fitting line is known as the regression line, and it can be expressed as an equation of the form $x = c + by$, where c is the intercept and b the slope.

The correlation coefficient squared (r^2) indicates how much of the variance in y is explained by x. So if x correlates with y 0.6, then 0.36 (36%) of the variance in y is explained by the variance in x.

Always bear in mind the aphorism 'Correlation does not equal causation': if variables A and B are correlated, one cannot say that A causes B. It could be that B causes A, or they may both be related to some other factor that produces the variation in A and B. Some examples: absenteeism and job satisfaction are negatively correlated, but one cannot conclude that low job satisfaction causes absenteeism; it is possible that being absent a lot causes the feelings of low job satisfaction. The positive correlation between foot size and height does not mean that having a large foot makes you grow; foot size and overall height are both caused by a common genetic factor. However, correlations are used to predict one variable from another. Knowing someone's foot size, one can predict how tall they are better than one could if you did not know their foot size.

Partial correlation is used when the correlation between two variables may arise because both are correlated with a third variable. Partial correlation is a technique which allows you to examine the correlation between two variables when the effect of the third variable has been partialled out.

Multiple regression refers to using more than one variable to predict the dependent variable. Job satisfaction is correlated with pay and with level of occupation. So one can predict job satisfaction from pay and one can predict it from job level; but one may get a better prediction if one uses both pay and job level as predictors. So one would have an equation of the form:

job satisfaction = pay (multiplied by a) + level of job (multiplied by b)

Each predictor variable is multiplied by a weighting, reflecting its importance in determining the dependent, or predicted, variable. The weighting is known as the regression coefficient for that variable. In multiple regression analysis, one investigates which variables add to one's ability to predict the dependent variable, and the weighting they should have.

17.2 Obtaining a scattergram

To get a scattergram between two variables, select from the menu

```
Graphs
        Scatter . . .
```

The option Simple will be the default offered, so click the Define button, which opens a dialogue box in which you can specify which variable is to be on the y axis and which on the x axis. Pressing the Titles button allows you to give a title to the graph. An example of the syntax is shown in Figure 17.1.

```
GRAPH
   /SCATTERPLOT(BIVAR)=att1 WITH att2
   /MISSING=LISTWISE
   /TITLE= 'Scattergram of att1 versus att2'.
```

Figure 17.1   *Example of syntax for obtaining a scatterplot*

When the syntax is run, the scatterplot will be created in the Chart Carousel described more fully in chapter 10. To see the graph, click on the Chart Carousel icon and a chart window will be opened and the plot displayed. An example is illustrated in Figure 17.2.

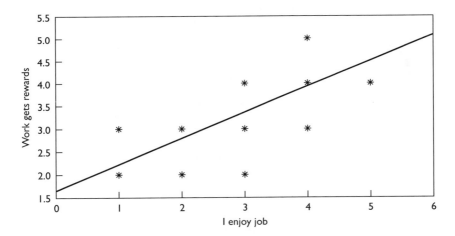

Figure 17.2   *Example of a scattergram*

You can separate the plots for subgroups of respondents: for example, one could plot att1 versus att2 for all the respondents in salesq, but have the data for females indicated by a different marker from those used to plot males' data. This is achieved by entering sex as the variable in the Set Markers By text box.

If you wish the graph to include the best-fitting straight line, while viewing the scattergram press the Edit button and then select from the menu bar

```
Chart
     Options
```

In the dialogue box revealed, there is a section entitled Fit line. Click on the Total option and then on the button marked Fit Options. You will then be faced with the screen shown in Figure 17.3: select the Linear Regression option.

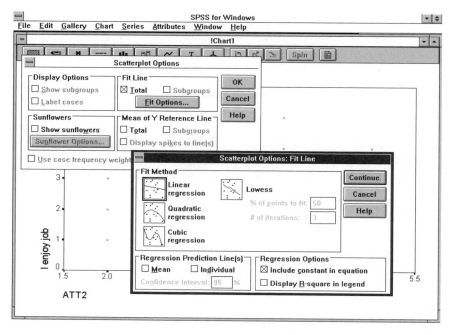

Figure 17.3   *The screen presented from Chart/Options for obtaining the best-fitting straight line in a scattergram*

17.3 Parametric (Pearson) and rank (Spearman) correlation

To obtain the correlation coefficient between two variables, select from the menus

```
Statistics
      Correlate
            Bivariate
```

The variables to be analysed have to be inserted in the Variables list in the usual manner. Specify which correlation coefficients you require (Pearson, Kendall's tau or Spearman rank) by checking the relevant alternatives in the Correlation Coefficients area of the dialogue box. You can ask for the correlation between all possible pairings of three or more variables simply by inserting all the variables into the Variables list.

SPSS indicates, unless you specify otherwise, whether a correlation is significant by printing asterisks: * indicates significant at the 0.05 level, and ** significant at the 0.01 level. If you want the actual significance levels to be displayed in the printout, check the Display Actual Significance Level box in the Bivariate Correlations dialogue box. This was done in order to obtain the display illustrated in Figure 17.4. The significance of a correlation is by default presented in the output using a non-directional (two-tailed) probability. If you have predicted in advance the direction of the relationship between the variables, you are entitled to use a directional (one-tailed) probability, and this can be requested in the Bivariate Correlations dialogue box.

Requesting Pearson correlations yields the output illustrated in Figure 17.4, where the correlations between scores on sales_2, att1, att2 and att3 in the salesq file were requested. Take care when reading the output on correlations. Many people confuse the correlation coefficient and the probability (significance) level. The correlation coefficient is not labelled, just printed out. In Figure 17.4, the correlation between sales_2 and att2 is $-.4136$. (Do not forget the minus sign indicates a negative correlation.) The number in brackets below the correlation coefficient is the number of cases used; in this example it is 22. The numbers given after $p=$ is not the correlation but the probability of the correlation having arisen by chance. If this p value is less than 0.05, the correlation is statistically significant. In Figure 17.4, for sales_2 and att2, $p = .056$, which indicates a non-significant correlation because it is greater than 0.05 or 0.01. On the other hand, the correlation between att1 and att2 is .7001, and $p = .000$, which indicates a highly significant correlation as .000 is less than 0.05 or 0.01.

The Correlations procedure will exclude any case which has missing data on either of the variables being correlated. This is referred to as Exclude Cases Pairwise. If you are requesting a number of correlations, with three or more variables entered in the Variables list, you can ask SPSS to exclude from all the analyses any case that has a missing value on any of the variables: this is Exclude Cases Listwise, and is available via the Options button of the Bivariate Correlations dialogue box.

Spearman rank correlations are displayed as shown in Figure 17.5. The correlation coefficient is shown (.6843 in Figure 17.5), then the number of cases (22 in the example), and then the significance or probability level (.000 in Figure 17.5). If this Sig (significance) value is less than 0.05, the correlation is statistically significant. In Figure 17.5, Sig = .000, which indicates a significant correlation because 0.000 is less than 0.05 or 0.01.

17.4 Obtaining means and standard deviations of the variables being correlated

To have the mean and standard deviations of the scores on the variables being correlated shown in the printout, select the Options button from

```
CORRELATIONS
  /VARIABLES=sales_2 att1 att2 att3
  /PRINT=TWOTAIL SIG
  /MISSING=PAIRWISE .

                        - -  Correlation Coefficients  - -

                SALES_2       ATT1        ATT2        ATT3

SALES_2         1.0000      -.3063      -.4136       .2675
              (    22)     (    22)    (    22)     (    22)
               P= .        P= .166     P= .056     P= .229

ATT1            -.3063      1.0000       .7001      -.7654
              (    22)     (    22)    (    22)     (    22)
               P= .166     P= .        P= .000     P= .000

ATT2            -.4136       .7001      1.0000      -.6483
              (    22)     (    22)    (    22)     (    22)
               P= .056     P= .000     P= .        P= .001

ATT3             .2675      -.7654      -.6483      1.0000
              (    22)     (    22)    (    22)     (    22)
               P= .229     P= .000     P= .001     P= .

(Coefficient / (Cases) / 2-tailed Significance)

  " . " is printed if a coefficient cannot be computed
```

Figure 17.4   *Output from the correlation procedure showing Pearson correlation coefficients*

```
NONPAR CORR
  /VARIABLES=att1 att2
  /PRINT=SPEARMAN TWOTAIL SIG
  /MISSING=PAIRWISE .

 -S P E A R M A N   C O R R E L A T I O N   C O E F F I C I E N T S-

ATT2               .6843
              N(    22)
              Sig .000

                  ATT1

(Coefficient / (Cases) / 2-tailed Significance)

  " . " is printed if a coefficient cannot be computed
```

Figure 17.5   *Output from the correlation procedure showing Spearman rank correlation coefficient*

the Bivariate Correlations dialogue box and check the Means and Standard Deviations box. This will add into the syntax the line

/STATISTICS DESCRIPTIVES

and when the procedure is run a list, such as that shown in Figure 17.6, will be given before the correlation coefficient table.

```
Variable     Cases        Mean        Std Dev
ATT1           22        2.5455        1.1010
ATT2           22        3.0909         .9211
```

Figure 17.6 *Example of statistics obtained within the Correlations procedure*

17.5 Partial correlation

The correlation between two variables may arise because both are correlated with a third variable. Partial correlation is a technique which allows you to examine the correlation between two variables when the effect of other variable(s) has been partialled out. Partial correlation analysis is obtained from the menu

```
Statistics
     Correlate
          Partial
```

Enter into the Variables list the two variables to be correlated, and into the Controlling For: list the control variables, the ones whose influence on the correlation between the two variables is to be partialled out.

To obtain the means and standard deviations on each variable, and/or a matrix showing the zero-order correlations between all the variables, request them via the Options button. (A zero-order correlation is the usual correlation, with no partialling out for the effects of a control variable.)

Figure 17.7 illustrates the output from the Partial Correlations procedure. In this example, the correlation between sales_2 and att2 was examined, with sales_1 as the control variable. The correlation is shown (.0600) with the degrees of freedom used in the calculation (19) and the probability value ($p = .796$ indicates the correlation is not significant).

Previously, in Figure 17.4, the correlation between sales_2 and att2 was found to be -0.4136. But now, in Figure 17.7, after the effect of sales_1 has been partialled out, the correlation is only 0.0600. This suggests that the original correlation value was spurious, and arose because att2 correlates with sales_1 and sales_1 and sales_2 are highly correlated. Once the effects of sales_1 are removed by the partial correlation procedure, the low correlation between att2 and sales_2 is revealed.

17.6 Multiple regression

In multiple regression, you use a number of independent variables to predict the dependent variable. For example, you can predict sales_1 from cust (number of customers visited), since the correlation between these two variables is 0.7266, significant at the 0.001 level. But will the prediction be better if you also consider the person's response to the att1,

```
PARTIAL CORR
  /VARIABLES= sales_2 att2 BY sales_1
  /SIGNIFICANCE=TWOTAIL
  /MISSING=LISTWISE .


- P A R T I A L   C O R R E L A T I O N   C O E F F I C I E N T S -

Controlling for..    SALES_1

               SALES_2         ATT2

SALES_2        1.0000          .0600
               (    0)       (   19)
               P= .          P= .796

ATT2            .0600         1.0000
               (   19)       (    0)
               P= .796        P= .

(Coefficient / (D.F.) / 2-tailed Significance)

" . " is printed if a coefficient cannot be computed
```

Figure 17.7   *Output from the partial correlation procedure*

att2 and att3 questions? It is with this type of problem that multiple regression is concerned.

Multiple regression is obtained by selecting

```
Statistics
      Regression
            Linear
```

This opens the Linear Regression dialogue box shown in Figure 17.8. Enter the dependent variable in the Dependent box, and the predictor variables in the Independent box using the normal procedure of clicking on the variables in the source list and then on the appropriate arrow button.

You can specify the regression method to be used from Enter, Stepwise, Forward, Backward and Remove. Stepwise is probably the most frequently used method, although Enter is the default and enters all the variables in one step. Forward enters variables one at a time depending on whether they meet statistical criteria, Backward enters all the variables and then removes them one at a time depending on a removal criterion, while Stepwise, which is a combination of forward and backward procedures, examines each variable for entry or removal. Remove means that variables in a block are removed in one step. It is possible to specify one method for one block of variables and another method for another block; to do this, you have to create a second block of predictor variables by clicking on the Next button and then enter the predictor variables for this set. To move between the blocks of variables, use the Previous and Next buttons.

Various statistics can be requested from the Statistics button of Figure 17.8. When it is clicked, a dialogue box is revealed allowing various

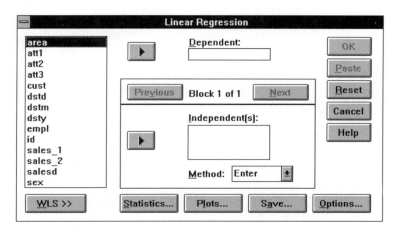

Figure 17.8   *The Linear Regression dialogue box*

```
REGRESSION
  /DESCRIPTIVES MEAN STDDEV CORR SIG N
  /MISSING LISTWISE
  /STATISTICS COEFF OUTS R ANOVA
  /CRITERIA=PIN(.05) POUT(.10)
  /NOORIGIN
  /DEPENDENT sales_1
  /METHOD=ENTER cust att1 att2 att3  .
```

     * * * *   M U L T I P L E   R E G R E S S I O N   * * * *

Listwise Deletion of Missing Data

	Mean	Std Devi	Label
SALES_1	5859.623	2324.296	
CUST	50.818	17.012	Number customer visits
ATT1	2.545	1.101	I enjoy job
ATT2	3.091	.921	work gets rewards
ATT3	3.409	1.182	wish a different job

N of Cases =   22

Correlation, 1-tailed Sig:

	SALES_1	CUST	ATT1	ATT2	ATT3
SALES_1	1.000	.727	-.273	-.437	.274
	.	.000	.109	.021	.109
CUST	.727	1.000	-.330	-.516	.269
	.000	.	.067	.007	.113
ATT1	-.273	-.330	1.000	.700	-.765
	.109	.067	.	.000	.000
ATT2	-.437	-.516	.700	1.000	-.648
	.021	.007	.000	.	.001
ATT3	.274	.269	-.765	-.648	1.000
	.109	.113	.000	.001	.

Continued on next page

```
        * * * *   M U L T I P L E   R E G R E S S I O N   * * * *

Equation Number 1    Dependent Variable..    SALES_1

  Descriptive Statistics are printed on Page    70

Block Number   1.  Method:  Enter  CUST     ATT1     ATT2     ATT3


Variable(s) Entered on Step Number
     1..    ATT3      wish a different job
     2..    CUST      Number customer visits
     3..    ATT2      work gets rewards
     4..    ATT1      I enjoy job


Multiple R              .73362
R Square                .53820
Adjusted R Square       .42954
Standard Error     1755.50691

Analysis of Variance
                    DF      Sum of Squares       Mean Square
Regression           4        61058696.52776    15264674.13194
Residual            17        52390676.44811     3081804.49695

F =        4.95316       Signif F =   .0078


------------------ Variables in the Equation ------------------

Variable             B          SE B         Beta          T    Sig T
CUST          94.089513    26.412297      .688644      3.562   .0024
ATT1         188.651933   594.574534      .089360       .317   .7549
ATT2        -186.742951   664.802598     -.074007      -.281   .7822
ATT3         214.419185   521.545812      .109001       .411   .6861
(Constant)   444.191264  4131.188962                    .108   .9156


End Block Number   1   All requested variables entered.
```

Figure 17.9 *Output from REGRESSION with the Enter method*

options to be requested. If you select Descriptives, the output will
include the means and standard deviations of the variables being analysed as well as a correlation matrix, as shown in Figure 17.9, which
illustrates the output from multiple regression when sales_1 was the
dependent variable, and cust, att1, att2 and att3 were used as predictor
(independent) variables.

The Plots button will allow you to obtain a scatterplot of the dependent variable (Dependnt in the source variable list) with standardized
predicted values or one of a number of other predicted or residual
variables which are calculated by the Regression procedure. These newly
calculated variables can be saved from the Save button and its associated
dialogue box.

The Options button permits you to alter the criteria used when the
stepwise, forward or backward methods are used, by inserting your own
values for *F* or for the probability of *F*. You can also force the suppression
of a constant term in the regression equation, by deselecting the Include
Constant in Equation option.

The WLS button in the Linear Regression dialogue box allows you to obtain a weighted least-squares model.

The program will exclude from the analysis any case that has a missing value on any of the variables being analysed; this is referred to as Exclude Cases Listwise. You can have any missing values replaced with the mean of the scores on that variable, or you can ask the program to calculate correlations for all cases which have no missing value for the two variables being correlated (Exclude Cases Pairwise). These alternative treatments for missing values are obtained from the Options button of the Linear Regression dialogue box.

The first part of Figure 17.9 shows means and standard deviations of the variables included in the analysis, and this is followed by the correlations between them all with one-tailed significance levels. After this table of correlations, the dependent variable is identified as sales_1, and the multiple regression method used is shown as 'Enter'.

After listing the predictor variables that were entered into the equation, it gives the Multiple R (.73362 in Figure 17.9) which is the correlation between the predictor variables combined and the dependent variable. R square indicates the proportion of the variability in the dependent variable which is accounted for by the multiple regression equation. The figure labelled 'Adjusted R Square' is an estimate of R^2 for the population (rather than the sample from which the data was obtained), and includes a correction for shrinkage.

The analysis of variance table shown in Figure 17.9 shows the sum of squares explained by the regression equation and the 'residual' sum of squares. The residual sum of squares is the variability in the dependent variable which is left unexplained by the regression equation. The F statistic (4.95316 in Figure 17.9) is obtained by dividing the Mean Square regression by the Mean Square residual. If F is significant (the probability value labelled, Signif of F, is less than 0.05), one can conclude that R^2 is significantly different from zero. This means that one can assume there is a linear relationship between the predictor and the dependent variables and that the regression equation allows you to predict the dependent variable at greater than chance level.

The final part of Figure 17.9 lists the predictor variables and some statistics associated with each one. B is the regression coefficient for the variable. In the present example, we have a regression equation like this:

sales_1 = cust($w1$) + att1($w2$) + att2($w3$) + att3($w4$)

The values of $w1$, $w2$, etc. are regression coefficients and determine how much weight is given to each of the predictor variables; the last section of Figure 17.9 shows the regression coefficients (B) for each predictor variable. It is important to realize that these B values do not show how important each predictor variable is; the relative importance is shown when the B values have been transformed into standard scores, when they are referred to as beta. These are included in the printout and indicate that cust (with beta = .688644) has much more influence on the dependent variable, sales_1, than do att1, att2 or att3. It is worth remembering that the beta coefficients obtained depend on the independent variables which have been used in the analysis, and have no absolute value.

The final columns of this part of the output show T values and their probabilities (Sig T). These indicate whether the regression coefficients for each variable are greater than zero. In Figure 17.9, the T values for att1, att2 and att3 are not significant, so one would conclude that these

```
REGRESSION
  /MISSING LISTWISE
  /STATISTICS COEFF OUTS R ANOVA
  /CRITERIA=PIN(.05) POUT(.10)
  /NOORIGIN
  /DEPENDENT sales_1
  /METHOD=STEPWISE cust att1 att2 att3  .


              * * * *   M U L T I P L E   R E G R E S S I O N   * * * *

Listwise Deletion of Missing Data

Equation Number 1     Dependent Variable..   SALES_1

Block Number 1. Method: Stepwise  Criteria PIN .0500 POUT .1000
    CUST       ATT1       ATT2       ATT3


Variable(s) Entered on Step Number
    1..    CUST       Number customer visits

Multiple R              .72664
R Square                .52801
Adjusted R Square       .50441
Standard Error     1636.25617

Analysis of Variance
                    DF      Sum of Squares       Mean Square
Regression           1      59902687.69741     59902687.69741
Residual            20      53546685.27847      2677334.26392

F =      22.37400      Signif F =  .0001


------------------ Variables in the Equation ------------------

Variable             B          SE B        Beta        T   Sig T

CUST           99.281605    20.989251     .726645     4.730  .0001
(Constant)    814.312508  1122.233677                  .726  .4765


------------- Variables not in the Equation -------------

Variable     Beta In  Partial  Min Toler        T  Sig T

ATT1         -.037411 -.051403   .891058     -.224  .8249
ATT2         -.085159 -.106216   .734255     -.466  .6468
ATT3          .084479  .118426   .927525      .520  .6092


End Block Number   1   PIN =     .050 Limits reached.
```

Figure 17.10 *Output from REGRESSION with the Stepwise method*

variables do not add to the ability to predict sales_1. The T value for cust is significant ($p = .0024$), so this does predict sales_1.

The final row of the table, labelled (constant), refers to the intercept of the regression line. The T value indicates whether it is significantly different from zero.

Some idea of the way that the multiple regression method affects the output can be seen by comparing Figure 17.9 with Figure 17.10 which shows the output of analysing the same variables as in Figure 17.9 but using the Stepwise method rather than Enter. The variable cust is entered into the regression equation at step 1 and the Beta value shown. Those variables not entered are then listed with the beta values they would have if they were entered. The non-significant T values shown in the column headed Sig T indicate that none of the variables would add to the predictive power of the equation, and so the process terminates without adding them in. Stepwise produces output which is simpler to interpret than Enter. In this example, the two methods produce very similar outcomes: only cust, of the four variables included, predicts sales_1.

17.7 Chapter summary

- When calculating correlations, always plot the two variables in a scattergram to see whether there is evidence of a curvilinear relationship. Use Graph /Scatter to obtain the scattergram.
- Take care when reading the output on correlations and do not confuse the figures for the correlation coefficient with those for the probability (significance) level.
- Obtain the mean and standard deviations of the variables being correlated from the Options button of the Bivariate Correlations dialogue box.
- Partial correlation allows you to examine the correlation between two variables when the effect of a third variable has been partialled out.
- Multiple regression uses a number of independent variables to predict the dependent variable. The Enter method forces all the predictor variables to be included in the analysis. The Stepwise method is more often used.

ANALYSING NOMINAL AND ORDINAL DATA

18.1 Non-parametric analyses

Non-parametric tests are used when the data does not lend itself to parametric statistical analysis because it is nominal or rank data, or is skewed, or the groups show unequal variance. In this chapter only the more commonly used ones are considered, but others will be found in the same menu as those described here.

It is important to distinguish between dealing with nominal (frequency) data and dealing with ordinal data. If you have counted the number of cases or people who appear in certain categories, the data is nominal and the chi-square test, the binomial test, or the McNemar test are appropriate. If the data has been measured on an ordinal scale or consists of ranks, there are a number of tests which allow you to compare the sets of rankings. Section 2.9 gives guidance on deciding which analysis to use.

18.2 Obtaining the non-parametric tests

The chi-square test for independent samples is used when you have a table showing the number of people categorized according to independent variables such as the number of people who are male and come from the North, who are female from the North, who are male from the South, or are female from the South. If the data forms a table like this, with different people appearing in each of the possible categories, then the SPSS procedure needed is Crosstabs with the subcommand for obtaining the chi-square for independent samples. The procedure is described in section 14.5.

All other non-parametric tests except rank correlation (see section 17.3) are obtained from the menu

```
Statistics
    Nonparametric Tests
```

which offers the options listed below.

- Chi-square   Note that this is the one-sample chi-square. The more common chi-square for testing the association between two categorical variables is found under Statistics /Summarize /Crosstabs.
- Binomial   The binomial test is used when the data forms two categories (such as male and female), and compares the observed frequency of cases in each category with the frequency expected from the binomial distribution.
- Runs   The runs test examines whether a sequence of two alternative values is in a random order.
- 1 sample K-S   K–S stands for Kolmogorov–Smirnov. The test is used to determine whether a sample set of scores come from a specified distribution such as normal or uniform.
- 2 Independent samples   The dialogue box revealed by selecting this entry offers the Mann–Whitney, Moses extreme reactions, Kolmogorov–Smirnov two sample, and Wald–Wolfowitz runs tests.
- K Independent samples   This has the Kruskal–Wallis and median tests.
- 2 Related samples   This includes the Wilcoxon, sign, and also the McNemar tests.
- K Related samples   This provides the Friedman and Cochran's Q tests, and Kendall's W (the coefficient of concordance) which is used to measure the relation among three or more sets of rankings. It can be seen as a measure of rank correlation but with three or more sets of data rather than just two. Unlike the correlation coefficient, W can only vary between 0 and 1.

Each set of tests has its own dialogue box in which the particular test is selected and the variables to be analysed are specified in the conventional manner of highlighting the variable name in the source list and clicking on the arrow button. Not all the tests available will be described here, as once you are familiar with the way the system operates and how to use the Help facility, there should be little difficulty in making appropriate decisions for specifying the test required.

The various tests allow you to obtain the mean, standard deviation, lowest and highest scores and number of cases for the variables being analysed by selecting the Options button and then, in the Statistics area of the dialogue box that appears, selecting Descriptive.

MISSING VALUES IN NON-PARAMETRIC TESTS   The Options button of the dialogue box for each test allows you to specify how missing values should be treated. The default is Exclude Cases Test-by-test, which means that where you have requested a number of tests to be done, as each test is carried out any cases that have missing values on the variable being analysed are excluded. The alternative is Exclude Cases Listwise: if this is selected, cases with a missing value on any of the variables inserted into the Test Variable List box are excluded from all analyses.

18.3 One-sample chi-square

Do not confuse this with the two-sample chi-square, obtained from the Crosstabs procedure! The one-sample chi-square test is used to test a hypothesis such as 'Suicide rate varies significantly from month to month'. If the hypothesis is false, the suicide rate will be the same for every one of the twelve months. The one-sample chi-square can be used to compare observed suicide rates per month with what would be expected if the rate were equal for all months.

SPSS will assume that you are comparing the observed distribution with an expected distribution in which the cases are spread equally across the categories. This can be altered, using the Values area in the Expected Values part of the dialogue box. So you can compare the observed distribution of suicides with that expected if January had twice as many suicides as August, and all other months had an equal rate mid-way between the January and August ones. The way to achieve this is to enter a value for each category in the Values text box and click on Add. You must enter the values in the order corresponding to the ascending order of the categories for the variable being tested.

To run this test, select

```
Statistics
     Nonparametric Tests
          Chi-square
```

This opens the appropriate dialogue box. Insert a variable into the Test Variable List box. By default, each value of score on the variable generates its own category, but you can specify the range of values to be used by stating the lower and upper values. In this way you could exclude cases which had a score outside the range you specify.

Figure 18.1 shows the results of applying a one-sample chi-square on the employer variable in salesq, to see whether the number of respondents from all three employers differs from what would be expected if each employer had an equal number. The categories of employer are listed, with the number of cases for each (Cases Observed). The expected frequencies which would occur if all employers had had an equal number of cases is shown in the column headed Expected. The Residual column shows the difference between the observed and the expected values. The final lines show the value of chi-square, the degrees of freedom (df) and the probability level. In this example, chi-square is not significant, as the probability shown (.8338) is larger than 0.05.

18.4 Two matched groups: Wilcoxon test

If you have carried out a within-subjects experiment, and have two scores for each subject, the Wilcoxon test is used to see whether there is a

```
NPAR TEST
  /CHISQUARE=empl
  /EXPECTED=EQUAL
  /MISSING ANALYSIS.

- - - - - Chi-square Test

    EMPL        employer

                              Cases
                    Category  Observed  Expected   Residual

    Jones and Son       1         8       7.33        .67
    Smith and Co        2         8       7.33        .67
    Tomkins             3         6       7.33      -1.33
                                 --
                    Total        22

        Chi-Square            D.F.          Significance
          .3636                2               .8338

-----------------------------------------------------------
```

Figure 18.1   *Output from the one-sample chi-square test*

significant difference between the subjects' scores under the two conditions.

It involves calculating the differences between the scores for each subject, and ranking the difference scores, giving rank 1 to the smallest difference etc., but ignoring the sign of the difference. Any subjects where the difference score is 0 are dropped from the analysis. The + or − signs of the difference scores are assigned to the rank values, and the sum of the rank-values obtained for the + and − signed ranks separately.

The Wilcoxon test rests on the argument that if there is no difference between the two sets of scores, the sum of the ranks for + differences will be about the same as the sum of the ranks for the − differences. If the sums of + differences are very dissimilar to the sum of the − differences, then it is likely there is a reliable difference between the two sets of scores.

The dialogue box offering the Wilcoxon test also includes the sign test, used to establish that two conditions are different when the two members of each pair can be ranked, and the McNemar test for the significance of changes which is a form of two-sample chi-square for repeated measures.

To obtain the Wilcoxon test, select from the menu

```
Statistics
    Nonparametric Tests
        2 Related Samples
```

In the dialogue box, indicate the two variables to be compared by clicking on each of them; the first one will appear under Current Selections Variable 1:, and the second one will appear as Variable 2. To insert these into the Paired Variables list, click on the right-pointing arrow button: the two variables will then be shown as a linked pair. You can create further pairs in the same way. Figure 18.2 shows the output for a Wilcoxon test to compare the scores on att1 and att2 of the respondents in salesq.

The printout shows how many cases had att2 score less than (Lt) att1 scores, how many had att2 greater than (Gt) att1, and how many were tied (i.e. the scores on att1 and att2 were the same). It gives also the mean rank for those situations where the scores were not tied. The test yields a z value, and this together with the relevant probability level is provided in the output. In this instance, probability is less than 0.05, so you can conclude there is a significant difference between the scores on att1 and att2.

```
NPAR TEST
  /WILCOXON=att1  WITH att2 (PAIRED)
  /MISSING ANALYSIS.


- - - - - Wilcoxon Matched-pairs Signed-ranks Test

        ATT1
 with ATT2
      Mean Rank    Cases
          8.50         3   - Ranks  (ATT2 Lt ATT1)
          9.11        14   + Ranks  (ATT2 Gt ATT1)
                       5     Ties   (ATT2 Eq ATT1)
                      --
                      22     Total

        Z =    -2.4142              2-tailed P =  .0158
```

Figure 18.2   *Output from the Wilcoxon test*

18.5 Three or more matched groups: Friedman test

This is used to compare three or more related sets of scores. A table is created where each row is the data for one subject, and the data within each row is ranked. The sum of ranks (T) for each column is calculated. The test is concerned with establishing whether the rank totals of each column differ more than would be expected by chance; if there were no difference between the sets of scores, the rank totals would be more or less the same.

The test is available by selecting from the menu

```
Statistics
      Nonparametric Tests
            K Related Samples
```

In the dialogue box presented, specify the variables to be compared, by clicking on the variable names and then on the right-pointing arrow. The output is shown in Figure 18.3, the test having been used to compare the scores on att1, att2 and att3.

The Friedman test ranks the scores on the variables for each respondent separately, and calculates the mean of these rank scores for each variable. These means are shown in the printout, with a chi-square statistic, degrees of freedom and significance (probability) level. In Figure 18.3, the significance value is less than 0.05 and so you would conclude there is a significant difference between the scores on the three variables.

```
NPAR TESTS
  /FRIEDMAN = att1 att2 att3
  /MISSING LISTWISE.

- - - - - Friedman Two-way ANOVA

    Mean Rank    Variable
        1.55     ATT1
        2.14     ATT2
        2.32     ATT3

        Cases         Chi-Square        D.F.    Significance
          22            7.1818           2          .0276
-------------------------------------------------------------
```

Figure 18.3   *Output from the Friedman test*

The Cochran Q test, also available from this dialogue box, is used for analysing nominal data from three or more matched groups or repeated measures.

18.6 Two independent groups: Mann–Whitney

The Mann–Whitney compares the scores on a specified variable of two independent groups. The scores of the two groups are ranked as one set, the sum of the rank values of each subgroup is found and a U statistic is then calculated. The Mann–Whitney is in the group of tests accessed by selecting from the menu

```
Statistics
      Nonparametric Tests
            2 Independent Samples
```

In the dialogue box, specify the variable to be analysed and then indicate the variable to be used to create the two groups of respondents whose scores are to be compared. This is done by inserting the variable name in the Grouping Variable box and specifying which groups you need by clicking on the Define Groups button. Suppose we want to compare the scores on sales_1 of the respondents in salesq from the employers 1 and 3. Enter the variable name empl into the Grouping variable box, click the Define Groups button, and then enter 1 into the box labelled Group 1, and 3 into the box labelled Group 2.

Figure 18.4 shows the result of using the Mann–Whitney to compare scores on sales_1 for respondents of employer 1 and employer 3. The average rank of each group is shown in the table, as are a value for U and a value for z with the associated two-tailed probability. In this example, the probability is less than .05, indicating that there is a significant difference between sales_1 scores for employers 1 and 3.

The Mann–Whitney procedure also carries out the Wilcoxon Rank Sum test, and the output shows the value of W and its associated probability.

The Moses extreme reactions, Kolmogorov–Smirnov two sample, and Wald–Wolfowitz runs tests are also available.

```
NPAR TESTS
  /M-W= sales_1   BY empl(1 3)
  /MISSING ANALYSIS.

- - - - - Mann-Whitney U - Wilcoxon Rank Sum W Test

      SALES
  by EMPLOYER
     Mean Rank      Cases
         5.38          8   EMPL = 1   Jones and Son
        10.33          6   EMPL = 3   Tomkins
                      --
                      14   Total

                             EXACT              Corrected for Ties
         U           W      2-tailed P         Z       2-tailed P
        7.0        62.0      .0293           -2.1947      .0282

------------------------------------------------------------------
```

Figure 18.4   *Output from the Mann–Whitney test*

18.7 Three or more independent groups: Kruskal–Wallis

Kruskal–Wallis is used to compare the scores on a variable of more than two independent groups. It is found under

```
Statistics
     Nonparametric Tests
          K Independent Samples
```

In the dialogue box, specify a Grouping Variable by selecting a variable from the source list and inserting it in the Grouping Variable box. You then have to define the range of the grouping variable by clicking on the Define Range button, which opens a dialogue box in which you enter the values corresponding to the lowest and highest scores on the grouping variable. For example, to compare the scores on cust for the respondents of the three employers in the salesq set of data, remember that the employers were coded as 1, 2 or 3. So in the Several Independent

Samples: Define Range box, you would enter 1 as the Minimum and 3 as the Maximum.

The output from the Kruskal–Wallis test is shown in Figure 18.5. The data on customer visits has been ranked, and the mean rank for each employer is given in the table. Two chi-square values are shown below the table, the second one having been corrected for tied ranks. Probability values are provided, so in Figure 18.5 one can see that there is a significant difference between the customer visits of the three employers, as the probability value (.0040) is less than 0.05.

```
NPAR TESTS
  /K-W=cust    BY empl(1 3)
  /MISSING ANALYSIS.

- - - - - Kruskal-Wallis 1-way ANOVA

     CUST        customers visited
  by EMPLOYER
     Mean Rank      Cases
         9.00          8    EMPL = 1    Jones and Son
         8.38          8    EMPL = 2    Smith and Co
        19.00          6    EMPL = 3    Tomkins
                      --
                      22    Total

                                           Corrected for Ties
    CASES     Chi-Square  Significance   Chi-Square  Significance
     22         11.0425        .0040       11.0550         .0040
------------------------------------------------------------------
```

Figure 18.5   *Output from the Kruskal–Wallis test*

The median test, which is also available from the dialogue box offering the Kruskal–Wallis is used to test whether three or more independent groups have been drawn from populations with equal medians.

18.8 Chapter summary

- Non-parametric tests are used when the data does not fulfil the assumptions required by the parametric tests: it is nominal or rank data, or is skewed, or the groups show unequal variance.
- The chi-square test for independent samples is obtained from the Statistics /Summarize /Crosstabs procedure, not from Non-parametric tests.
- Rank correlation is obtained from Statistics /Correlations.
- All other non-parametric tests are obtained from Statistics /Non-parametric Tests.

ASSESSING TEST RELIABILITY

19.1 The concept of test reliability

Many studies in the social sciences involve assessing some attribute of the respondents. In the data file salesq, for example, there is data on the sales performance of those who completed the questionnaire and on their responses to three attitude statements. Whenever attributes of people are measured, it is necessary to consider the validity and reliability of the measuring instrument. Validity means 'Does the test measure what it claims to measure?' and is assessed by comparing the test with a 'true' measure of the attribute.

Reliability refers to the consistency of the results. There are a number of types of reliability. Test–retest reliability means that people obtain the same scores if they take the test twice. It can be assessed by giving the test to the same people on two occasions and correlating the two sets of scores. (In practice, to prevent the respondents simply remembering the answers they gave the first time, you may have two versions of the test with slightly different items. The two versions are known as parallel forms.)

Inter-scorer and inter-administrator reliability mean that the test gives the same results whoever is marking or administering it.

Another aspect of reliability is ensuring that all the items measure 'the same thing'. This can be assessed by comparing the scores on any item with the total score on all the items. If one item does not correlate with the total score, it is eliminated so the test has homogeneity of items. Another procedure is to divide the test into two halves and see how far the scores on each half correlate. This 'split-half' reliability indicates the internal consistency of the test.

But there are many ways you can construct the two halves. If you had a test of 40 items, you could take the first 20 and the final 20 or you could take the odd-numbered ones and then the even-numbered ones, or you could take items 1–10 and 21–30 as one half with the others forming the other half and so on. Perhaps the best thing would be to take every possible way of forming two halves, correlate the scores of the halves and then find the average of the correlations. This is essentially what Cronbach's alpha does and is one of the standard ways of expressing a test's reliability.

High reliability in all senses is not always a 'good thing'. High inter-scorer agreement is always desirable, but high item homogeneity is not. If you are measuring intelligence, you want to be sure that all aspects of intelligence are tested, and so you will not want all the items to show a very high correlation with each other.

You may ask what is an acceptable level of reliability, but there is no simple answer. For tests of cognitive ability (such as intelligence tests), reliability coefficients of about 0.8 are usually expected and for ability tests should not be below 0.7. But tests of personality often have much lower values, partly because personality is a broader construct. The issue of test reliability is complex, and you should consult a text on psychometric testing such as Kline (1993).

19.2 Assessing test reliability with SPSS: RELIABILITY

To obtain Cronbach's alpha and other indications of the reliability of a test select

```
Statistics
     Scale
          Reliability Analysis
```

In the dialogue box revealed, identify the items in the test from the list of variables by clicking on them and then on the right-pointing arrow button so the variables appear in the list to the right, headed Items. Alternative models for assessing reliability can be chosen from the drop-down menu entitled Model. An example of the output is shown in Figure 19.1. Note that alpha here is negative, and this indicates that the model is inappropriate. The reason for this is that the scores on att3 in the file salesq are negatively related to those on att1 and att2. Consequently, they were recoded to be consistent with the scoring of att1 and att2 using the

```
RELIABILITY
  /VARIABLES=att1 att2 att3
  /FORMAT=NOLABELS
  /SCALE(ALPHA)=ALL/MODEL=ALPHA.

*** Method 1 (space saver) will be used for this analysis ***

R E L I A B I L I T Y   A N A L Y S I S  -  S C A L E  (A L P H A)

Reliability Coefficients
N of Cases =      22.0                    N of Items =   3

Alpha =   -2.0176
```

Figure 19.1   *Syntax and output from RELIABILITY. The negative value indicates the model is inappropriate*

recode procedure described in section 12.6. The scores on att3 were
recoded into the new variable att3rc, and the reliability procedure was
then run again. The syntax and output can be seen in Figure 19.2.

```
EXECUTE .
RELIABILITY
  /VARIABLES=att1 att2 att3rc
  /FORMAT=NOLABELS
  /SCALE(ALPHA)=ALL/MODEL=ALPHA.

*** Method 1 (space saver) will be used for this analysis ***

R E L I A B I L I T Y   A N A L Y S I S - S C A L E (A L P H A)

Reliability Coefficients
N of Cases =     22.0                    N of Items =  3

Alpha =    .8737
```

Figure 19.2 *Syntax and output from RELIABILITY after one variable has been recoded*

Pressing the Statistics button from the original Reliability Analysis
dialogue box reveals the box shown in Figure 19.3, from which you can
request a number of useful statistics. The type of output obtained when
statistics are requested is shown in Figure 19.4. The first section shows
the means and standard deviations on each item obtained by selecting
Descriptives for Item from Figure 19.3. This is followed by the correlations between the items, as Inter-Item Correlations were asked for. The
figures described as Statistics for Scale show the overall mean score,
variance and standard deviation if the scores on the separate items (att1,
att2 and att3rc) were added together to make a single scale. They are
given if you ask for Descriptives for Scale. By asking for Summaries
Means, one obtains the mean of the means for the separate items, which

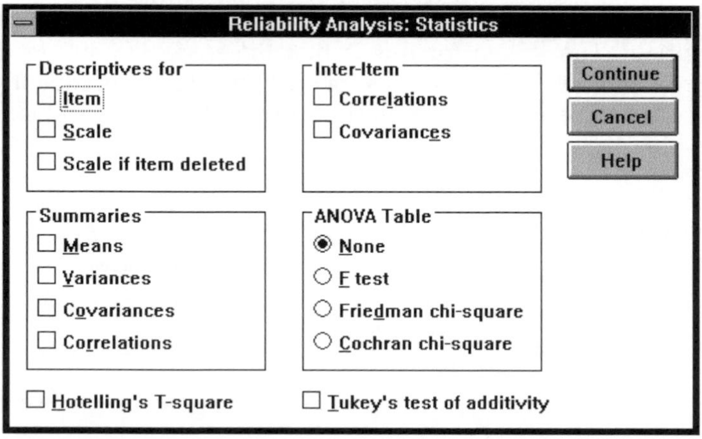

Figure 19.3 *The Reliability Analysis: Statistics dialogue box*

is given in the section headed Item Means of Figure 19.4. This also prints out the range of the item means, and their variance.

```
RELIABILITY
  /VARIABLES=att1 att2 att3rc
  /FORMAT=NOLABELS
  /SCALE(ALPHA)=ALL/MODEL=ALPHA
  /STATISTICS=DESCRIPTIVE SCALE CORR
  /SUMMARY=MEANS .

**Method 2(covariance matrix) will be used for this analysis**

R E L I A B I L I T Y   A N A L Y S I S - S C A L E (A L P H A)

                             Mean         Std Dev       Cases
     1.    ATT1              2.5455        1.1010        22.0
     2.    ATT2              3.0909         .9211        22.0
     3.    ATT3RC            2.5909        1.1816        22.0

                    Correlation Matrix

                ATT1          ATT2          ATT3RC
     ATT1       1.0000
     ATT2        .7001        1.0000
     ATT3RC      .7654         .6483        1.0000

          N of Cases =        22.0

                                             N of
     Statistics for  Mean    Variance    Std Dev  Variables
            Scale    8.2273    8.2792     2.8774       3

     Item Means    Mean  Minimum  Maximum Range  Max/Min   Variance
                 2.7424   2.5455   3.0909 .5455   1.2143      .0916

     Reliability Coefficients      3 items

     Alpha =    .8737            Standardized item alpha =    .8774
```

Figure 19.4 *Example of statistics obtained using Reliability/Statistics*

The ANOVA Table section of Figure 19.3 lets you select an analysis of variance. The *F*-test produces a repeated-measures ANOVA table. If the items are in the form of ranks, you can select Friedman chi-square, and if they are all dichotomies, you can select Cochran chi-square. Hotelling's *T* square test can be used to test the hypothesis that the item means are equal, while Tukey's test of additivity is used to test the assumption that there is no multiplicative interaction among the items.

19.3 Chapter summary

- Reliability refers to the consistency of the results on different items in a test.
- Use the Reliability procedure to obtain Cronbach's alpha.

20

FACTOR ANALYSIS

20.1 Basic principles of factor analysis

Factor analysis is a technique or more accurately a family of techniques which aim to simplify complex sets of data by analysing the correlations between them. The underlying principles are explained in texts such as Stevens (1996). A simple coverage is provided by Kline (1994), and this chapter relies heavily on his exposition.

Given a set of scores on a number of variables, the correlation between each of the variables can be calculated and yields a correlation matrix such as is shown in the upper part of Figure 20.3. In the example data used in this chapter, 300 respondents answered 10 questions labelled att1 to att10. In Figure 20.3, the correlations between the responses to each question are shown: for example, the correlation between att1 and att2 is .36788, and the correlation between att2 and att3 is .74843.

Factor analysis is designed to simplify the correlation matrix and reveal the small number of factors which can explain the correlations. A component or a factor explains the variance in the intercorrelation matrix, and the amount of variance explained is known as the eigenvalue for the factor.

A factor loading is the correlation of a variable with a factor. A loading of 0.3 or more is frequently taken as meaningful when interpreting a factor. So when deciding what a factor signifies, one looks to see which variables have loadings of 0.3 or above. Communality is the proportion of the variance in each variable which the factors explain; the higher it is, the more the factors explain the variable's variance.

Exploratory factor analysis is employed to identify the main constructs which will explain the intercorrelation matrix, and is the most common usage. Confirmatory factor analysis is where one tests whether hypothesized factor loadings fit an observed intercorrelation matrix.

There are a number of considerations to bear in mind before carrying out factor analysis. First, the outcome depends on the variables which have been measured and the respondents who yielded the data. Secondly, the number of respondents should not be less than 100, and there should be at least twice as many respondents as variables. So if you are measuring 60 variables you need at least 120 respondents. Both the number of respondents and the ratio of respondents to variables should be as large as possible. Thirdly, the respondents should be heterogeneous on the abilities or measures being studied.

As mentioned above, there are many different types of factor analysis and you should have previously decided which particular procedures you mean to follow. (Those described in this chapter are only an illustration and not necessarily those relevant to your specific problem.)

In carrying out exploratory factor analysis, Kline recommends that one should first of all perform a principal components analysis. This is a form of analysis which derives as many components as there are variables, although the amount of variance explained by each component will decrease as more components are extracted. It is a consequence of the nature of principal components analysis that it will yield a large general factor first. The components obtained in a principal components analysis are uncorrelated and emerge in decreasing order of the amount of variance explained. Although one initially obtains as many components as there are variables, the aim of factor analysis is to explain the matrix with as few factors as possible. The number to extract can be determined if one obtains a scree plot; an example is shown in Figure 20.4. A scree plot shows the eigenvalues plotted against the number of the components. One looks at the plot to find where the line changes slope, where the 'elbow' is. In Figure 20.4 it is between the factor numbers 2 and 3, so one would take 2 as the number of factors to be extracted.

Once the principal components analysis has indicated the number of factors to extract, a common factor analysis is run with the number of factors set to the value obtained from the principal components analysis. There are many alternative types of analysis which can be chosen; 'In general principal factor analysis is an adequate method' (Kline, 1994: 54). Kline recommends running the analysis with rotation of factors; again, there are alternative methods of rotation but he recommends using the Varimax method: 'where an orthogonal simple structure rotation is desired, Varimax should be applied' (1994: 68).

However, it is not necessary for the factors to be orthogonal, and there can be advantages in having oblique or correlated factors. 'If an oblique rotation gives a better simple structure then the Direct Oblimin package is the one to use' (Kline, 1994: 76).

20.2 Obtaining a factor analysis

From the menu select

```
Statistics
    Data Reduction
        Factor
```

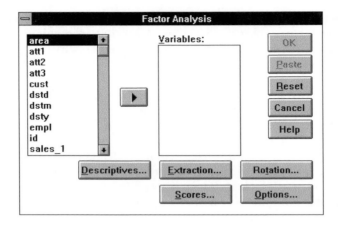

Figure 20.1   *Dialogue Box for Factor Analysis*

This opens the dialogue box shown in Figure 20.1. Identify the variables to be included in the analysis by selecting them and pressing the button with the right arrow. Clicking the Extraction button reveals another dialogue box, shown in Figure 20.2, in which you can choose from the drop-down menu the method to use; principal components is the default. A scree plot is requested by clicking on the labelled button.

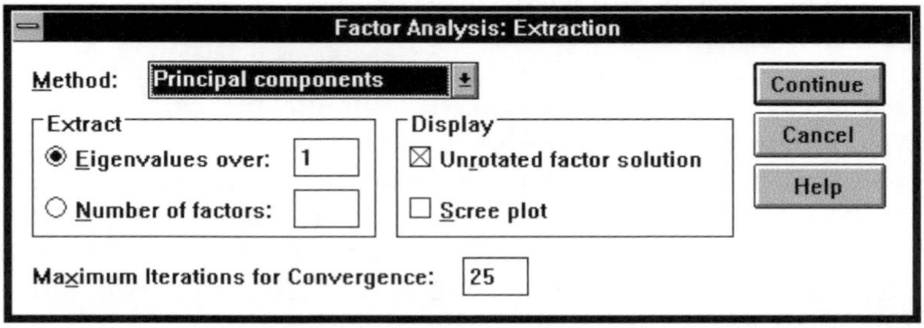

Figure 20.2   *The Factor Analysis: Extraction dialogue box*

The syntax and output from a principal components analysis is illustrated in Figure 20.3. The first section of output illustrates the intercorrelations between the scores on each of the variables, and this is followed by the Initial statistics. Principal components will begin with the same number of components as variables, as shown in the left-hand part of the table. The right-hand part shows the eigenvalues and percentage of variance explained by each of the factors. The total of the eigenvalues equals the number of variables, and the percentage of variance explained is calculated from the eigenvalues: the eigenvalue for the factor is divided by the sum of the eigenvalues and multiplied by 100.

The scree chart was plotted and is shown in Figure 20.4. The Factor Matrix in Figure 20.3 shows the loading of each of the variables on each of the two factors which were extracted. The final section shows the communality for each variable: this is the proportion of variance in each variable which the factors explain. So in Figure 20.3, the two factors explain 0.49327 of the variance in the scores on att1.

The principal components analysis indicated that two factors underlie the scores on variables att1 to att10, so a simple factor analysis with two factors to be extracted was run. From the dialogue box of Figure 20.2, the Principal-axis method was selected from the Method drop-down menu and the Number of Factors to extract was set at 2 by clicking the radio button and typing 2 into the text box. From the dialogue box shown in Figure 20.1 the Rotation button was used to reveal a box allowing various rotation methods to be chosen, and Varimax was selected. The syntax and output is shown in Figure 20.5.

The output is similar to that from principal components (Figure 20.3), since the principal axis method of factor analysis is identical to principal components analysis with one exception (Kline, 1994: 36). In principal components, a value of 1 is inserted in the diagonal of the intercorrelation matrix, but in the principal axis method an estimate of communality is used. This is why the first tables of Figure 20.3 and

```
FACTOR
    /VARIABLES att1 att2 att3 att4 att5 att6 att7 att8 att9 att10  /MISSING
    LISTWISE /ANALYSIS att1 att2 att3 att4 att5 att6 att7 att8 att9 att10
    /PRINT INITIAL CORRELATION EXTRACTION
    /PLOT EIGEN
    /CRITERIA MINEIGEN(1) ITERATE(25)
    /EXTRACTION PC
    /ROTATION NOROTATE .


 - - - - - -  F A C T O R   A N A L Y S I S  - - - - - -

Analysis number 1   Listwise deletion of cases with missing values

Correlation Matrix:

          ATT1     ATT2     ATT3     ATT4     ATT5     ATT6     ATT7
ATT1  1.00000
ATT2   .36788  1.00000
ATT3   .32731   .74843  1.00000
ATT4   .35025   .75944   .62652  1.00000
ATT5   .43122   .41091   .42031   .41322  1.00000
ATT6   .38892   .84113   .67955   .74812   .40282  1.00000
ATT7   .36873   .24842   .27273   .27992   .52084   .26594  1.00000
ATT8   .35552   .27454   .35496   .23764   .42545   .31047   .31993
ATT9   .34013   .71422   .71106   .67178   .3694    .72067   .35057
ATT10  .47638   .70737   .67700   .68357   .48575   .71017   .34506


          ATT8     ATT9    ATT10
ATT8  1.00000
ATT9   .35494  1.00000
ATT10  .27640   .74809  1.00000
```

Continued on next page

```
Extraction 1 for analysis 1, Principal Components Analysis (PC)

Initial Statistics:

Variable Communality * Factor  Eigenvalue  Pct of Var   Cum Pct
                     *
  ATT1    1.00000   *    1      5.48437       54.8        54.8
  ATT2    1.00000   *    2      1.35172       13.5        68.4
  ATT3    1.00000   *    3       .71823        7.2        75.5
  ATT4    1.00000   *    4       .65299        6.5        82.1
  ATT5    1.00000   *    5       .48630        4.9        86.9
  ATT6    1.00000   *    6       .38758        3.9        90.8
  ATT7    1.00000   *    7       .32178        3.2        94.0
  ATT8    1.00000   *    8       .25310        2.5        96.6
  ATT9    1.00000   *    9       .20084        2.0        98.6
  ATT10   1.00000   *   10       .14309        1.4       100.0


Hi-Res Chart  # 4:Factor scree plot

PC    extracted   2 factors.

Factor Matrix:

              Factor  1       Factor  2
  ATT1         .56425          .41821
  ATT2         .86867         -.29915
  ATT3         .82204         -.18822
  ATT4         .82143         -.25255
  ATT5         .62894          .50888
  ATT6         .86389         -.25923
  ATT7         .48648          .60648
  ATT8         .48051          .49977
  ATT9         .84459         -.18142
  ATT10        .85916         -.10708

Final Statistics:

Variable Communality * Factor  Eigenvalue  Pct of Var   Cum Pct
                     *
  ATT1     .49327   *    1      5.48437       54.8        54.8
  ATT2     .84408   *    2      1.35172       13.5        68.4
  ATT3     .71117   *
  ATT4     .73852   *
  ATT5     .65452   *
  ATT6     .81350   *
  ATT7     .60449   *
  ATT8     .48066   *
  ATT9     .74625   *
  ATT10    .74963   *


Skipping  rotation   1 for extraction   1 in analysis  1
```

Figure 20.3 *Output from a principal components analysis*

Figure 20.5 are identical except that the communality values for each variable are less than 1 in Figure 20.5. The factor matrix and Final Statistics sections of Figures 20.3 and 20.5 of course differ. The result of the Varimax rotation is then presented, showing the loading on each of the factors for each of the variables under the heading Rotated Factor Matrix.

If oblique rather than orthogonal factor rotation is used, you select Direct Oblimin instead of Varimax in the dialogue box revealed by selecting the Rotation button of Figure 20.1. The syntax and output following oblimin rotation is shown in Figure 20.6. The section headed Pattern Matrix shows the coefficients used to express standardized

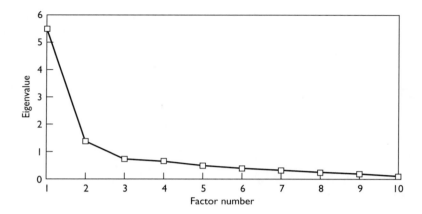

Figure 20.4   *Example of a scree plot*

```
FACTOR
   /VARIABLES att1 att2 att3 att4 att5 att6 att7 att8 att9 att10   /MISSING
   LISTWISE /ANALYSIS att1 att2 att3 att4 att5 att6 att7 att8 att9 att10
   /PRINT INITIAL EXTRACTION ROTATION
   /CRITERIA FACTORS(2) ITERATE(25)
   /EXTRACTION PAF
   /CRITERIA ITERATE(25)
   /ROTATION VARIMAX .
```

```
- - - - - -   F A C T O R   A N A L Y S I S   - - - - - -
```

Analysis number 1   Listwise deletion of cases with missing values

Extraction   1 for analysis   1, Principal Axis Factoring (PAF)

Initial Statistics:

Variable	Communality	*	Factor	Eigenvalue	Pct of Var	Cum Pct
ATT1	.33352	*	1	5.48437	54.8	54.8
ATT2	.78959	*	2	1.35172	13.5	68.4
ATT3	.64650	*	3	.71823	7.2	75.5
ATT4	.65032	*	4	.65299	6.5	82.1
ATT5	.45916	*	5	.48630	4.9	86.9
ATT6	.75982	*	6	.38758	3.9	90.8
ATT7	.33339	*	7	.32178	3.2	94.0
ATT8	.29287	*	8	.25310	2.5	96.6
ATT9	.69869	*	9	.20084	2.0	98.6
ATT10	.69892	*	10	.14309	1.4	100.0

PAF   extracted   2 factors.   8 iterations required.

Factor Matrix:

	Factor 1	Factor 2
ATT1	.51046	.30770
ATT2	.87272	-.27059
ATT3	.79532	-.12251
ATT4	.79962	-.18171
ATT5	.59593	.49214
ATT6	.85966	-.22141
ATT7	.44434	.47835
ATT8	.42799	.32936
ATT9	.82425	-.12305
ATT10	.83967	-.03956

Continued on next page

```
Final Statistics:

Variable Communality * Factor  Eigenvalue   Pct of Var   Cum Pct
                     *
ATT1        .35525   *    1     5.15331        51.5        51.5
ATT2        .83485   *    2      .86116         8.6        60.1
ATT3        .64754   *
ATT4        .67241   *
ATT5        .59734   *
ATT6        .78805   *
ATT7        .42626   *
ATT8        .29165   *
ATT9        .69453   *
ATT10       .70660   *
```

VARIMAX rotation 1 for extraction 1 in analysis 1 – Kaiser Normalization.

VARIMAX converged in 3 iterations.

Rotated Factor Matrix:

```
              Factor  1      Factor  2
ATT1            .28000         .52616
ATT2            .88781         .21598
ATT3            .74535         .30330
ATT4            .77945         .25470
ATT5            .25862         .72832
ATT6            .85136         .25148
ATT7            .13563         .63864
ATT8            .19811         .50240
ATT9            .77046         .31768
ATT10           .74081         .39724
```

Factor Transformation Matrix:

```
              Factor  1      Factor  2

Factor  1       .85807         .51353
Factor  2      -.51353         .85807
```

Figure 20.5   *Syntax and output for factor analysis with varimax rotation*

observed variables in terms of the factors, but the section headed Structure Matrix is the correlation between variables and factors and is used to interpret the factors. The Factor Correlation matrix shows the correlation between the factors. (Varimax, which yielded Figure 20.5, produces just one factor matrix whereas oblimin, which yielded Figure 20.6, produces both a pattern matrix and a structure matrix. This is because with orthogonal factors, as in varimax, the pattern matrix and the structure matrix are the same.)

In deciding whether to use orthogonal or oblique factor rotation, one can apply orthogonal rotation and see whether it provides a simple structure solution. Kline (1994: 65) maintains that the overriding criterion of simple structure is that each factor should have a few high loadings, with the rest being zero or close to zero. On this criterion, the solution shown in Figure 20.5 is superior to that shown in Figure 20.6, since those variables which load at 0.3 or above on factor 1 (att2, att3, att4, att6, att 9 and att 10) all load less than 0.4 on factor 2, whereas the variables that have low loadings on factor 1 (att 1, att 5, att 7 and att 8) all have quite high loadings (above 0.5) on factor 2. In Figure 20.6, however, the

```
FACTOR
    /VARIABLES att1 att2 att3 att4 att5 att6 att7 att8 att9 att10   /MISSING
    LISTWISE /ANALYSIS att1 att2 att3 att4 att5 att6 att7 att8 att9 att10
    /PRINT INITIAL EXTRACTION ROTATION
    /CRITERIA FACTORS(2) ITERATE(25)
    /EXTRACTION PAF
    /CRITERIA ITERATE(25) DELTA(0)
    /ROTATION OBLIMIN .
```

OBLIMIN rotation 1 for extraction 1 in analysis 1 - Kaiser Normalization.

OBLIMIN converged in 4 iterations.

Pattern Matrix:

	Factor 1	Factor 2
ATT1	.12827	.51022
ATT2	.97050	-.10068
ATT3	.76742	.05980
ATT4	.82678	-.01138
ATT5	.02441	.75800
ATT6	.91343	-.04405
ATT7	-.08684	.70123
ATT8	.04025	.51496
ATT9	.79165	.06675
ATT10	.72556	.17278

Structure Matrix:

	Factor 1	Factor 2
ATT1	.43414	.58712
ATT2	.91014	.48113
ATT3	.80327	.51987
ATT4	.81996	.48427
ATT5	.47882	.77263
ATT6	.88702	.50354
ATT7	.33354	.64917
ATT8	.34896	.53908
ATT9	.83167	.54134
ATT10	.82914	.60775

Factor Correlation Matrix:

	Factor 1	Factor 2
Factor 1	1.00000	
Factor 2	.59949	1.00000

Figure 20.6   *Syntax and excerpt of the output for factor analysis with oblimin rotation*

loadings shown in the Structure Matrix table are less clear-cut: all items are loading over 0.3 on both factors. In this instance, therefore, one would stop at the orthogonal, varimax procedure.

20.3 Adding factor scores to the data file

It is possible to have the factor scores for each case added to the active data file by pressing the Scores button of Figure 20.1 and checking the Save as variables option. There are alternative ways in which the factor scores are calculated: use the Help button to gain information about them. If you use this procedure, a new variable for each factor is added to the data in the data window. To preserve these factor scores it is necessary to save the modified data file to disk.

20.4 Chapter summary

- For factor analysis the number of respondents should not be less than 100, and there should be at least twice as many respondents as variables. The respondents should be heterogeneous on the abilities or measures being studied.
- Perform a principal components analysis first. The number of factors to extract can be determined from a scree plot.
- Then run a common factor analysis with the number of factors set to the value obtained from the principal components analysis.
- To obtain an orthogonal simple structure rotation use Varimax. If an oblique rotation is needed, use Direct Oblimin.

OBTAINING NEAT PRINTOUTS

21.1 Obtaining a clean output (.lst) file

If you wish to use the .lst file for presenting the results of your analysis, you will need a 'clean' version of the file, containing just the results you want. There are various ways of obtaining a clean .lst file. The simplest way is to start with a syntax file which is perfect so that it runs without error, then open a new output file (File /New /Output) and make it the designated window by clicking on the ! button. Run the commands in the syntax file and only a clean version of the output will be placed in the output window. An alternative is to edit the .lst file, either within SPSS or by importing it into a word processor as described in section 7.8.

Either of the techniques mentioned above involves editing or reformatting the output. Another way of obtaining a clean and tidy printout of the results of your analysis is to use the REPORT procedure.

21.2 Generating tables using REPORT

Earlier versions of the Report facility were of such complexity that few will have bothered to use it, as similar results could be obtained by importing the output file into a word processor and editing and formatting it there. In SPSS for Windows, an attempt has been made to provide a front-end which makes it feasible to consider using Report to provide presentation tables of the data and of the results of the analyses.

A data file includes the data organized into cases, and in many situations the case corresponds to a person. When dealing with the results of a survey, where one has obtained responses from a number of different types of respondent, one may well want to produce tables showing the responses of each subgroup of respondents (males and females, different age groups, different socio-economic groups, etc.) on some or all of the variables that were measured. Using Report, one can obtain tables that show the data from each subgroup of respondents, and/or the summary statistics of each subgroup (such as the mean or median response), with the table organized so that the various subgroups are divided from each other. The statistics for the whole set of data, referred to as grand totals, can also be shown. An example is shown in Figure 21.1.

```
SORT CASES  BY sex (A) .
Report
  /FORMAT= CHWRAP(ON) PREVIEW(OFF) CHALIGN(BOTTOM)   BRKSPACE(-1)
  UNDERSCORE(ON)
  ONEBREAKCOLUMN(OFF) CHDSPACE(1)  SUMSPACE(0)  AUTOMATIC  NOLIST
  PAGE(1) MISSING'.' LENGTH(1, 99999) ALIGN(LEFT) TSPACE(1) FTSPACE(1)
  MARGINS(1,36)
  /TITLE=
  LEFT 'Mean sales by sex'
  RIGHT 'Page )PAGE'
   /VARIABLES
 sales_1  (VALUES)  (RIGHT)  (OFFSET(0)) (8)
 sales_2  (VALUES)  (RIGHT) (OFFSET(0))(8)
  /MISSING=LIST
 /BREAK (TOTAL) 'Grand Total' (SKIP(1)) /SUMMARY
 MEAN( sales_1) SKIP(1) MEAN( sales_2 )    'Mean'
 /SUMMARY  VALIDN( sales_1) VALIDN( sales_2 )    'N'
 /BREAK    sex  (LABELS)  (LEFT) (OFFSET(5))(16)(SKIP(1))
 /SUMMARY MEAN( sales_1) SKIP(1) MEAN( sales_2 )    'Mean'
  /SUMMARY  VALIDN( sales_1) VALIDN( sales_2 )    'N' .
```

Mean sales by sex	Page	1
SEX	SALES_1	SALES_2
male		
	5950.64	6411.54
N	10	10
female		
	5724.00	6278.20
N	11	11
3		
	6441.38	6388.32
N	1	1
Grand Total		
Mean	5859.62	6343.81
N	22	22

Figure 21.1   *Example of a table obtained using the REPORT procedure*

The Report facility is obtained from

```
Statistics
     Summarize
          Report Summaries in Rows ...
```

A dialogue box shown in Figure 21.2 is presented. Specify which variables are to be shown in the tables by selecting variables from the list in the left-hand box and inserting them into the Data Columns box by clicking on the right-pointing arrow in the usual way.

Report is usually used to get the data broken down into subgroups, and you specify the variables to be used to create the subgroups by entering the variables into the Break Columns box: select the appropriate

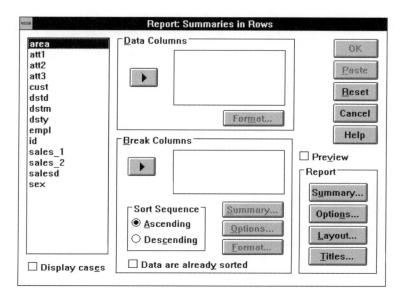

Figure 21.2 *The Report dialogue box*

variable(s) from the left-hand list of variables, and enter them into the Break Columns box by clicking on the arrow to the left of the Break Columns box. Suppose we wanted the data for males and females in salesq to be tabulated separately, then sex would be a Break Column variable. One can select ascending or descending order of levels of each Break Column variable by making the appropriate selection in the Sort Sequence box. Remember the data will be sorted according to the values of the variables in the data file. In salesq, 1 represents male and 2 represents female, so an ascending order will put the 1s (males) before the 2s (females). To have those with a sex score of 2 put first, one would select the Descending sort sequence.

If you wish to have statistics of the subgroups you have specified (e.g. for males and females in salesq), select the variable in the Break Columns list of variables, and then select Summary from the Break Columns area (not from the Report area). Another box is presented (Report: Summary Lines For), and you can indicate which statistics you want, including sum, mean, number of cases, standard deviation and others. The Percentage Above, Percentage Below and Percentage Inside options allow you to ask for the percentage of cases above, below, or between specified values that you type into the boxes to the right of these entries. When you have made your selection, click on Continue.

To set the line spacing between break categories, between break headings and summary statistics, or to set it so that each break category is on a separate page, select a variable in the Break Columns list of variables and then select Options in the Break Columns area (not in the Report section of the box).

When Report is used to produce a table in which the data is broken down by subgroups, there are headings for each subgrouping, referred to as break column headings. These can be modified if one selects Format from the Break Columns section (not in the Report section of the box).

To specify the headings of the data columns, the alignment of the column headings, the width of the columns, whether the table shows the numbers or the value labels, select a variable in the Data Columns list of variables in the Report: Summaries in Rows dialogue box. (You created this list by selecting variables from the variable list and inserting them into Data Columns.) Click on Format . . . in the Data Columns area of the Report dialogue box. This reveals a dialogue box in which you can type in a heading for the column. If you leave it blank, the variable label is used, and is wrapped to fit the column width. You can type in a fresh heading, but must use Ctrl+Enter at the end of each line if you want it to occupy more than one line. The column heading can be right-aligned, centred or left-aligned by selecting appropriately from the Column Title Justification drop-down list. (Click on the down-pointing arrow to reveal the list.)

The column width can be set by typing a number into the Column Width box. If you leave this blank, a default value will be used, and this varies according to whether or not you have specified a column heading and the data that the column will contain. If you do not specify a column heading, the variable name is used as the heading, and the width of the column will be set to the length of the longest word in the variable label. If you do specify a column heading, the column width is set to the length of the longest line in the heading. If the data is to be displayed as value labels (i.e. words, not the code numbers), then the column width is set to the length of the longest value label.

The program will try to make allowances if you specify a column width which is too short for the data you want shown; for example, numbers will be converted to scientific notation or be replaced by asterisks if you specify a width less than six characters and the figures are too long for that. If you find these happening, you will need to increase the column width.

The Column Content area allows you to say whether you want the table to show numbers or value labels.

The position of the data within the column is selected from the area headed Value Position within Column. By default, numbers are right aligned and words are left aligned with the column edge. One can specify how many character positions to offset the data from the edge of the columns or select the Centred within Column option.

You may wish to obtain statistics on the whole set of data in addition to the various subgroups. These are requested by using the buttons in the

Report area of the Report: Summaries in Rows dialogue box. To obtain statistics on the whole set of data, select the Summary button.

The margins of the table generated by Report and the number of lines per page can be specified by selecting the Layout button from the Report area of the Report: Summaries in Rows dialogue box. This box also allows you to align the table within the margins you have set. *Note* that if you specify a width that is insufficient for the report table, it will not be generated.

21.3 Page headers and footers in REPORT

To specify the titles you want printed on each page of the Report, or the message you want printed at the foot of each page, select the Titles . . . button from the Report area of the Report: Summaries in Rows dialogue box (Figure 21.2) to reveal the Report: Titles dialogue box. You can type in page titles for the left, centre, or right of the page. If you want a title to occupy more than one line, type in the text you want for Left, Center or Right position, and then click on Next in the upper right of the Report: Titles dialogue box.

To have the date or the page number as a title or footer, click on DATE or TIME in the Special Variables box in the lower left of the Report: Titles dialogue box. Decide where you want the date or time to appear: left, centre, or right, and at the top (title) or foot of the page, and click on the right-pointing arrow adjacent to the appropriate text box heading.

You can have variable names included in titles and footers. Select the variable name from the list in the Report: Titles dialogue box, and click on the right-pointing arrow next to Left, Center or Right for the page title or page footer. The variable name will be inserted in the appropriate text box.

To specify the number of lines between headers and the Report table and between the bottom of the Report table and any page footer, select the Layout button from the Report area of the Report: Summaries in Rows dialogue box.

The titles and footers are left-aligned, right-aligned, or centred according to the report width or – if you have specified them in the Report layout box – the report margins. They may not align with the table, because the table is narrower than the margins you have set, but you can shift the position of the titles and footers by changing the margins.

21.4 Page numbering in REPORT

The pages of output from Report are numbered, and will start at 1 unless you alter this. To do so, select Options from the Report area of the Report: Summaries in Rows dialogue box shown in Figure 21.2. The dialogue box revealed includes an option entitled Number Pages From, and you can type in the value you require.

21.5 Missing data in REPORT

When dealing with a set of data, there are likely to be instances where some cases are incomplete: respondents have not provided data on one of the variables which you are tabulating with Report. By default, such cases are deleted from the report. To alter this, so that missing cases are included in the tabled Report, select Options from the Report area of the Report: Summaries in Rows dialogue box, and cancel Exclude Cases with Missing Values Listwise. If you indicate that you want cases where the data is missing to be included, they will be shown as a full stop, but you can specify a different character using the option Missing Values Appear As.

21.6 Saving the REPORT commands

When you have made the (numerous) selections for Report, you can paste them into a syntax window, and then save that file so you have a record of the commands which produced the layout. An example of the complex syntax is shown in Figure 21.1.

21.7 Chapter summary

- To obtain a clean .lst file, either create a perfect syntax file and run it into a new, empty output file or import the .lst file into a word processor and edit it.
- The REPORT procedure allows you to obtain tables of results laid out according to your specifications.

REFERENCES

Hinton, P.R. (1995) *Statistics Explained*. London: Routledge

Howell, D.C. (1992) *Statistical Methods for Psychology*. 3rd edn. Belmont, CA: Duxbury.

Kline, P. (1993) *The Handbook of Psychological Testing*. London: Routledge.

Kline, P. (1994) *An Easy Guide to Factor Analysis*. London: Routledge.

Stevens, J. (1996) *Applied Multivariate Statistics for the Social Sciences*. 3rd edn. Mahwah, NJ: Erlbaum.

INDEX